COASTAL CONVOYS 1939–1945

COASTAL CONVOYS 1939–1945

The Indestructible Highway

by

Nick Hewitt

Pen & Sword
MARITIME

First published in Great Britain in England by
Pen & Sword Maritime
an imprint of
Pen & Sword Books Ltd
47 Church Street
Barnsley
South Yorkshire
S70 2AS

ISBN 978 1 84415 861 4

A CIP catalogue record for this book is available from the British Library

Typeset in Sabon by
Phoenix Typesetting, Auldgirth, Dumfriesshire

Printed and bound in England by
CPI UK

Pen & Sword Books Ltd incorporates the Imprints of Pen & Sword Aviation, Pen & Sword Maritime, Pen & Sword Military, Wharncliffe Local History, Pen & Sword Select, Pen & Sword Military Classics and Leo Cooper.

For a complete list of Pen & Sword titles please contact
PEN & SWORD BOOKS LIMITED
47 Church Street, Barnsley, South Yorkshire, S70 2AS, England
E-mail: enquiries@pen-and-sword.co.uk
Website: www.pen-and-sword.co.uk

This book is dedicated to all those who served around Britain's coast during the Second World War.

Contents

Maps

Foreword

By Captain Richard Woodman

It is an extraordinary omission on the part of maritime historians of the Second World War that the coastal element of Britain's fight for her seaborne supply lines has been ignored. The central element of this struggle has been dignified by its own, distinct name: the Battle of the Atlantic, but in truth it was only a third of the overall problem facing Britain as she geared up for the long fight with the German-led Axis.

Once a convoy had reached one of the major ports, its ships, arriving in a large number, all had to be discharged and then loaded with military supplies for campaigns being fought in the Western Desert, the Far East and elsewhere. They also had to carry a continuous stream of exported goods, just as in peacetime, to maintain an economy strained to the limit by the need to pay for war. The internal rail and road systems were incapable of handling the level of traffic required and coastal shipping, already a major carrier of cargoes, had to be mustered in convoys, organized and escorted. To the small- and medium-sized coasters were added deep-water merchant ships carrying cargoes consigned to the east coast ports of England and Scotland, and this task was made all the more difficult after the early occupation of France, the Low Countries, Denmark and Norway.

Coal in particular, required in the south of England to fuel power stations and domestic fires, was needed at a rate of 40,000 tons a week and the supply to the power stations of southern England meant that colliers had to traverse the English Channel, under attack from occupied France, while the main routes threading through the coastal shoals of England's east coast, were easily interdicted by fast patrol boats armed with torpedoes, destroyers and aircraft, besides running terrible risks from mines. This backyard battle lacked the high profile of the struggle to secure ascendancy in the North Atlantic, employing as it did an unglamorous class of coasting merchantman. For the supporting Royal Navy it consisted of endless mine-sweeping, of patient attendance of large, slow-moving convoys of ageing ships, while all suffered the difficulties and dangers of navigating in shallow, tidal waters where the weather – both gales and fog – could make life miserable.

The first coastal convoy between the Thames and the Firth of Forth sailed on 6 September 1939, a day after the very first ocean convoy of the war, and the last attacks came shortly before the German surrender; they were an essential component of the absolutely vital network of supply routes by which victory was finally achieved.

In this splendid account Nick Hewitt places the elements that made up this dreary, excoriating war in their proper place in our history. The naval organization, the air cover and the military resources to protect 'the trade' are all covered in his analysis, giving us a glimpse into the complexities of warfare and the difficulties of co-ordination, command and control. So too are the fighting elements of this story, of German air, surface, long-range artillery and – towards the war's end – submarine attacks on coastal convoys. But neither does he neglect the little colliers of the so-called 'Coal-Scuttle Brigade', the salt-caked and dirty coasters of Masefield's famous phrase, or the obscure tenders of Trinity House which, like the Royal Navy's minesweepers, played their important part in keeping these narrow sea lanes open. Nor does he neglect the authentic voice of the men who achieved all this, forgotten men whose voices have not been heard until culled from the archives of the Imperial War Museum and the National Archives.

Too often dismissed as a mere amorphous collection of 'freighters' or 'coasters', the author gives these nondescript vessels of Britain's once huge Merchant Navy, along with their hard-bitten crews, their rightful place amid the fighting services in the front line.

Richard Woodman.

Acknowledgements

In August 2006 I was interviewed about the Channel Convoys for the BBC television series *Coast*. As a historian of the Second World War at sea I was aware of their existence, but I had never really given much thought to what it was like to take those battered little ships up and down the war channel twice a week. In preparing for *Coast* it soon became clear that precious few authors had either, and so this book was born.

I am particularly grateful for the support I have received from friends and colleagues at the Imperial War Museum, notably Brad King, the Director of HMS *Belfast*, for his enthusiasm and encouragement. Material from the incomparable IWM collections forms much of the content of this book, and I am grateful to Rod Suddaby, Tony Richards and Simon Offord in the Department of Documents; everyone in the Department of Printed Books; Margaret Brooks and Richard McDonagh of the Sound Archive; Hilary Roberts, Glyn Biesty and all of 'Team Digital' in the Photograph Archive; and Jenny Wood and Pauline Allwright in the Department of Art. Experiencing the IWM as a 'user' was a privilege, and made me all the more grateful for the expertise and commitment to public service found across the Museum, and in the Collections Division in particular.

The service provided by the National Archives was, as always, outstanding, even at a time of extensive refurbishment, and all authors should give thanks that this immense and 'user-friendly' treasure trove exists.

Particular thanks are due to Henry Wilson and all at Pen and Sword for taking a chance with a first-time author, and Peter Hart, a friend and a fine historian, without whose advice my original proposal might never have got as far as Henry's desk.

As the book progressed I discovered that 'precious few others' did not mean 'no one at all.' One book in particular deserves special mention: Julian Foynes' extraordinary self-published study, *The Battle of the East Coast*. My own book takes a different, and I hope complementary, approach to Julian's, but his rigorously researched work was always helpful. I am grateful to Julian for permission to quote where required.

Another grateful mention goes to the late Arnold Hague, one of the foremost Naval Historians of the Second World War, and the extraordinary collection of material assembled by him in collaboration with the late John

K. Burgess and Don Kindell. After his death this material was generously made available by his widow Gill, and assembled by Mike Holdaway into a remarkable online database. Covering every convoy route operated by the Allies during the Second World War, it is available to researchers at www.convoyweb.org.uk.

I am grateful for permission to use material from the 'WW2 People's War' online archive of wartime memories contributed by members of the public and gathered by the BBC. The archive can be found at www.bbc.co.uk/ww2peopleswar.

A special mention goes to Richard Woodman, for me the definitive historian of the Merchant Navy, who generously agreed to write my foreword when I had the pleasure of meeting him in December 2007, as well as providing encouragement and advice, and permission to quote from his works *The Real Cruel Sea* and *Keepers of the Sea*.

Few first-time authors enjoy the services of a talented professional graphic designer, and special thanks are also due to Karen Balme, for generously agreeing to produce my maps.

Closer to home I am grateful to my family, especially my children Cerys and Daniel for their wonderful enthusiasm, their mother Vivienne, my own mother Ros and my father Terry Hewitt M.Ed, for many years Lecturer in Geography at the Roehampton Institute, for his advice regarding the importance of coastal shipping to the pre-war British economy. In no particular order this book also owes much to Dörthe Gruttmann, Patrick Mummery, Derek Tolfree, Katherine Campbell, Andrea Buffery, Ben Ledden, Kees Helder, Keith Lowe, Hayley Newman and Matt Rowan. Many names will inevitably be missed, and I hope they will accept this general expression of thanks. Mistakes are, of course, my responsibility alone.

Finally this book would never have appeared without my wonderful partner Ngaire; despite her own academic commitments, she has found time to be my unpaid proofreader, research assistant, editor and agent, and at all times my absolute rock.

Note for Readers

Times

This book conforms to naval custom and avoids any confusion between a.m. and p.m. by using the 24-hour clock throughout, except where participants are quoted verbatim.

Convoy Numbering

The FN/FS series of convoys described throughout this book ran in series of 1–100 and then started again. This can make the task of the reader (and the historian) infinitely more frustrating! I have therefore used throughout the numbering system devised by the late Arnold Hague, which adds an extra number at the front for each sequence of 100 convoys. Thus the 34th convoy of the fourth sequence becomes FN434.

Spelling and Grammar

Because many of the accounts and other documents quoted in this book were not written or recorded for publication, words and punctuation necessary to make them comprehensible and easy to read have sometimes been omitted by their authors. Alternatively the spelling or grammar is faulty. I have therefore occasionally taken the liberty of making small changes to assist with narrative flow. When I have added words to help the sense I have placed them in [square] brackets, and when words have been omitted I have marked the omission by inserting ellipses. Such intrusions have been kept to an absolute minimum.

Use of German

German motor torpedo boats (*schnellboote*, or *S-boote*) have been referred to throughout this book by their British designation as 'E-boats', in common with contemporary British accounts quoted. German unit designations and ranks have where possible been rendered in the original German, as in *1. Schnellbooteflotilla*.

Prologue

Manny's War, 17 March 1941

The SS *Daphné II*, a 1,970 ton French coaster, was inching her way up the British coast from London to Leith. *Daphné II* had been taken over by the British following France's capitulation in 1940 but was still manned by most of her original crew and still under the command of a Frenchman, Captain Lovarn. On this trip she was 'in ballast', an empty hull being relocated to collect cargo.

Amongst that crew was Emmanuel 'Manny' Raud, a nineteen-year-old seaman from the town of Séné, in Brittany. Although young, Manny was a veteran of the war at sea. A merchant sailor since he was sixteen, he had already been in action at Dunkirk, where the *Daphné* had been attacked by German dive-bombers while delivering ammunition to the encircled troops. Joining General de Gaulle's Free French had been an easy decision after that.

Since the summer of 1940 the *Daphné* had been employed on the convoys running up and down the British east coast: arduous and dangerous work, as Manny relates in his own words:

> As soon as we are empty, off we go back again. We are in a convoy, and we used to drop anchor just outside Southend, and we used to wait some time, twenty-four hours, sometimes thirty-six hours to form a convoy and then we used to go. We used to lose . . . a lot of ships . . . We were under attack all the time, at sea first of all we had the mines . . . In the bad weather they used to break and go [free]. Of course during the day it wasn't bad because you could see them we used to shoot at them and sink them. But in the night we couldn't see them . . . then in the day time we had the planes, the planes used to come over . . . they used to come in between the two lines of ships and . . . we couldn't fire at them, if we fired at them we fired at the ship on the other side so we had to wait . . . They used to go for the biggest; usually they used to go for petrol tankers or something . . . they used to go up.[1]

By March 1941 the most feared threat on the east coast were German motor torpedo boats, know to the British as E-boats. The waters off East Anglia and The Wash had become known as 'E-boat Alley' and by the time the *Daphné* sailed with FN434 Manny had already had one unpleasant encounter:

> Then of course in the winter night was the motor torpedo boat, those were really nasty . . . It was really difficult especially if it was foggy . . . but one night, I remember, this particular night we were leading the convoy . . . those motor torpedo boats came in, they knew the time of the tides, the speed of the convoy roughly about five or six knots or something maximum because we had some very slow ships . . . they must have come along before us, between the convoy and England and stop engine, motor torpedo boat is not very big, in the night . . . you miss it. The destroyer send a signal, and all ships, all at once, turn full circle to put our back to the ships. By that time of course the Germans realised what we were doing, they fire their torpedoes don't they, boom boom boom boom! Of course by turning the ship there wasn't much they could miss, they did sink, I don't know how many, four or five, you can't tell in the night. They fired their torpedo and off they went.[2]

Against this potent weapon the *Daphné* could muster one antiquated 75mm gun and some light weapons, manned by three French Army gunners supported by the ship's crew. But when the *Daphné* sailed on 17 March, Manny's mind was on something else entirely: leave! When the ship reached Leith she was to have a long-overdue boiler clean. Two weeks in dry dock meant two weeks leave for her exhausted crew.

Captain Lovarn had warned the crew that once the ship went into dry dock no washing would be possible, and so Manny had carefully washed and ironed all his clothes. Neatly tied up in his locker ready for shore was everything he owned: 'I had all my shirts washed and ironed, my handkerchiefs, my socks, my shoes polished, everything was all in my wardrobe. It was all tied up so for two weeks I wouldn't have to do any washing.'[3]

At 2000 hours on 17 March Manny came off watch. Unable to sleep he lay in his bunk, reading, until at midnight his cabin mate came down and warned him that he would be back on watch again in just a few hours:

> He said to me, 'Manny, you know you're going to be on duty in four hours, I think you should get some sleep . . . it's a lovely night, beautiful moonlight, full moon, the sea is calm, you can see miles away, no problem. Turn the light off and let's go to sleep.' I did exactly what he said, turned the light off, and off we went, off to sleep.[4]

By this time the *Daphné* was well inside E-boat Alley, steaming off the Humber River through placid seas at a speed of 10 knots, a gentle breeze from the north-east the only disturbance. Captain Lovarn was on the bridge with the Second Mate and the duty watch. Without warning the ship was rocked by an explosion. A torpedo had struck her on the port side in an empty hold. No E-boat had been sighted and no engines heard, and it seems likely that the German commander had followed a common tactic of anchoring in the convoy lane, engines stopped or idling gently. The *Daphné* started to sink by the stern on an even keel:

> Boom! Everything went dark. [I] jumped out of my bed and tried to come out on the bridge . . . as we came to try to go up the ladder on to the bridge, no way! Water was pouring down, gallons . . . of water were coming down, and the water was coming up to your feet, once or twice we tried to go up the ladder but the pressure was so hard it just pushed you back, so you fall back again and then you try again. We all looked at each other . . . there must have been eight of us left in there, because the others were on duty on the bridge or in the engine room . . . we really there and then thought that . . . the ship was already sunk, we were going down with the ship, no way we could come up.[5]

Miraculously the inrush of water slowed and stopped, possibly as the *Daphné* righted herself as she settled, and Manny and his messmates could see the night sky through the hatch. Emerging from the warm fug of the mess deck to the cold night air was a shock. Manny's habit of sleeping almost naked was one he was starting to regret. 'Now can you imagine I've got nothing on me except my underpants, one o'clock in the morning, March 1941, believe me it was cold. The bridge is iron isn't it? My feet? I couldn't feel them!'[6]

On deck Manny and his comrades searched in vain for a lifeboat. The *Daphné* was badly damaged. All her hatches were blown, the steering gear was wrecked and the engines were unserviceable. The deck was buckled and several plates had sprung, letting in the cold North Sea waters. In addition the port side lifeboat had been destroyed in the explosion. Captain Lovarn assessed the damage and concluded that his ship was doomed. In the time it took Manny and his comrades to fight their way through the onrushing water to the deck, Lovarn ordered the remaining starboard boat away, dangerously overloaded with eighteen men. Fortunately fear of E-boats coupled with the boredom of earlier North Sea trips, which may have involved hours paralysed in fog banks, had caused the men to build their own salvation. 'Luckily for us . . . months before . . . we built ourselves a raft with oil drums . . . I think it was six of the oil drums, we had a plank of wood across, tied up with rope, and we built it on the top . . . we said 'good job we had that, it's the only thing we have left.'[7]

However the raft was lashed in place and no one had anything to cut it free, so Manny made his way below again to find a fire axe. On his way back he heard a noise from a cabin. Closer inspection revealed that the door had buckled in the explosion so Manny smashed it down with the fire axe he had just retrieved. He found the ship's elderly Chief Engineer, dazed, crawling on the deck on his hands and knees, searching for his glasses and passport. As Manny helped the man up the ladders, he heard yet another noise.

> I heard somebody calling me, and it was the donkeyman, his name is Michel . . . I went down to see him, his cabin was on top of the engine room and the porthole was open and I could see him. I said 'what you doing there Michel?' He said, 'Manny I can't get out, I can't open the door, I can't move.' I said 'no, no the door is jammed with the explosion.' Anyhow I didn't know what to do because the ship is sinking under my feet, everyone is going to go and I shall be left on my own in a minute . . . I had a few words with him, and I put my hand through the porthole and I shook hands with him. I said '*au revoir* Michel', I don't know exactly what I said. And I remember his last words to me, I'll never forget. He said, 'when you go back to France, do me a favour, go and see my wife and my two children', he had two daughters. I said, 'yes I will', and of course I shook hands with him, there was nothing else I could do. And I went back to the raft.[8]

Distraught at having to leave Michel to certain death, Manny returned to the deck, where someone else had managed to cut the raft free. One by one Manny and his comrades boarded the flimsy craft, their legs hanging over the side and their feet dangling in the freezing water. Then there began a desperate struggle to push the raft clear of the *Daphné* before the suction of the sinking ship pulled it down.

> When we're all . . . settled we said, OK, we have to push ourselves away from the ship, because the torpedo had been just behind us there and the water was still going into the ship, and of course there was suction, and the hole was so flipping big we thought we might go in there as well! I said, 'when we say push we all have to push together', one guy was on the front he had his knife ready and he cut the rope to let it go and we all pushed together and we just managed to clear the ship.[9]

The *Daphné* men watched anxiously as ship after ship passed them by. Finally, and probably against orders, one of the last ships in the convoy stopped and they wearily clambered aboard, so cold they could barely grip the rungs of the rope ladder. On board, Manny was finally given some clothes. Donated by a kindly wireless operator well over six feet tall, they enveloped Manny but were none the less welcome for that. Then they were taken to the warmth and safety of the wardroom, where Manny finally began to relax from his ordeal: 'We [were] all joking, we said, "oh well that's OK, we're OK now, we'll be OK in a minute." . . . I saw the steward come in with the tray in his hand and the teapot, coming down to put [it] on the table, and the alarm went!'[10]

The escort had signalled that another E-boat was stalking the convoy.

> I said, 'well this is it, it's only a matter of time' and I mean that boat is doing about thirty-five knots . . . we could do maximum of seven or eight. I was told

> then to go on deck and pass ammunition to the gun in the back. And then we doubled the men in the engine room, instead of two we had four, all you could hear . . . was the shovels shoveling the coal and the smoke coming up, and we were going like a lizard you know, instead of going straight we [zigzagged]. And then we waited for the bridge, we loaded the gun . . . and suddenly we were told to fire the gun and we fired . . . and I was passing . . . the shells into the gun. We went on for some time, maybe half an hour, maybe more, I don't know, because this torpedo boat was really catching up on us. But with a bit of luck that English destroyer who went a long way away after the [first] torpedo boat, he must have heard the gun or seen the flash because he was coming back to see what was happening and I think . . . the E-boat people must have seen the warship as well and decided it's time to go and they turned around and went back.[11]

Thankfully this was the end of the battle for Manny Raud. The following day he was landed in Hartlepool and handed over to the care of the Red Cross. Returning to sea in the coaster *L'Armenier,* he spent another year in the merchant service on coastal convoys before joining the Free French Navy in 1942. He married a British girl and settled in England after the war.

Manny's story has a happy postscript. According to Captain Lovarn's official report, Michel the donkeyman's cries for help were heard from the lifeboat. After handing thirteen of his crew over to the trawler *Kingston Olivine*, Lovarn turned the boat back to try and help him. When he returned to the *Daphné* he discovered that Michel had already been rescued by men from the destroyer HMS *Versatile,* who managed to pull him through the porthole.[12]

The *Daphné* herself could not be allowed to sink in the narrow congested waters of the 'war channel', the east coast convoy route which ran between the shore and the miles of British defensive minefields. The *Kingston Olivine* fixed a tow and she was painstakingly hauled inshore, eventually being beached at Cleethorpes.

This is just one story from the coastal convoys. By the end of the war more than 100,000 had been made from the Thames Estuary to Scottish ports and back again, plodding painfully through the dangerous waters of the east coast. Still more had braved the hazards of the English Channel. Hundreds were sunk or damaged, victims of attack by German aircraft, mines, E-boats and submarines. Over the years, historians have written of spectacular convoy battles in the Atlantic, or the grim Arctic convoys to Russia and the desperate efforts to get supplies through to the besieged island of Malta. But little attention has been given to what Captain Stephen Roskill, the official historian of the war at sea, has called 'the absolute necessity to maintain the flow of shipping up and down the east coast and . . . along the English Channel'.[13]

Richard Woodman, one of the foremost historians of the Merchant Navy during the Second World War, has written that 'the coasters' war was as gruelling as that in the Atlantic' and is 'one of the many disregarded elements in Britain's maritime struggle'.[14] But why were these ships and men forced to run this gauntlet at all? The coastwise trade was not the source of tanks, guns and aircraft from the United States, or food and manpower from the colonies. The answer is simple but far from exotic. Mostly it was all about coal.

Notes

1 Imperial War Museum Sound Record (henceforth IWM Sound) 20135 Raud, Emmanuel.
2 Ibid.
3 Ibid.
4 Ibid.
5 Ibid.
6 Ibid.
7 Ibid.
8 Ibid. The 'donkeyman' operated a small auxiliary steam boiler known as a 'donkey boiler'. This was used to supply steam to machinery used when the ship was in harbour and the main boilers were shut down.
9 Ibid.
10 Ibid.
11 Ibid.
12 National Archives (henceforth NA) ADM 199/2136 Survivors' Reports: Merchant Vessels 1 March 1941 to 30 April 1941
13 Roskill, Captain S.W., *The War at Sea*, vol. I, HMSO, London, 1954, p. 321.
14 Woodman, Richard, *The Real Cruel Sea: the Merchant Navy in the Battle of the Atlantic 1939–1943*, John Murray, London, 2004, pp. 57–8.

Chapter 1

Time and Tide: British Coastal Trade

Dirty British coaster with a salt-caked smoke-stack
Butting through the Channel in the mad March days,
With a cargo of Tyne coal,
Road-rail, pig-lead,
Firewood, iron-ware, and cheap tin toys.

John Masefield, 'Cargoes', 1903

Despite her small size and relatively unchallenging topography, Britain had always been a prisoner of her geography.

In the north lay the great resource centres, the most important of which for our story was coal. In 1924 there were 2,481 mines in Britain. Some were in the Midlands, but these were relatively new fields, immature industries not yet being exploited to their full potential. Far more important were the fields of Scotland, Durham and Northumberland, which formed the 'Great North Coalfield', the filthy, noisy, pulsating heart of the north-east. 'Few industries were more characteristically British, whether one considers the wide distribution of the coal fields, the numbers employed, or the position which coal occupied in the internal and external trade of the country.'[1]

Far away to the south lay the busy ports and population centres. Around forty-five ports benefited from the extraordinary riches of the north-east, but foremost amongst them was London, the single largest consumption point for not only fuel, but also foodstuffs and raw materials. The capital's appetite for coal was voracious and ever expanding. Between 1700 and 1936 London's coal need increased from a modest 500,000 tons a year to a staggering 10,250,000 tons for her gas, electricity, water, sewage, transportation and hydraulic power.[2]

The only way this volume of supplies could be met was by using the sea. Britain is a small irregularly shaped island with a high proportion of coastline to land mass. This coastline is broken up by an impressive range of navigable rivers penetrating deep inland. From the earliest of times this combination had made coastal shipping an economically attractive means of moving goods around the country. As early as 1776, Adam Smith wrote in

The Wealth of Nations that: 'It required only six or eight men to bring by water to London the same quantity of goods which would otherwise require fifty broad wheeled wagons driven by a hundred men and drawn by four hundred horses.'[3]

Professor T.S. Willan wrote in 1938 that the sea was 'merely a river around England, a river with peculiar dangers, peculiar traditions and peculiar advantages'.[4] By the time he wrote this, the east coast coal traffic had dominated trade on this 'river' for two centuries. Two thirds of coasters transported coal, and many of the east coast ports carried out little or no direct foreign trade at all. Even the coming of the canals and later the railways, which revolutionized inland transport, made only limited inroads into the importance of the coaster, although the flashy newcomers have perhaps resulted in the humble little ships being underestimated or ignored in accounts of the development of the transport network during this period.

Life on the colliers was hard and demanding. Coal was a filthy cargo, as the following account of 'coaling ship' by John Batten, the radio operator on one Second World War collier, vividly illustrates:

> What the devil is that racket? I jump out of my bunk, where I've slept a long comfortable sleep until 7:30 a.m., and peer out of my door. I am driven back by swirling clouds of coal dust, rising from the after holds, and already depositing a layer of dirt on my paintwork. There's a noise like a ton of rock bouncing on a corrugated iron roof, men shouting, trucks rumbling up overhead. I pull my door to quickly. We're a collier now. Half an hour later I'm brought a cup of tea. It has a skin of dust on top. When I walk along the boatdeck to go down to the saloon I leave footprints in the coal dust already thickly settled there . . . There's coal in our porridge, and in our steak and potatoes . . . In the galley the thick canvas blackout curtains are drawn, and the cook is wiping the sweat from his face, but he has time to point to a layer of coal-dust lying on a joint of beef. He shakes his head: 'It's everywhere,' he says, finally, hopelessly.[5]

William Hopper was a seaman on a collier before the war: 'We used to sleep, eat, live in coal dust and we used to get what we called "trimmers' eyes", which was your eyes get black on the lids, and if we were going ashore we used to spend hours rubbing butter on to try to get rid of [it].[6]

One consequence of this environment was that coal was a specialist cargo. A collier covered in coal dust could hardly be filled with fresh fruit on the way back north, and colliers invariably returned home empty, or 'in ballast' – carrying makeweight loads like stones purely to stabilise the ship. This meant that work on the colliers was tough economically as well as physically, with all profits having to be made on a one-way cargo, ideally with money left over to buy ballast for the return voyage.

By 1939, coastal shipping had already been through some severe trials.

Most recent had been the suffering endured during the Great Depression of 1929–36. Heavy industry during this period was highly interdependent, and one of the most catastrophically hit was coal mining, upon which the coaster men depended for their livelihood. Ships were laid up and their crews dispersed to the dole queues, to join the men from the coal mines, steel mills and shipyards. The closure of shipyards in turn resulted in no new coasters being built for many years. Engineer William Lind was lucky enough to be working during this period, but the minority of employed men were sometimes ruthlessly exploited:

> My first coaster was the SS *Jolly Guy* of Watford Lines. I had to take my watch, be my own greaser and also fireman, and dump my own ashes on six-hour watches. In the end I had to pack the job in . . . shipping was in the doldrums. No stipulated regulations governed working hours . . . annual leave and sick leave were unknown quantities. If you asked for leave of any description you took the sack with it.[7]

Henry Fellingham was a sixteen-year-old apprentice with the Cardiff-based shipping company E.T. Radcliffe at the height of the Depression in 1934. Conditions were almost unbelievably harsh. He was paid just £5 for his first year of work, rising to a paltry £8 for his second, £12 for his third and £15 for his fourth. From this subsistence allowance, National Insurance payments were deducted.

Food on board was appalling, particularly on long voyages:

> The food was really very poor. For one thing we had no ice box, no refrigerator, and we used to carry about three days . . . fresh meat and after that you went on salt tack [salted beef and pork], which is not much different to sailing ship days, so it was a tough company, and I think my father actually put me in it to break me, because he didn't want me to go to sea really.[8]

Although in theory a trainee officer, Henry was taught almost nothing, and used as cheap labour throughout his apprenticeship: 'The only time I ever got into the chart room was to scrub the deck.'[9] He was frequently ordered to work unpaid overtime, and on his first trip to sea Henry fell into the hold and broke his hip, an injury which forced him ashore for six months. Despite these hardships, almost incomprehensible to the modern reader, Henry actually enjoyed his life: 'We enjoyed ourselves in that we had no real responsibilities, we were all young, we were healthy, and although the food was so bad it was surprising how healthy we were.'[10]

The injustices heaped on merchant sailors like Henry Fellingham, whether in coastal or deep waters, are too many to list here.[11] One alone should, perhaps, be singled out for attention: the pay of a merchant seaman stopped as soon as his ship was sunk. Dreadful enough in peacetime, in wartime this practice was undoubtedly what Richard Woodman has called 'a scandalous abuse and appalling injustice'.[12]

The industrial recovery sparked in part by rearmament brought salvation for the coastal trade, and by the outbreak of the Second World War it had gone a long way towards resuming its traditional, understated importance.

The ships of this trade were incredibly varied. Some were substantial cargo vessels – 'liners' in the true sense of the word in that they spent their working lives making regular trips from one port to another, following the same 'line' week after week. These were not colliers; they carried general cargo and even passengers – the most obvious examples in coastal waters were the ferries to the continent, Ireland, and the Isle of Man. Some were small versions of the ocean cargo liners, well equipped and appointed, operated by larger companies which provided uniforms for officers. Others were far smaller and more basic.

Further down the coaster pecking order were the 'tramp' ships, so called not because of their unkempt appearance but because they 'tramped' from port to port picking up bulk cargo where they could find it. Invariably in coastal waters this was coal, but within the limitations of this dirty cargo they would carry other materials when they could: cement, stone and grain were other favourites. Tramps came in all shapes and sizes – older ships were steam powered, abbreviated to 'SS' in the ship's title, newer models tended to be diesel-engined motor vessels (MV). By 1939 small coastal fuel tankers were also starting to appear.

But by far the most common ships in coastal waters were the purpose-built colliers. One contemporary account paints a vivid picture of these charismatic little ships:

> Any description covering them all is impossible, yet there is a type that is very common. A squat tubby little ship, somewhere between 150 feet and 250 feet in length, with a low fo'c'sle, bridge amidships and engines right aft. Between the fo'c'sle and the bridge there is little freeboard. At sea the decks seem to be awash and, indeed, in rough weather, they are . . . from end to end of the gaping holds there is no obstruction to delay the stevedores – nothing to impede the grabs with which coal is usually discharged.[13]

Colliers on the return leg frequently sailed without ballast, a consequence of the slender profit margins of many coastal shipping concerns. The engines were placed right aft in the forlorn hope that the weight would force the screw down into the water even when empty, but despite this many colliers were appalling sea boats:

> She . . . 'milestoned' continually. This was an alarming phenomenon caused by the bow rising and the stern being kept down by the weight aft and the drag of the screw causing the bow to hang in the air and finally come down, not in

the trough but across the next wave. This jarred her from stem to stern and was just like striking solid rock. The credulous newcomer to the coast was told that there were actual milestones in the channel as an aid to navigation and the ship was continually scraping over them.[14]

Accommodation on these basic little ships left much to be desired although the usual courtesies of rank were observed as far as possible: officers had tiny cabins to themselves whilst crew shared a crowded mess. Official accounts tend to be stoic:

> These quarters, reached by steep narrow ladders, are not spacious, but there is room to move in them when men have acquired the habit of living in confined spaces. Getting around the table in the messroom in order to sit down may sometimes not be easy. Tall men must move their heads warily. The stoves are capable of producing the temperature desired but in warm weather ventilation is difficult.[15]

William Merryweather served on a small collier with typically challenging accommodation:

> The SS *Kylebank* . . . she was a small coaler of 600 tons . . . we were stationed right in the bow, we had a coal stove, there was very little room to move about and you virtually had to be stripped out to manage to live in there. [It was] like living in a greenhouse with the heat on. [16]

Perhaps the most damning indictment of coaster accommodation comes from an anonymous Trinity House pilot working on the east coast, who was deeply shocked at what he found and saw no reason to hide his disgust from a visiting journalist:

> I've seen slums ashore . . . but until I started this job I'd never seen slums at sea, having always been in well-found deep water ships . . . Slums ashore are bad, but slums at sea are worse . . . I could never have believed that men should live in such conditions. They destroy the men's self respect, until they don't care how they live . . . The ship owners are at fault. The coasting vessels are the worst, but it's bad in some of the deep-water tramps too. The public have no idea of the situation.[17]

Perhaps the most distinctive of the coastal colliers were the so-called 'flat-irons', purpose-built ships with low silhouettes, hinged funnels and telescopic masts to allow them to pass under London's bridges and go further upriver than normal ships: 'Long, low colliers with hardly any bridge to them like barges with engines. They have a big carrying capacity, and are dreadfully uncomfortable in rough weather. On their little bridge you're smothered with spray on a windy day, and in a storm it's much worse.'[18]

Capable of no general description were those vessels lumped together as 'estuarial craft', small boats capable of carrying cargo far upriver but also capable of going to sea in coastal waters. Mostly these were small motor vessels or motorized barges. Perhaps the most romantic were the Thames spritsail barges, graceful sailing workhorses, a few of which can still be seen making their stately way upriver loaded with corporate party-goers.

Some coastal shipping lines were large businesses. The Kent-based shipping firm F.T. Everard and Sons operated a fleet of coasters and small tankers before the Second World War, many sporting the company's eccentric themed names ending in 'ity': *Asperity, Angularity, Summity, Sincerity* and so forth. Others were much smaller firms, and some were simply single shipowner-operator concerns. William Merryweather's *Kylebank* was a typical family run collier:

> There was only about half a dozen on the boat, four of which were the same family, the other was a cook and the other was a chap that had been attached to us as a crew member . . . the family were Welsh . . . We travelled mainly from Plymouth to the Thames to pick up cement to take to Newcastle, from where we took coal on up to Leith, the port of Edinburgh.[19]

The story of the coastal convoys is not just one of coasters. Other participants will enter and leave the narrative. Ocean-going freighters were forced by circumstances to enter the narrow seas, and the testimonies of those who manned them will be found here. The men of the fishing fleet also found themselves caught up in the coastal battle, and their stories will appear from time to time, as will those of the soldiers, sailors and airmen who fought to protect the convoys, and occasionally those who fought to destroy them. But at the heart of the story, always, lie the little coasters, and the men who served in them. What sort of men were they? In a nutshell, they were as diverse as their ships:

> The men of the coasters are of a type. Some have come in middle age from the deep seas. Many more served their time in deep-sea ships but have returned to the coast on which they were bred. Not a few, particularly in the smaller tramps and estuarial craft, have served in narrow waters all their lives. Whether they have come to it to be nearer their homes and families, have left it only temporarily to gain wider experience, or have never left it, the coast sets its mark on them. They think in terms of tides. Their lives are ruled by tides. Their prosperity, their domestic plans, their standing with their fellows, are influenced by catching tides or missing them.[20]

Some coaster men spent their lives trading only between the ports of the British Isles. Others took part in what was known as the 'home trade', working in and out of ports on the Continent, across the other side of the Channel or the North Sea. Whatever their speciality, most stuck to the same route, year on year. The routine attracted them, and the short journeys: 'they follow the sea, but they go no more a-roving.'[21]

This predictable routine inspired a degree of contempt from their fellow seafarers. Coasters were known derisively as 'weekly boats' by sailors in big ocean-going freighters, as their crews only signed on 'articles' for a week at a time – the Articles of Agreement were the nearest thing a merchant sailor had to a contract. John Batten joined his coaster straight from a deep-sea ship:

> I'd seen lots of coasters in my few years at sea. Each time I'd been down the North Sea I'd seen them, small, mostly dirty and rusty, slow, smoking like anything . . . 'Scufflers' we used to scornfully call them. We'd look down on their rusty decks as we passed, supreme on our elevated main-deck, often nearly as high as their funnel. We'd see the un-uniformed officers on the bridge, maybe a man in a shiny suit and a bowler hat. 'Scruffy little coaster' we'd say.[22]

What many deep-water sailors completely failed to appreciate was the degree of skill required for coastal seamanship. J.W. Booth, a naval signalman serving on coastal colliers during the Second World War, recalled the coaster men dealing with patronizing comments in typically robust style:

> Deep sea men professed to despise coasters, the traditional jibe being 'what do you do if you lose sight of the land?' The answer was 'the same as you do if you see it. Shit myself.' I never saw a coaster officer on the sea but deep sea men on the coast were usually nervous wrecks.[23]

The deep-water sailor may have had to master the glamorous black arts of astronavigation, but he only navigated the treacherous waters of the tidal estuary or the shallow harbour mouth at the beginning and end of his journey, and when he did so he had a local pilot to help him. Such tricky, potentially fatal, inshore navigation was bread and butter for the coaster man, who often had to act as his own pilot:

> The master of a coaster probably has fewer people to help him than any other master mariner. He is nearly always in waters requiring very careful navigation. In the ports, which he enters or leaves every few days, his ship is commonly assigned the most inaccessible berth, so that his ability to handle her is being continually tested . . . he must bring his ship up crowded rivers, swing her in just sufficient space, and fit her smoothly . . . between two other ships into a space of quay no more than a foot or two above her length. He

> must do this by day and night and very frequently . . . no man remains the master of a coaster unless he is master of the art of handling ships.[24]

Foul weather was another occupational hazard in coastal waters. Thick fog in the Channel or North Sea could bring careers, and lives, rapidly to an end, and sometimes the coaster men were faced with no alternative but to anchor until it passed. It was not uncommon for them to wait for hours or even days at a time before it was safe to proceed. John Batten was fog-bound for forty hours:

> The quietness of the morning, accentuated by the fog, is broken. A couple of score anchors splash into the shallow coastal water, their chains ripping over the windlasses and shattering the silence. We can't go any further until the fog clears. The whole convoy is waiting now for the blanket that covers the North Sea to lift . . . The sun had gone, the sea was a flat light grey calm. Soon the dark shapes that had been ships ahead and astern of us faded out. We were quite alone in the fog.[25]

Winter gales in the North Sea, too, were as bad as anything that deep waters had to offer, as J.W. Booth recalled:

> On one trip we had a full gale from the north west and took three days to reach the Tyne instead of the usual thirty-six hours. We were on a 3,000-ton collier with the engine aft and she pitched heavily in a big head sea. From midnight to 4am one night I only logged one buoy. They were only about five miles apart, but with the wind and tide against us a speed of some eight knots through the water was only about one and a bit over the ground, and we were virtually bouncing up and down in the same hole.[26]

Foul weather, of course, was not restricted to coastal waters, but the deep-water sailor at least had the option of 'riding it out' in open water – the coaster man was never more than a few miles from some hazardous stretch of coastline.

Specialists were few and far between in the coasters. Many would only carry engineers, working twelve-hour shifts alone in their gloomy caverns, tending noisy, stinking and often elderly and temperamental machinery. Some ships carried no cook, and the ship's company were expected to buy and prepare their own food – many 'went to sea with a pie and a pint [or] . . . lived out of a frying pan, mainly on eggs and bacon'.[27]

Often, the only man with a sprinkling of semi-formal navigation and signals training would be the Captain, and even he could not be relied upon to be so equipped. In one early east coast convoy it was found that one very experienced captain could not read Morse code; another skipper, when hailed, 'said he did not know how to signal'.[28]

This, then, was the coastal shipping trade before the Second World War – an eclectic mix of ships and at times an unconventional group of men, about to be thrown into the maelstrom of total war. The coaster men were no strangers to war. For as long as there had been coastal shipping, the trade and its skilled seamen had always been a strategic asset, valued and threatened in equal measure in wartime. As early as 1691 the men of the colliers were immune from the attentions of the dreaded Press Gang, despite the resulting protests from the Navy about being deprived of such fine seamen.[29] According to one account, in 1800 the Admiralty described the men of the colliers as 'the finest seamen under the British flag and their life . . . the hardest known to the seas'.[30]

In 1778 the coastal coal trade was famously subjected to the unwelcome attentions of the American naval hero John Paul Jones, who during his country's War of Independence attempted to enter the Cumbrian port of Whitehaven and set fire to several hundred colliers lying at anchor there. No evidence exists that anything other than minor damage was done, and it has been suggested that Jones and his men were more interested in infiltrating the defences of a local inn rather than the harbour, but the fact remains that the humble colliers were seen as a worthwhile target.[31]

The First World War saw the trade's greatest trial yet: the first systematic attempt to destroy British coastal trade using that formidable new weapon of the industrial age, the submarine. This is not the place for a detailed examination of the long and complex war fought between the Royal Navy and Germany's U-boats during the First World War. It peaked between February and April 1917, when well over a million tons of British merchant shipping – more than 500 ships – was sunk, much of it in coastal waters.[32]

For coastal trade, the importance of the First World War lies in the measures which were put in place to take the advantage away from the U-boats. The new weapons and tactics which were developed would eventually ensure not only that the U-boats were defeated in the First World War, but also that British coastal waters would become a 'no-go' area for them for much of the Second.

The introduction of convoys – steaming merchant vessels in groups escorted by warships – was the first and most important development, although their adoption was a gradual process. Convoys had been used with some success in earlier wars; however it was felt in some quarters that the poor station-keeping of merchant skippers might lead to collisions and losses, that there were insufficient escorts, that any prowling U-boat would be treated to what modern tacticians would call a 'target-rich' environment, and that it was too defensive a tactic.

However as 1917 went by a number of factors made convoys a more practical option, and support for their introduction began to grow. Most importantly, merchant ship production had begun to increase dramatically and still more ships had been begged, borrowed or stolen, with former hulks and superannuated sailing vessels being salvaged from the scrapheap and pressed into service. Policy makers felt more confident that if a convoy was attacked and destroyed or lost ships due to collisions, the losses could be made good almost immediately.

Extra escorts were also available – first destroyers transferred from the battle fleet, then American destroyers based in Ireland, and other small ships built specifically for anti-submarine work. Any U-boat encountering a convoy would be sure of a warm reception. After trials in the spring, regular convoys were organized in late May. Even so this was initially applied only to ocean traffic and it was not until early 1918 that coastal traffic started to be so organized as well. Increasingly frustrated U-boat commanders started to find themselves staring out across empty waters.

Having taken the necessary steps to protect shipping, the Allies started to look at ways of striking back. At the beginning of the war any submarine had been difficult to find, and a submerged submarine had been almost impossible to attack. By the war's final year a *smorgasbord* of new technology had made them increasingly vulnerable and twenty-four U-boats were sunk between August and October 1918.[33]

Mines were used in ever greater numbers, a huge field being deployed across the entrances to German North Sea naval bases. Another, the Dover Barrage, was sown across the Straits of Dover. Poor-quality mines and inefficient laying meant it was some time before it became effective, but the concept was basically sound and eventually led to twelve U-boats being sunk between November 1917 and May 1918. This effectively closed the Straits to all but the most determined U-boat commander.[34] Another field, the more ambitious but less effective Northern Barrage, was strung out between the Orkneys and the Norwegian coast. Further coastal fields served to protect British ports and coastal shipping.

Shore-based direction-finding stations tracked U-boat movements by taking bearings on their radio transmissions. Underwater microphones known as hydrophones were deployed to find submarines, and a new variation on the mine which could be deployed in response to a contact and fused to go off at a pre-set depth was being fitted to escort ships. This device was, of course, eventually christened the depth charge. At first these were simply dropped over the side; later, throwing devices became common.

Aeroplanes and airships were deployed against U-boats in ever greater numbers. During the last six months of the war, nearly 600 aircraft of all types flew 83,807 hours on patrol. They sighted 167 U-boats, and attacked 115.[35] Although they rarely sank one, U-boat commanders soon learned to keep a healthy distance (or more accurately depth) from their unwelcome attentions.

Finally, ASDIC submarine-detection equipment, which detected the range and depth of a submerged submarine by bouncing soundwaves off its hull, producing the 'ping' beloved of Hollywood, made its first appearance at the end of 1918.[36] Sinking submerged U-boats was still very difficult, but it was becoming easier to force them down and keep them down, and a submerged submarine being stalked by warships was virtually impotent.

The general pattern of shipping losses to the end of the First World War was one of steady decline. Conversely, U-boat losses started to rise. The crisis was past. On 11 November 1918 the Armistice was declared and Germany's submarines surrendered. Britain's coastal shipping had passed its first great test.

This brief overview was never intended to be a detailed account of the war against the U-boats in 1914–1918. It merely gives a flavour of it, and perhaps serves to point out that the coaster men were no strangers to war. Indeed, such was the age of many of them that in 1939 a proportion would almost certainly have served in the earlier conflict. However, before this story moves on, it is important to re-emphasize the vital lessons which had been learned.

Firstly, and most importantly, convoys were seen as the 'magic bullet', the obvious and immediate panacea to a submarine offensive should Europe fall into another conflict. Never again would Britain suffer such a fatal delay in introducing them in waters within reach of the U-boats.

Secondly, the Royal Navy was confident that offensive tactics based around new equipment developed at the end of the First World War, particularly ASDIC, could make coastal waters a virtual no-go area for U-boats. Lamentably, the vital contribution of aircraft to this success was rather overlooked once the war had ended.

Thirdly, the Straits of Dover could be barred by an effective mine barrage stretched between the friendly shore on either side, forcing U-boats to pass around the north of Scotland to reach their patrol areas and making the Channel a safe haven for shipping.

These deductions were doubtless true. Unfortunately, the predators in the new conflict would be very different indeed, but whatever the threat, the coasters had no choice but to keep on plodding along their well-worn paths up and down the North Sea and the Channel. Transporting goods by sea in 1939 was not some sort of luxury add-on, easily supplanted by other methods when danger loomed. The sea had been an essential part of Britain's internal communications network for hundreds of years and alternatives were not easy to find. Certainly the rail and road networks of the day could not have coped with such a sudden and dramatic increase in the amount of freight to be carried.

Shipping simply had to get through. The 'river around England' was about to be transformed into the 'indestructible highway'.

Notes

1. Hancock, W.K. (ed.), *UK Civil Series – Coal*, HMSO, London, 1976, p. 10.
2. Ibid., p. 34.
3. Hewitt, Terry, M.Ed, unpublished lecture notes on coastal shipping (henceforth Hewitt, *Coastal Shipping*), pp. 1-3.

4. Willan, Professor T.S., *The English Coasting Trade 1600–1750*, Manchester, 1938, quoted in Hewitt, *Coastal Shipping*.
5. Batten, John, *Dirty Little Collier*, Hutchinson, London, undated, pp. 13–14.
6. IWM Sound 10800: Hopper, William.
7. IWM Docs 99/43/1: Lind, W.
8. IWM Sound 11509: Fellingham, Henry.
9. Ibid.
10. Ibid.
11. Richard Woodman's magnificent *The Real Cruel Sea: The Merchant Navy in the Battle of the Atlantic 1939–1943*, John Murray, London, 2004, contains fascinating detail about the life of the merchant sailor before and during the Second World War.
12. Woodman, *The Real Cruel Sea* p. 30. It should probably be pointed out that if they worked for a good employer on board a modern ship, merchant seamen might stand a chance of being paid more and enjoying better living conditions than their Royal Navy equivalents. This was, however, by no means guaranteed.
13. *British Coaster 1939–1945*, HMSO, 1947, p. 15.
14. *IWM Docs 91/17/1: Booth, J.W.*, p. 18.
15. *British Coaster 1939–1945*, p. 17.
16. IWM Sound 1250: Merryweather, William.
17. IWM Docs 85/10/1 Rutter, Major O., p. 72.
18. Batten, *Dirty Little Collier*, p. 33.
19. IWM Sound 1250: Merryweather, William.
20. *British Coaster 1939–1945*, p. 6.
21. Ibid., p. 7.
22. Batten, *Dirty Little Collier*, p. 7.
23. IWM Docs 91/17/1 Booth, J.W., p. 27.
24. *British Coaster 1939–1945*, pp. 6–7.
25. Batten, *Dirty Little Collier*, p. 73.
26. IWM Docs 91/17/1; Booth, J.W., p. 18.
27. *British Coaster 1939–1945*, p. 10.
28. Foynes, J.P., *Battle of the East Coast*, published by the author, 1994, p. 8.
29. Rodger, N.A.M., *The Command of the Ocean*, Penguin, London, 2005, p. 207.
30. *British Coaster 1939–1945*, p. 5.
31. See the BBC television programme *Coast*, first aired 4 July 2007, BBC1.
32. Terraine, John, *Business in Great Waters*, Wordsworth, Ware, 1999, p. 17. German submarines were known as *Unterseebooten*, or 'under sea boats'. This was abbreviated by both sides to 'U-boat'.
33. Grove, Eric J. (ed.), *The Defeat of the Enemy Attack on Shipping 1939–1945*, London, Navy Records Society, 1997, p. 5.
34. Ibid., p. 13.
35. Ibid., pp. 7–8.

36. ASDIC was supposedly an acronym for the Anti-Submarine Detection Investigation Committee. However no evidence for such a body has ever been found and the definition was apparently made up by the Admiralty in response to a question by the Oxford English Dictionary in 1939. Today the technology is known as sonar.

Chapter 2
Storm Clouds

1939

When war finally came, on 3 September 1939, it followed months of increased tension, and for many it was no surprise. Britain was well prepared for the war she thought she was going to have to fight in coastal waters. Believing that it would be essentially a replay of 1914–1918, a number of factors were assumed and were, to be fair, perfectly applicable at the beginning of the war. France was an ally and the French coast could reasonably be assumed to be friendly. As in 1914–1918, therefore, the Channel could be closed to hostile shipping with relative ease by stretching mines and barriers from one friendly shore to another. Mines and patrolling warships – the 'Northern Patrol' – could close or at least interdict the northern exits from the North Sea as well. U-boats, the principle perceived threat, could be defeated by introducing convoys at the earliest opportunity, equipping merchant ships to defend themselves as far as possible, and by the aggressive use of technology developed during the earlier conflict, notably escorts equipped with depth charges and ASDIC. These were the building blocks of trade protection in coastal waters and Britain began to assemble them as soon as she could.

The Convoys

Above all else, the most important building block for the protection of merchant shipping was placing it in convoys. In anticipation of this, as early as 26 August merchant shipping was placed under Admiralty control. It is important to realize that this did not give the government the right to determine routes or cargoes. Merchant shipping was still a privately owned and run industry, and Britain's economic survival was dependent on the continuation of trade. Shipping required for military purposes still had to be chartered by the government or purchased directly by the Ministry of Shipping, which was later merged with the Ministry of Transport to become the Ministry of War Transport in 1941.[1]

However the new powers did give the Admiralty the all-important authority to place ships in convoy, whether their owners liked it or not. Specifically, the administration of merchant shipping was carried out by the Trade Division of the Admiralty, who organized escorts, routes and orders for convoys. To facilitate this, the Trade Division installed Naval Control Service (NCS) officers with small staffs in all ports used by United Kingdom shipping, wherever in the world, before the outbreak of war. In some cases, the authoritative title of 'Naval Control Service' implied a grandeur far removed from the truth. John Batten remembered reporting to one NCS office in the north-east:

> Naval Control has two small, bare rooms over a sweet shop in a side street of the town. There were two Lieutenant Commanders there, one about sixty, the other younger. They handed me the route and late information about the navigational warnings and so on, and the ship's clearance certificate. It all seemed pretty bleak and remote from some of the Naval Control places I've seen, where the best rooms in all the good hotels have been taken over and red-faced Commanders and Sub-Lieutenants lounge in well padded armchairs with an army of Wrens to do their bidding.[2]

This 'army of Wrens' was the Womens' Royal Naval Service, or WRNS. One member was 2nd Officer Penny Martin, who in 1940 found herself somewhat reluctantly working for the NCS rather than in some more adventurous field:

> When asked if I could type, I foolishly said, 'Oh yes and I can take shorthand too!' which instantly decided my future. 'Ah!' the recruiter said, 'Then of course you'll be a writer' and added that probably I'd be sent to Yeovilton or St Merryn in Cornwall, where a new Fleet Air Arm Station was opening up. So I returned home and waited, and waited. I saw the dentist – had a physical . . . collected clothes . . . I finally got my draft notice on 18 July and the next day I set out to join the Navy – but not to St Merryn (which still wasn't completed) but to the Royal Navy College at Dartmouth, where I was to be secretary to the Naval Control Service Officer – a 'dugout' Navy Lieutenant Commander called Dodgson.[3]

The first convoys began on the east coast. We have already seen how maintaining the supply of coal was a vital requirement, not a luxury, and by 1939 the capital alone needed a minimum 40,000 tons of coal per week. Although the management of the railways believed that in wartime the needs of London and the south could be met by their network, this expectation, in the understated words of one official history of the period, 'turned out to be ill-founded'.[4] Neither was road transport up to the task: in 1939 the so-called 'Great North Road' was just a two-lane highway funnelling through congested mediaeval market towns. And so the scruffy, hard-worked little

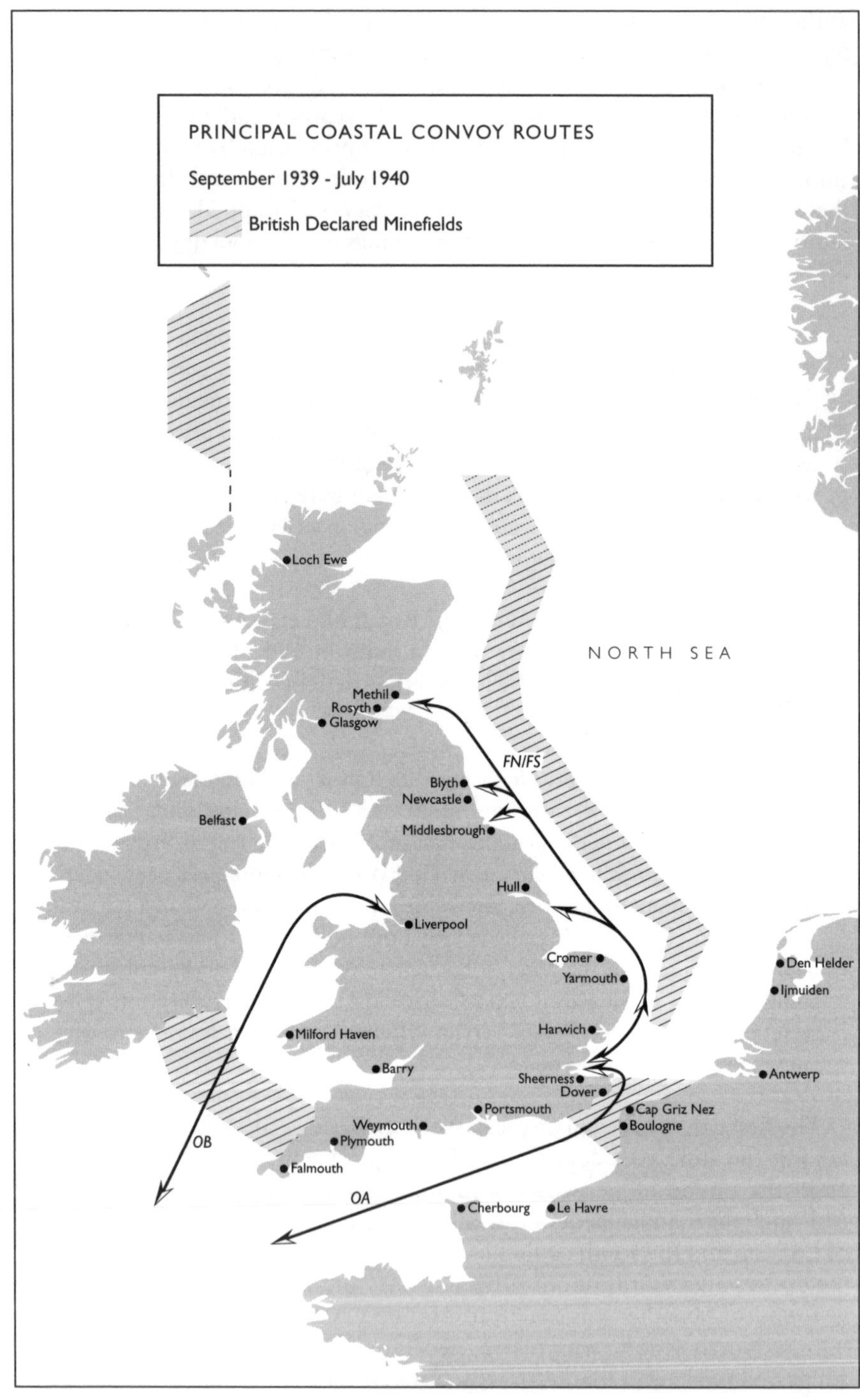
PRINCIPAL COASTAL CONVOY ROUTES
September 1939 - July 1940
British Declared Minefields
NORTH SEA
Loch Ewe
Methil
Rosyth
Glasgow
FN/FS
Blyth
Newcastle
Middlesbrough
Belfast
Hull
Liverpool
Cromer
Yarmouth
Den Helder
Ijmuiden
Harwich
Milford Haven
Barry
Sheerness
Dover
Antwerp
Portsmouth
Cap Griz Nez
Boulogne
Weymouth
Plymouth
OB
Falmouth
OA
Cherbourg
Le Havre

colliers were organized for defence in anticipation of a renewed U-boat threat identical to that faced down and ultimately defeated in 1918. It was time to build the 'indestructible highway'.

The southern convoy assembly area was the Thames Estuary, off Southend, where the famous pier was taken over by the Royal Navy 'for the duration' and the Naval Control Service headquarters was established in a row of houses on Royal Terrace, which overlooked it. Naval personnel found local billets, which on the whole were good, as Signalman J.W. Booth remembered: 'Many of our hostesses were seaside landladies and, as Southend was closed to casual visitors at the time, it was us or nothing and most of them made the best of a bad job.' [5]

In the north the ships formed up off Methil, a coal port on the Firth of Forth, where the locals were equally generous to their unexpected guests:

> In Methil on the Forth we were in civvy billets, easily the best I ever had. The landladies there were miners' wives, many with sons also down the pit, and although taking in sailors was surely unprofitable the way they treated us, they regarded it as their war effort . . . On one occasion a couple of our lads were being barracked a bit by some noisy locals. Before they could react their host stepped across and floored the noisiest one remarking with an air of finality 'that'll be enough about Sassenachs, these lads are wi' me!'[6]

As the east coast convoys started and finished in the Forth, they were designated 'FN' (Forth-North) or 'FS' (Forth-South) convoys. Each convoy had its own individual number, and each series of numbers started again after 100.[7] Ships joined from, or departed to, various ports as the convoy made its way along the coast, and the number of ships which finished a 'run' was rarely the same as the number which started.

The desperate need for coal meant that the east coast convoys were run on an incredibly tight turnaround from the very beginning, with two FN and two FS convoys expected to be at sea at any given time. For operational purposes they were given reusable codes: Agent and Arena for the southbound convoys and Booty and Pilot for the northbound.[8] The first FN and FS convoys assembled off Methil and Southend on 6 September 1939, just three days after the outbreak of war.

Convoy work did not come easily to the independently minded merchant skippers, whose instincts tended to encourage them to stay as far from other ships as possible, not stick to them like glue. William Hopper was Merchant Navy through and through. He had been educated by the Trinity House Marine School in Hull and first went to sea at the age of fifteen. By 1939 he was a deck officer on the 6,500-ton SS *Larpool*:

> It was quite a thing to learn how to keep station in convoy; it's something we'd never done before. Maybe twenty, thirty ships, no lights, you're all right in the

daytime but in the night time when we changed watches on the bridge you had to be up with the other officer about fifteen minutes before his eyesight was used to the darkness and he could pick the ships out.[9]

Unlike the east coast, Channel waters were seen as relatively safe in 1939, within easy reach of friendly naval bases on both shores and constantly patrolled. The Thames Estuary was arguably the world's busiest seaway at the time, and the Port of London handled a third of British foreign trade – closing such a vital artery to traffic was inconceivable and unnecessary. So on 7 September, one day after the first east coast convoys, another series began from the Thames, steaming westbound through the Channel. The south coast convoys were coded 'OA', for 'outbound – Route A'. A parallel series, originating from Liverpool, were coded 'OB'. While an OA convoy remained in British waters, coasters would tag along like children following a circus parade, leaving and joining as the convoy passed the multitude of small ports which they served, enjoying the luxury of armed escort while they could. In the Channel, before the coasters left, the OA convoys could be huge, numbering as many as fifty ships.

OA convoys consisted only of ships capable of steaming between 9 knots and 14.9 knots. They were escorted as far as a point roughly 750 nautical miles west of Land's End and out of the anticipated U-boat danger area. Here they dispersed and ships proceeded independently to their various destinations.[10] Michael Marwood was a professional Royal Navy officer who had spent two years in the Mediterranean as a Midshipman, before returning to the UK to spend what should have been another year training as a Sub Lieutenant. The world crisis meant that instead, he was promoted to Acting Sub Lieutenant after just a few weeks and joined the destroyer HMS *Antelope* as Navigating Officer on 22 August 1939. At Portland twelve days later 'we received the message: "Special telegram TOTAL GERMANY" which meant we were at war.' *Antelope* escorted OA1 out to the Atlantic, a pretty amateurish affair:

Unlike the disciplined formations of later convoys with proper intercommunication facilities, the first convoys were just a rabble of ships steering in the same direction with us, while we, with our high speed, careered about protecting them, like a sheepdog with its flock. We rigged up a batch of messdeck loudspeakers and amplifiers in order to talk to the ships!'[11]

U-boats were the great, perhaps the only, concern in those early days: 'We dropped so many depth charges on targets detected by our Asdic equipment that might have been U-Boats but which were actually wrecks on the seabed, that we had to proceed to Portsmouth to restock.'[12]

It is important to realize that convoys were only a suitable defence against submarines, which were almost immobile under the water, and lightly armed and vulnerable above it. The First World War had shown how almost any purpose-built escort vessel (and better still, an effective aircraft) was capable of keeping a submarine down and even sinking it. As it was not possible to give every merchant ship an escort, grouping them together with the available warships made sense. Furthermore, U-boats then had to seek out the convoy, and thus, by default, its escort, exposing themselves to the risk of being sunk.

However, dispersing the merchant ships once the convoys had passed out of range of U-boats was an equally valid tactic. In 1939, the main threat in deep waters were the German Navy's surface raiders, of which the famous 'pocket battleships' were perhaps the best known.[13] For a surface raider, with its long-range heavy guns and high speed, a convoy and its lightly armed anti-submarine escort amounted to the same thing: targets. Better to force these lone wolves to expend precious fuel and supplies combing the seas for individual ships, than present them with twenty or thirty gift-wrapped with a destroyer or two thrown in for good measure.

The Commodores

Each convoy was controlled by a naval Commodore carried in one of the merchant ships, whose job was to try and ensure that the merchant skippers maintained the right speed and course and obeyed convoy instructions. These remarkable men and their staffs were another important building block of trade protection.

All volunteers, the commodores were either retired naval officers, or experienced merchant skippers, some of whom also held a rank in the Royal Naval Reserve (RNR). On the longer oceanic convoy routes that were eventually established to worldwide destinations, commodores were often former admirals of very advanced age, formidable individuals determined to help and prepared to take a drop in rank to 'do their bit'. The coastal convoys usually had to make do with a RNR Commander or Lieutenant Commander, invariably over sixty years of age and ineligible for a return to front-line duty.[14] The coaster men sometimes viewed them suspiciously as 'neither fish nor fowl', and worse, as extra bodies to accommodate and mouths to feed, and it could be hard to win their respect:

> Our old man keeps a private list of his own of Commodores, and stars them. Those who get the convoys up quickly have the most stars. The dawdlers, as he styles some of them, who are sticklers for a timetable and never a moment ahead of time, have one or no stars . . . it's a great topic among coasting skippers, the way convoys get north or south. They say Commodores are held in check by Admiralty officials who know little of the conditions, that valuable hours are wasted at sea when ships might be under the coal tips because of officialdom's insistence on keeping to their schedule.[15]

Undoubtedly it was hard for the more experienced (or irritable) coaster skippers to share their bridges with a stranger, particularly one with gold braid around his cuffs, and some did their best to make the newcomers feel unwelcome. Some commodores, however, were more than capable of giving the coaster skippers a run for their money in the truculence stakes, and surely won themselves a few friends amongst the coaster skippers in the process: 'One red bearded, piratical looking Commodore drafted [signals] like business letters . . . Once when an escort ventured to suggest that he was off course he made a polite reply beginning "My dear Sir, I would have you know that there are on this bridge at present no less than four master mariners."'[16]

On another occasion, when asked for his ETA (Estimated Time of Arrival), the same Commodore startled the Senior Officer Escort (SOE) with:

> I hope that we shall not be late,
> My sweetheart's waiting at the Gate,
> According to my ETA,
> We reach the boom at noon today.[17]

Each Commodore had a small staff of naval signalmen. These were often, like J.W. Booth, 'Hostilities Only' naval personnel who had signed up for the duration of the war. Given the circumstances they often arrived with very limited training and no experience:

> Technical training consisted of learning International Code flags and their significance in the Merchant Ships' Signals Book (Mersig). We also learned the Morse Code and the semaphore alphabet and did practical exercises reading a morse lamp at up to ten words a minute and semaphore at about twenty. The first half of each class was made with the Chief Yeoman facing the class and the second half with his back to us. One of our Chiefs was a fat man and as he wasn't that fussy about stretching out his arms one could just see two flags flapping about and not much else. He answered all complaints by saying that if you could read his semaphore you could read anyone's.[18]

DEMS

Other newcomers sent by the Admiralty were those who arrived to provide the coasters with another important building block: the ability, albeit limited, to defend themselves. The process of providing armament for merchant ships began in June 1939, three months before merchant shipping was placed under Admiralty control, and was carried out by a special section of the Admiralty Trade Division, known as the Defensively Equipped

Merchant Ships (DEMS) section. Naval reservists sent to this section wore DEMS shoulder flashes, and were consequently known as 'Dems' gunners.

In theory every merchant ship was to be adequately protected against submarines and aircraft. Against the former, each ship was supposed to be fitted with one low-angle gun of 3-inch, 4-inch or 6-inch calibre. These had to be mounted aft as forward-mounted weapons were considered 'offensive' under international law, and made ships vulnerable to being sunk without warning. Such faintly ludicrous distinctions seem anachronistic in a conflict characterized by the use of unrestricted submarine warfare almost from the outset.

The guns themselves were usually of 1914–1918 vintage, having been removed from scrapped warships and stored in the years before the war. Some men greeted their arrival with gratitude, presumably on the grounds that any form of defence was better than nothing. William Hopper was one such individual who was determined to look on the bright side: 'We had a 4-inch gun fitted . . . it seemed to be something because up to that time all we had was two rifles . . . First World War as well, not that they'd be any good.'[19]

Others saw the incongruous presence of an antiquated naval gun mounted high and visible on the poop deck as an unnecessary provocation, particularly when Merchant Navy men were expected to assist the DEMS gunners in manning it. Amongst them were the crew of Joseph Wharton's *Clan Alpine*. Like many ships that traded with the Indian subcontinent, a number of the sailors were Indian seamen, known as 'lascars' – a word derived from the Persian word for sailor, *lashkar*. Understandably, some of them failed to see how this was in any way 'their' war, and were reluctant to risk drowning for the sake of a remote chance of hitting back:

> We went down to Newport and we had our gun, a 4-inch gun, fitted there, a Japanese gun from the First World War. And our Indian crew went on strike for danger money so it was decreed that the company would break the strike by getting officers, apprentices and junior engineers from the other ships lying in Princes and Queens Dock, and we got them on board and we sailed the ship ourselves. The apprentices, being small fry, we were stuck down in the stokehold shovelling coal. Anyway thank goodness we just got as far as Greenock and we anchored off there and the native crew came back a little chastened but the company had to give in to them, which was right and fair really because it wasn't their war.[20]

Other merchant sailors were less reluctant to man the armament, and not always for purely patriotic reasons. James Currie was a poorly paid cadet who greatly appreciated the extra sixpence a day that came to him with his Gunner's Certificate, 'a fortune for a Cadet.'[21]

In the beginning the gunners were sometimes, like the Commodore's signals staff, seen as an unnecessary nuisance. Once they joined a ship they had to sign articles similar to the merchant sailors, and the ship then had to take responsibility for feeding and paying them, although the cost of the latter could be recouped by shipowners from the Admiralty. Often without a commissioned officer to look after their interests, Signalman J.W. Booth felt that the lot of the gunners was even harder than his own:

> They were much more at the whim of merchant skippers than we were . . . We once did a trip to the Tyne on a dreadful Baron [a shipping company] boat where the food was awful and the gunners' quarters so cramped and filthy that we refused to sleep there and used the saloon settees . . . [they] had become demoralised and made no effort to improve their lot.[22]

It was not impossible for maltreated gunners to 'improve their lot.' A DEMS Petty Officer from a different ship told Booth that when faced with similar circumstances he had 'Exercised his right to insist on the hoisting of the DEMS flag. This was an international code flag which, when hoisted in harbour, means "the DEMS officer is required on board". The officer boarded the ship and heard the complaints, inspected the quarters and withdrew the gunners.[23]

The offending ship was not allowed to sail until improvements had been made, which leads to some interesting conclusions about just how bad the offending quarters must have been to justify tying up vitally needed tonnage in harbour in the desperate circumstances of wartime.

DEMS training lasted eight weeks in total following which the new recruit could be afloat within hours. From 1941 it was overseen by the redoubtable Admiral Sir Frederick Dreyer, as Inspector of Merchant Navy Gunnery: 'His great drive and experience, his readiness to cut through red tape and his unique position in relation to the Prime Minister, meant that his appointment gave considerable impetus to DEMS training.'[24]

Amongst Dreyer's innovations were the 'Dome' anti-aircraft gunnery training devices, which many veterans remember with varying degrees of affection and resentment, as any time in port was often accompanied by a refresher session. The Dome threw the image of an aircraft onto a curved ceiling accompanied by the sound of aircraft engines. Trainee gunners had to take aim and their success (or otherwise) was indicated to the instructor by a spot of light visible only to him.

Dreyer also recruited two gunnery commanders whose role was to interview officers from sunk or damaged merchant ships, and establish the latest German methods of attack and the effectiveness of Allied countermeasures. The result was the remarkable series of Merchant Navy Survivors' Reports, which form the basis for much of this book.

At the beginning, DEMS armament was not restricted to conventional guns, which were often in short supply. A plethora of stop-gap devices appeared, mostly emanating from the Admiralty's ominously titled Directorate of Miscellaneous Weapon Development at Weston-super-Mare, and were handed over to the long-suffering merchant crews and DEMS gunners to make the best of.

Cadet James Currie was exposed to a number of these 'miscellaneous weapons' in exchange for his sixpence. Amongst his favourites were the PAC (parachute aerial cable), 'lethal to ship's personnel in a strong wind', Marlin and Hotchkiss 'peashooter' machine guns and the FAM (fast aerial mine), a rocket fired from a steel channel trailing a wire with a grenade at one end. The optimistic idea was that an aircraft hit the wire and the grenade slid along it towards the aircraft, to explode on contact: 'chance is a wonderful thing'.[25] However his favourite by far was the Holman Projector:

> Now this beauty, a Holman Projector, a steel tube two inches diameter and thirty inches long. The idea was to hold a grenade, pull the pin and drop the grenade into the tube – now to fire the grenade into the air, steam or air pressure was used. Alas there were some disastrous results. On one ship the weapon was sighted abaft the ship's funnel . . . the grenade was duly plopped into the tube and the steam turned on, of course the steam pressure was insufficient and the grenade simply flopped out of the tube. Sadly personnel were killed and it didn't do the funnel any good.[26]

As the war went on, more and better conventional armament became available and some of the more outlandish contraptions used by DEMS were consigned to the dustbin of history. The arrival of 20mm Oerlikon and 40mm Bofors quick-firing guns much later in the war eventually gave the coasters teeth, although by this stage the threat from the air was much reduced.

According to the Official History of the War at Sea, approximately 5,500 ships required arming at the beginning of the war. The low-angle, anti-submarine guns were the first to be fitted and by the end of 1940 some 3,500 ships had been so equipped. By the end of the war a staggering 9,500 merchant ships had been armed with these weapons, and 50,000 anti-aircraft machine guns had also been fitted; 24,000 Royal Navy personnel had been recruited to man them, and 150,000 merchant sailors had received their gunner's certificates and sixpences to assist them.[27]

Ultimately the Royal Navy did not have enough men to meet demand and in February 1940 the Army were asked to make a contribution to DEMS. The result was the formation of the Maritime Royal Artillery, christened 'Churchill's Sharpshooters', which by March 1943 numbered six regiments, with a total strength of 170 officers and 14,000 other ranks.[28] Mixed Army and RN crews were common.

By the end of the war, 2,713 naval and 1,222 army DEMS gunners had lost their lives.

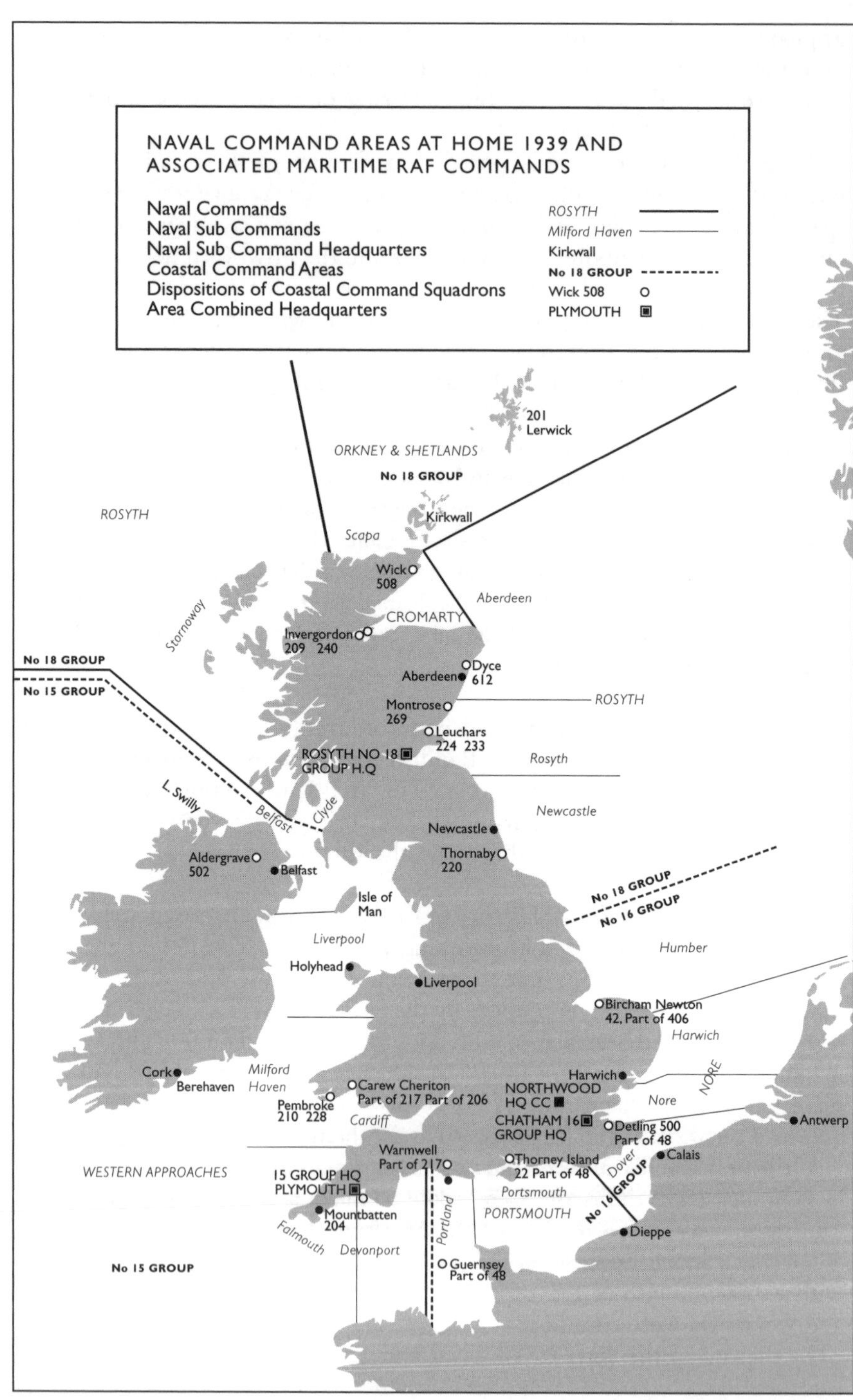
NAVAL COMMAND AREAS AT HOME 1939 AND ASSOCIATED MARITIME RAF COMMANDS
Naval Commands
Naval Sub Commands
Naval Sub Command Headquarters
Coastal Command Areas
Dispositions of Coastal Command Squadrons
Area Combined Headquarters
ROSYTH
Milford Haven
Kirkwall
No 18 GROUP
Wick 508
PLYMOUTH
201 Lerwick
ORKNEY & SHETLANDS
No 18 GROUP
ROSYTH
Kirkwall
Scapa
Wick 508
Aberdeen
Stornoway
CROMARTY
Invergordon 209 240
No 18 GROUP
No 15 GROUP
Dyce 612
Aberdeen
Montrose 269
ROSYTH
Leuchars 224 233
ROSYTH NO 18 GROUP H.Q
Rosyth
L. Swilly
Belfast
Clyde
Newcastle
Newcastle
Aldergrave 502
Belfast
Thornaby 220
No 18 GROUP
No 16 GROUP
Isle of Man
Liverpool
Humber
Holyhead
Liverpool
Bircham Newton 42, Part of 406
Harwich
Milford Haven
Cork
Berehaven
Harwich
NORE
Carew Cheriton Part of 217 Part of 206
NORTHWOOD HQ CC
Nore
Pembroke 210 228
Cardiff
CHATHAM 16 GROUP HQ
Detling 500 Part of 48
Antwerp
Warmwell Part of 217
Thorney Island 22 Part of 48
Dover
Calais
WESTERN APPROACHES
15 GROUP HQ PLYMOUTH
Portsmouth
No 16 GROUP
Mountbatten 204
Portland
PORTSMOUTH
Dieppe
Falmouth
Devonport
Guernsey Part of 48
No 15 GROUP

The Royal Navy

DEMS gunners, however valiant, were never going to be able to protect merchant ships alone. This burden would fall largely on the Royal Navy, perhaps the most important building block of all in the complex structure devised to protect coastal trade. The principal naval organisations concerned with the coastal convoys were the Nore Naval Command, which covered the Dover Straits and the southern North Sea, Rosyth Command (Northern North Sea), Portsmouth Command (Eastern Channel) and Western Approaches (Western Channel).

The principle escort forces were based at Portsmouth, Dover, Harwich and Rosyth. As the convoys proceeded around the coast they would be passed from command to command, as a relay team passes the baton, with additional escorts being bolted on as necessary in particularly high-risk areas or if a convoy was threatened.

Providing escorting warships was no easy task for the Admiralty at a time when the country was chronically short of them. In 1939 the Rosyth Escort Force consisted of eleven First World War vintage V&W Class destroyers manned almost entirely by reservists like G.R. Price, an architect until 1938 when this ceased to become a reserved occupation. He took the opportunity to fulfil a lifetime's ambition by going to sea and joined the Sussex Division of the Royal Naval Volunteer Reserve (RNVR), known as the 'Wavy Navy' due to the distinctive design of the officers' rank insignia.

The RNVR was the middle-class option for reserve service, often drawn from the ranks of naval sentimentalists and weekend yachtsmen, unlike the RNR, who were often professional seafarers from an entirely different social background. A common saying of the time, amusing on one level but deeply revealing of the class prejudice and stereotypes of the time, ran as follows:

> The RNR are sailors, trying to be gentlemen
> The RNVR are gentlemen, trying to be sailors
> And the RN are neither, trying to be both.

Price was part of the ship's company of the Rosyth-based destroyer HMS *Vanessa*. In July 1939, he arrived with several hundred other reservists to reactivate 'three or four very old and dirty destroyers' in time for the Fleet Review in July 1939. Lower deck life was something of a shock for this comfortably off young professional: 'The seamen's mess was on the upper deck and crowded. Each individual mess, which had one of the four corners of the area, was comprised of one Leading Seaman and eighteen seamen.'[29]

Having painted the ship, cleaned her and begun the process of 'working her up' into an efficient fleet unit, Price and his new comrades in arms steamed from Rosyth to Weymouth, where they were reviewed by the King.

There followed a month of intense training, after which they returned to the Clyde, where the ship was still lying on 3 September:

> The Bosun came into the Mess Deck about noon and asked if anyone could ride a bicycle. He got two offers and I and another VR found ourselves up the funnel painting out the flotilla markings. After that I was instructed to use the paint and paint the stern light grey and also the handrails up to Y Gun. War had really come upon us.[30]

Other old destroyers were based on the south coast and took the OA convoys out into the Atlantic. These too had their share of reservists amongst their ship's companies, like Sidney Bush, another one of the 1938 intake:

> My first sea-going ship was one of the old First World War destroyers, the *Witch*. We were working in co-operation with another V&W class destroyer, the *Wren*, going out from Plymouth, picking up a westbound convoy, taking it out to about ten degrees west, picking up an inbound convoy and taking it up-Channel to Dover, where we turned round, picked up yet another westbound convoy from the Downs, and peeled off when we were relieved to go back into Devonport for a couple of days layover.[31]

Sidney soon found that life in the Navy could be hard, particularly in the older ships with their basic 1914–1918 era facilities. Reservists could also find that they were treated as second-class citizens by the hard cases of the lower deck:

> I was the only reserve rating in that particular branch. I had a pig of a Yeoman who treated me very badly . . . conditions in the ship in those days were pretty basic. Our mess was two decks down, just about on the water line with only a small hatchway for escape should anything happen to the ship.[32]

Sidney eventually found companionship amongst the officers on the bridge, thanks to his education and background in commerce in the City of London. He does not record whether this made life amongst his messmates any easier, though it is hard to imagine that it would have increased his popularity. It is perhaps telling that both Sidney Bush and G.R. Price, with their middle-class, professional backgrounds, were both selected as officer candidates in 1940 and went on to command small warships.

In overall command of the convoy was the senior officer of the warship escort, or 'SOE'. Their relative youth and perceived inexperience could sometimes mean friction with the commodores, many of whom had command experience from the First World War. One unfortunate SOE fell foul of Commodore R.G. Thelwell RNR, a distinguished 1914–1918 destroyer officer, after describing him as displaying 'lack of care and attention' with regard to station-keeping. The SOE was put in his place in no uncertain terms by his own superior officer, who reminded him that 'The RNR Commodores are all very keen and men of much sea experience and now also have a considerable experience of East Coast convoys. Their navigational appliances and control over speed are severely limited. I consider Commanding Officers of escorts should be extremely chary of criticizing them in such strong terms.'[33]

Highly trained and disciplined naval officers could also find the ways of coaster skippers inordinately frustrating. A fairly typical comment is this from Captain Philip Ruck-Keen, the commanding officer of the 1st Destroyer Flotilla, in HMS *Blencathra*:

> When off Dungeness I discovered the convoy was in considerable disorder. There is no reason why this should have occurred other than laxity on the part of the Masters [in] paying attention to their station keeping. In spite of every effort the convoy was still something of a rabble by the time Dover was reached.[34]

The perspective of a coaster man, William Hopper, on this vexed question of station-keeping, is illuminating. Elderly colliers manned by men entirely unused to steaming in formation faced problems which young naval officers used to discipline and faster, more maneuverable ships could not begin to understand:

> At the time . . . when a coal burning cargo ship [was] at sea the duty of the fireman towards the end of the watch was to clean all the fires out and consequently the steam pressure would fall . . . so your revolutions would fall . . . We were there shouting to the engine room down the voicepipe 'put the revs up, put the revs up' as our speed was dropping down. So this was one feature which had to be changed in the coal burning ships. Throughout the four-hour watch the fireman would alternately clean one fire and then carry on throughout the watch. That was so that at the end of the watch there was no falling of steam pressure and your speed consequently dropping. But it was quite a thing to learn.[35]

A more sympathetic naval officer, Lieutenant Commander Garth Owles, was more inclined to place the blame for bad station-keeping on penny-pinching owners rather than hard-pressed masters: 'In many cases . . . the ships would be capable of higher speed if they were given more frequent overhauls, boiler cleans and dry docking . . . it is submitted that owners should be required to maintain their ships in such a state as to be capable of keeping station in a seven knot convoy.'[36]

The Commodore of the first northbound convoy to assemble off Southend on 6 September 1939, FN1, also demonstrated more understanding of the problems facing the coaster men. FN1 consisted of nineteen ships, a large and unwieldy number to handle although well short of the recommended maximum, thirty-five, and a long way from the enormous convoys of sixty or more ships which would eventually wend their way down the east coast:

> Visual signaling was very bad but it must be borne in mind that officers and crew in east coast trade have no previous experience of the art, and moreover in most of the little ships there is no-one to bend on flags, hoist them and fumble with the International Code except the Officer of the Watch who is usually preoccupied.[37]

Although the most effective, destroyers were by no means the only escorts made available to the coastal convoys at the beginning of the war. At Harwich another escort force consisting of modern sloops and corvettes provided reinforcements when necessary, and anti-aircraft cruisers based at Grimsby were also available. The latter were older ships, light cruisers built during the First World War, whose armament had been replaced by high-angle guns with more up-to-date fire-control equipment.

As the war went on, more modern and effective ships were added to the coastal escort forces, notably the Hunt-class anti-aircraft destroyers of which Ruck-Keen's *Blencathra* was one example: 'super little ships' according to one man who served in them.[38]

The Royal Naval Patrol Service

The trawlers and other auxiliary warships of the Royal Naval Patrol Service, used for a range of duties from minesweeping to general patrolling and anti-submarine work, provided further escorts. The RNPS, another important building block, was something of a 'Navy within a Navy'. It was formed at the beginning of the war by the simple expedient of calling up fishing trawlers, complete with their Royal Naval Reserve crews, and at first numbered around 600 ships and 6,000 men. Their depot, HMS *Europa,* was established in a municipal pleasure gardens in Lowestoft with the deeply unmilitaritistic title of 'The Sparrow's Nest'.[39]

These were men of the same ilk as the coaster skippers: tough, bloody-minded, professional seamen with their own way of doing things and their own rank and rate structure to match. RNPS trawlers were, for instance, commanded by a 'Skipper RNR', not a Lieutenant or Sub Lieutenant. War or no war, fishing was a hard life. Albert Ellington started when he was fourteen years old: 'You would go to Iceland for, say, twenty-eight days, you couldn't get a wash . . . the sweat of the steel used to drop into your bed, you didn't have a proper bed it was what they call a donkey's breakfast, just a bag full of straw.'[40] Albert saw RNR service as a break, 'a holiday away from fishing' for which he was paid the princely sum of thirty shillings a month. Naval discipline was nothing compared to the backbreaking grind of his 'real' job. He was called up to Sparrow's Nest in August 1939, and found to his embarrassment that he was not as well prepared as he should have been. 'Spit and Polish' had clearly not characterized his service in the Reserves:

> I came straight in from sea and the Board of Trade at Aberdeen said I had to report to Lowestoft the next morning in full uniform . . . I felt very bad because I didn't have the uniform . . . the little boys roundabout the street where I lived, I gave them a sailor's hat and a lanyard and half of my uniform I'd given away to little boys to play with . . . I got a Boy Scout's lanyard from someone and I'd got a Reserve's hat, I was in the Boys' Reserves when I was a boy and I put that on instead of the proper sailor's hat.[41]

By the time he reached the 'Nest' it was full to the brim with newly arrived reservists. 'There was so many sailors got into this place, we ripped all the seats out of the theatre and lay on the floor and my friend and I we slept on top of a billiard table, there was nowhere for us to go at that time.'[42] The following day he was sent off to Cardiff to pick up a trawler, which after landing her catch replaced her trawls with sweeping gear and became one of the overnight warships that characterised the RNPS.

John Chrisp was a 31-year-old regular Royal Navy man, who on the outbreak of war was appointed as Bosun in command of the Admiralty trawler *Jasper,* a purpose-built warship based on the standard fishing boat design. His job was to teach the newly arrived trawlermen their new job as quickly as possible: 'We were training skippers in antisubmarine warfare . . . we only had twenty-five crew, there was myself, a Chiefie RN stoker and an asdic rating, who were the only regular service . . . we took one skipper per month and exercised the trawlers at the entrance to the Firth of Forth with a small submarine, until war broke out.'[43]

John soon found out why the trawlermen, with their well-honed small-boat handling skills, were uniquely qualified for this job:

> When you have a small ship of about 600 tons with a gun for'ard and these depth charges aft, they were very difficult to handle, we only had one screw you see. And we had no radar and we had no gyro compass, so we were basically down to magnetic steering, and of course ship handling was different to when you were in destroyers with two propellers . . . they were a bit hectic when they got into rough seas.[44]

A sprinkling of Royal Navy senior rates were brought in to the RNPS to try to introduce a level of naval discipline, and the RN also provided technical specialists, in particular communications ratings. As the war went on the RNPS was filled with more and more RN personnel, many of them

Hostilities Only ratings for whom naval service was a mystery and who set no great store by the social niceties of pre-war inter-reservist prejudice. Jack Yeatman was one of them, a Telegraphist who volunteered for transfer to the RNPS later in the war after he completed his training. Serving in a trawler could be something of a culture shock:

> The ship I served in – HMS *Pearl*, formerly the *Dervish* of Hull – was a 600-ton, 160-foot long, coal-burning distant-water trawler, designed to operate in the Arctic fishing-grounds with a crew of twelve. As an Asdic Trawler escorting convoys and hunting U-Boats, we had forty-seven on board – twenty-two of us in the former fish-hold! And there was no communication below deck – you had to carry your meals along the open deck from the coal-fired Galley right aft to the Mess Deck up for'ard, which meant that, even in normal English Channel and North Atlantic weather, they often arrived in a 'modified condition with extra salt'. And of course the freshwater tanks were quite inadequate for the much larger crew, so that the washing of person and clothes at sea was strictly forbidden – there were only three tin wash-basins.[45]

Jack had transferred to the RNPS anticipating a career in minesweeping, and more money: trawler crews received an allowance known as 'hard-lying money' as recompense for the difficult conditions on board. However, when he arrived on board *Pearl* he found the ship was actually equipped for convoy escort duties on the south coast. The crew was a typical RNPS mix:

> The core of crew members came from the fishing communities, the numbers then being made up from RNR Reservists, ex-Merchant Seamen, and large numbers of Hostilities Only ratings – our Lower Deck included two university graduates and a Scottish bank manager – originally recruited into the Royal Navy and then seconded to the RNPS, or who, like me, had actually volunteered for transfer. It was indeed a transfer – the RNPS was nothing like the Navy proper! . . . In such small ships, the rigid RN distinctions of rank and rating were just not possible – everyone had to muck in as required.[46]

The diverse mix of ships and men which made up the RNPS, and the informal non-conformist nature of the service, led to its being dubbed 'Harry Tate's Navy' after a famous pre-war comedian whose trademark was his perpetual bewilderment by the trappings of the modern world.

Charles Stoakes was a RNVR 'amateur sailor' from Grimsby, now living somewhat incongruously in Luton, almost as far from the sea as it was possible to be. On the outbreak of war he reported to his local police station and a month later, on 4 October, he reported to HMS *Pembroke* in Chatham. After three weeks he was assigned to the RNPS and was told to report to Sparrow's Nest, from where he was posted to the minesweeping trawler *Lady Elsa*:

> The interior had been converted, and the exterior of the ship had been dressed for war with ancient guns, most of which had been used to fight World War One. There was a twelve-pounder gun, two Lewis machine guns and a twin Lewis gun aft. Possibly they would carry two, or perhaps four, depth charges in case they should make the acquaintance of a submarine. A lick of grey Admiralty paint and these ships were ready for war. All forty-three of them were now considered to be fighting ships. Prior to the outbreak of war the Admiralty had marked out a channel circling the British Isles, now called a main highway. It varied from a couple of miles wide in some parts to no more than a few hundred yards in others, all of which had to be constantly swept, the enemy laying mines as quickly as we cleared them.[47]

This, then, was the War Channel, the next building block of the defensive network, which was established to protect the coasters and a battleground for the next five years.

The War Channel

The Admiralty had learned during the First World War that defensive minelaying was an important means of protecting vulnerable coastal traffic from unwelcome enemy attention, and we have already seen how on the outbreak of war there was no reason to suppose that the overall strategic situation would differ from that which had prevailed twenty-two years before. So as soon as war broke out the Admiralty began to recreate the defensive fields, initially with mines of the conventional tethered variety, anchored to the seabed and requiring physical contact with the target ship to explode them. Both sides used other types of mine during the war, notably 'influence' mines of the magnetic, acoustic and pressure variety. These mines and the techniques used to counter them will be introduced as they appear.

First and foremost amongst the early minefields was the famous Dover Barrage, a network of deep and shallow minefields, cables, nets, surface patrols and submarine-detection loops stretched across the narrowest part of the English Channel – 10,000 mines went into the Dover Barrage. Other barrages were slowly introduced across the Bristol Channel, between the Outer Hebrides and the Faeroe Islands, and finally between the Faeroes and Iceland.

According to international law marine minefields had to be 'declared' if they posed a danger to merchant shipping. Deep fields aimed at submarines could remain secret or 'undeclared'. On the east coast a declared minefield was announced off the Yorkshire Coast as early as 27 September, at the same time as an undeclared deep field was laid in the same area. Initially these were paper tigers, with a relatively small number of very widely dispersed mines, but as the war progressed more fields were laid. By 23 December 1939, it was possible to declare an East Coast Mine Barrage running between the Thames Estuary and the Moray Firth.[48]

Between the Mine Barrage and the coast ran the narrow war channel, under a mile wide, and swept daily for both German and drifting 'friendly' mines. The men responsible for this monotonous yet deadly activity had a bitter little ditty which was the unofficial anthem of the east coast sweepers: 'Sweeping, sweeping, sweeping, always bloody well sweeping, from early in the morning until last thing at night.'[49]

Sub Lieutenant John Neale was an RNVR officer assigned to east coast sweepers at the beginning of the war after eight weeks' training:

> The flotilla was equipped with Oropesa sweeps, which consisted of two large winches on the quarterdeck with huge drums carrying specially serrated sweep wires with a breaking strain of thirty tons each. On the end of each wire was a multiplane otter [a board to keep the sweep away from the ship] which hung from an Oropesa float always referred to as 'Horace'. The otter streamed the wire in a long curve to one side of the ship and the correct depth near the stern was controlled by another multiplane called a 'kite'.[50]

Wartime propaganda led to the widespread belief that British mines became inert once their tethers had broken. This was completely untrue – drifting British mines remained lethal to the unwary, just like their German counterparts. Nevertheless the myth persists in the reminiscences of veterans of the war channel even today.

Many of the minesweepers were RNPS-crewed fishing trawlers, like the *John Stephen*. The typically diverse nature of this crew has been beautifully illustrated by a series of letters they wrote to Mollie Baker, who adopted the crew and sent them parcels of knitted clothing throughout the bitter winter of 1939.[51]

Thirty-four-year-old Skipper William Stewart RNR, or 'Skipper Bill', a career trawlerman, commanded the *John Stephen*: 'I sail skipper of a trawler in civil life so the only difference now is I'm sweeping for mines instead of for fish . . . we sweep for mines all day and patrol all night so the boys and myself are on top line.'[52] Amongst his crew of seventeen – 'one of the finest . . . in the patrol service' – were fishermen like Able Seaman Sam Gibbs, Bob Clarke, the wireless operator, a local government clerk in Birmingham – 'from city office to a fisherman's life is a bit too much of a change for my liking' – and a 22-year-old signalman who before the war had been a history teacher from London, 'one of nature's little gentlemen' according to his skipper.[53]

By 1940 the war channel had taken on the form that would characterize it for the next five years. It was marked by floating buoys at half-mile intervals each with its own distinctive arrangement of lights. It was divided into two lanes so that northbound and southbound convoys could pass, FS in the outer lane nearest the minefields, FN in the inner lane nearest the coast. Closer inshore was a shallow-water channel used for barges and small coasters sailing independently over short distances. The convoys followed fixed routes, code-named QZS for safe (QZ meant mined), which are frequently mentioned in the reports compiled by their escort commanders and commodores. QZS 148 ran from Southend to Yarmouth, QZS 288 from Yarmouth to Sheringham in Norfolk, QZS 152 from Sheringham to the River Humber and QZS 254 northbound from the Humber.[54]

Responsibility for maintaining this huge and complex network of buoys and lights lay largely with Trinity House, the General Lighthouse Authority for England and Wales since 1514. On the outbreak of war Trinity House was equipped with nine tenders to maintain more than sixty manned lightships and lighthouses, numerous unmanned offshore lights and buoys beyond count: 'up the East Coast . . . they used to call it Map Post Alley because it was all lights, buoy lights'.[55]

The Trinity House men were desperately exposed, whether swinging at anchor in a flimsy lightship or ploughing through the seas in a slow, unescorted tender, and were thus in the front line of the war in coastal waters from the beginning. The tenders were armed accordingly with DEMS crews and weapons, although employees of the Corporation did not see themselves as combatants: 'One master, Captain Stephens, conscientiously resigned the instant a gun was on his ship.'[56]

The East Coast Mine Barrage absorbed 35,000 mines by the end of the Second World War, 13.5 per cent of Britain's total mining effort, which ran to around 260,000 mines. Whether it justified such enormous expenditure of material and effort is open to debate. One contemporary source states unequivocally that 'there is no evidence that [it] had any appreciable effect upon the strategy or tactics of the enemy.'[57] Its effect on the morale of the beleaguered coaster men, for whom it provided at least an illusion of security, is impossible to calculate.

The Royal Air Force

One last building block remains to be described: the Royal Air Force's Coastal Command, which had responsibility for providing air cover over the convoys. At the beginning of the war Coastal Command was very much the 'Cinderella service' of the RAF, as it would remain for much of the war. Its well-documented struggle for more and better aircraft was a particular feature of the battle to protect the oceanic convoys which lie outside the scope of this book, but its effects could be seen in the sometimes empty skies over the coastal convoys as well.

In the interests of balance, the Royal Air Force view about this issue was that Coastal Command came a poor third to Bomber Command and Fighter

Command as a matter of strategic necessity. The Royal Navy was sufficiently strong at sea, so went the argument, that the RAF would be better employed concentrating on building up those areas in which Britain was demonstrably inferior to Germany.[58]

Coastal Command had only been formed in July 1936, and its primary function was unclear for some time afterwards, resulting in its operational development, equipment and training being severely handicapped. This was particularly true of its ability to track, force down and sink submarines, which was all but non-existent, despite the fact that the 1914–1918 experience had shown this to be highly effective: at the end of the war the Naval Staff had concluded that air escorts for convoys had been 'very successful as an anti-submarine measure'.[59]

This situation had not substantially changed by September 1939, despite the fact that the country was preparing for a war which it had every reason to expect would be a replay of the First World War – a war in which the U-boat was likely to become one of the principle maritime opponents.

Within Coastal Command, anti-submarine capability was downplayed in favour of prioritizing operations against surface raiders, which the RAF's own Official History called 'the greatest danger to our seaborne trade, in the official opinion of the Admiralty'.[60] Given this it is hard to explain Coastal Command's lamentable anti-surface strike capability: only two genuine torpedo-bomber squadrons both equipped with what the same work calls the 'completely out-of-date' Vickers Vildebeeste biplane, first flown in 1928. To make matters worse, only one of these squadrons was active in 1939.[61]

In December 1937, Coastal Command was finally informed that its primary role was 'trade protection, reconnaissance and co-operation with the Royal Navy'.[62] By September 1939, it had three operational groups to carry out this very broad and difficult role: 15 Group, based at Plymouth and responsible for the Western Approaches from the Atlantic, including the western Channel; 16 Group at Gillingham in Kent, responsible for the eastern Channel and southern North Sea, and 18 Group, at Donibristle in Fife, covering the northern North Sea and north-western approaches. The headquarters for Coastal Command itself was at Northwood, to the north-west of London. Together the three operational groups fielded some 296 aircraft. Most of these were Avro Anson reconnaissance aircraft, slow, short ranged and able to carry only a small and almost entirely useless 100-lb bomb.

This book is not the place to launch into an impassioned contribution to the debate about the state of maritime air power in 1939, and the hapless Anson provides a case study of the pitfalls of becoming involved with this subject. The Royal Navy's official historian describes the Anson as 'inadequate to the efficient execution of its function'.[63] The official historian of the RAF calls it 'excellent and highly reliable'.[64]

The bottom line was that the Royal Navy was reasonably well prepared for the anti-submarine campaign it thought it was going to have to fight in coastal waters. For whatever reasons, the Royal Air Force was arguably nowhere near ready for the same hypothetical scenario. In 1943 the Air Ministry produced a small book about the activities of Coastal Command during the first half of the war. Given this provenance, one can reasonably assume that the author was encouraged to put a positive 'spin' on proceedings. Despite this, the book is unintentionally illuminating about the state of maritime air cover at the beginning of the war, as the following brief excerpt relating to a convoy patrol in 1939 illustrates. The aircraft concerned are Tiger Moths, flimsy biplane trainers pressed into service to protect coastal shipping: 'Left patrol area . . . on account of deteriorating weather conditions . . . contents of bottom of pigeon's basket were blown back into cockpit, affecting eyes.'[65]

The same publication optimistically goes on to relate that 'the presence of an aircraft, even of a Moth, made it impossible for a U-boat to travel on the surface in daylight.'[66] Perhaps so, although the Moth's puny 20-lb bombs would barely have dented a U-boat's casing and almost any aircraft available to the Germans in 1939 would have made short work of it. Ultimately the unfortunate (and clearly courageous) Moth pilot had to rely on his carrier pigeon flying home and summoning a warship capable of actually harming the submarine, and his aircraft's endurance was so low that he would probably not have been able to keep the U-boat down for long enough to await its arrival.

Having said all this, after the first few months of the war in coastal waters the desperate state of Coastal Command's anti-submarine capability simply didn't matter. The Germans threw the 1914–1918 rule book out of the window and U-boats were almost never seen in coastal waters. What replaced them was a range of threats unlike anything encountered in the First World War. Almost from the very beginning, protecting coastal convoys in this new war was going to be a different game altogether.

Notes

1. Roskill, Captain S.W., *The War at Sea*, vol. I, HMSO, London, 1954, p. 21.
2. Batten, John, *Dirty Little* Collier, Hutchinson, London, undated, p. 71.
3. Courtesy of the Second World War Experience Centre, Leeds.
4. Hancock, W.K. (ed.), *History of the Second World War: UK Civil Series – Coal*, HMSO, 1951, p. 35.
5. IWM Docs 91/17/1 Booth, J.W., p. 10.
6. Ibid., pp. 10–11.
7. See 'Note for Readers' at the start of this book.
8. Foynes, J.P., *Battle of the East Coast*, published by the author, 1994, p. 3.
9. IWM Sound 10800 Hopper, William.

10. Grove, Eric J. (ed.), *The Defeat of the Enemy Attack on Shipping 1939–1945*, London, Navy Records Society, 1997, p. 30.
11. BBC PW A 1117964 Marwood, Michael.
12. Ibid.
13. The pocket battleships were *Graf Spee*, *Admiral Scheer* and *Deutschland* (later renamed *Lützow*).
14. Hague, Arnold, *The Allied Convoy System 1939–1945: Its Organisation, Defence and Operation*, Vanwell, 2000.
15. Batten, *Dirty Little Collier*, p. 41.
16. IWM Docs 91/17/1 Booth, J.W., p. 28.
17. Ibid.
18. Ibid, p. 8.
19. IWM Sound 10800 Hopper, William.
20. IWM Sound 13242 Wharton, Joseph.
21. BBC PW A9014807 Currie, James.
22. IWM Docs 91/17/1 Booth, J W, pp. 31–2.
23. Ibid, p. 32.
24. Slader, John, *The Fourth Service: Merchantmen at War 1939–1945*, Robert Hale, London, 1994.
25. BBC People's War (henceforth BBC PW), A9014807 Currie, James.
26. Ibid.
27. Roskill, *War at Sea*, vol. I, p. 22.
28. Slader, *Fourth Service*.
29. IWM Docs 04/2/1 Price, Lieutenant G.R.
30. Ibid.
31. IWM Sound 13300 Bush, Sydney.
32. Ibid.
33. NA: ADM 199/28 FN Convoys Reports 27 April 1940–22 June 1940.
34. NA: ADM 199/929 CE and CW Convoys Reports: 1941.
35. IWM Sound 10800 Hopper.
36. NA: ADM 199/929 CE and CW Convoys Reports: 1941.
37. NA: ADM 199/26 FN Convoy Reports September 1939–February 1940.
38. IWM Docs 01/39/1 Syms, Commander James Anthony, DSC, RN.
39. Lund, Paul and Ludlam, Harry, *Trawlers go to War*, New English Library, London, 1971, pp. 9–10.
40. IWM Sound 13120 Ellington, Albert.
41. Ibid.
42. Ibid.
43. IWM Sound 16843 Chrisp, John.
44. Ibid.
45. BBC PW A4189098 Yeatman, Jack.
46. Ibid.
47. BBC PW A8017102 Stoakes, Charles.
48. Grove, *The Defeat of the Enemy Attack on Shipping*, p. 151.

49. IWM Docs 92/50/1: Neale, Lieutenant Commander J.K., p. 24.
50. Ibid., p. 5. 'Oropesa' minesweeping was named after HMT *Oropesa*, the trawler which first tested the equipment during the First World War.
51. IWM Docs 88/42/1 Baker, Mrs M.
52. Ibid.
53. Ibid.
54. Foynes, J.P., *Battle of the East Coast*, published by the author, 1994, p. 3.
55. IWM Sound 12424, Bird, Richard.
56. Woodman, Richard, *Keepers of the Sea: The Story of the Trinity House Yachts and Tenders*, Chaffcutter Books, Ware, 2005, p. 138.
57. Grove, *The Defeat of the Enemy Attack on Shipping*, pp. 152-3.
58. Richards, Denis, *Royal Air Force 1939–1945*, vol. 1: The Fight at Odds, HMSO, London, 1974, p. 55.
59. Grove, *The Defeat of the Enemy Attack on Shipping*, p. 9.
60. Richards, *Royal Air Force 1939–1945*, vol. 1, p. 56.
61. Ibid.
62. Grove, *The Defeat of the Enemy Attack on Shipping*, p. 74.
63. Roskill, *War at Sea*, vol 1, p. 36.
64. Richards, *Royal Air Force 1939–1945*, vol. 1, p. 56.
65. *Coastal Command*, HMSO, London, 1943, p. 56.
66. Ibid., p. 56.

Chapter 3
Not so 'Phoney' War

3 September 1939 to 30 April 1940

Joseph Wharton was a nineteen-year-old apprentice with the Clan Line shipping company and had just returned to coastal waters from India in the *Clan Alpine*. Leaving Tilbury for Glasgow on 3 September he saw a grim sign that war was imminent:

> We passed a German ship in the Irish Sea, the *Hugo Stinnes*, and she had a great bone in her teeth, a great bow wave and smoke was pouring out her funnels and she was trying to get back to Germany or some neutral port or whatever . . . when we docked in Glasgow that fateful Sunday morning there we heard the Prime Minister on the radio and that was it.[1]

The German Navy, the *Kriegsmarine*, had been given its first war order by Adolf Hitler on 31 August:

> If England and France open hostilities against Germany . . . damage should be done to enemy forces and their economic sources of supply as far as resources allow . . . in its warfare on merchant shipping the Navy is to concentrate on England.[2]

The next day Germany invaded Poland without declaring war, prompting Britain and France to issue ultimatums which military weakness and geographical realities, combined with lack of political will, prevented them from enforcing. These expired on 3 September, and the Allies declared war at 1115. Less than ten hours later the submarine *U30* sank the liner *Athenia,* jerking Aberdeen fisherman and naval reservist John Harwood from his peacetime existence to a new life in the RNPS in fairly typical fashion:

> I was fishing off the Minch, and was changing grounds to a position off the Butt of Lewis when I heard on my wireless that the liner *Athenia* had been torpedoed by a U-boat. The same day I saw a number of ships making for Cape Wrath. I knew then that it was war, and made tracks for home. I didn't

see any other ships making their way to Buchan Ness, so I decided to go on to harbour at Aberdeen. It was packed with ships all awaiting mobilization. Within a week I was sent to the Nest to await an appointment.[3]

The period that followed has become known as the 'Phoney War'. On the Franco-German borders, the armies glowered at each other from their fortifications. German aircraft bombed Poland, while Allied aircraft dropped leaflets. But as far as coastal shipping was concerned, 'There was no phoney war,' as one Royal Navy seaman bitterly commented, any more than there was for the unfortunate Poles.[4]

Initial indications were that Germany was about to embark on the type of war against trade that Britain expected, although in many respects she was even less well prepared. *Kommodore* Karl Dönitz, the talented and inspirational Flag Officer commanding the *Kriegsmarine*'s U-boats, was painfully aware that he had insufficient operational U-boats, just fifty-seven, to be anything more than 'a petty annoyance' to the British and unable to play 'anything like an important part in the war against Britain's commerce'.[5] By his own estimates, Germany required at least 300 to replicate the kind of strategic campaign she had waged in 1917–1918. His superior, *Großadmiral* Erich Raeder, wrote after the war that:

Granting that in the short period since 1935 we had built up a well organised and excellently trained submarine arm, it was still too weak to have any decisive effect. And our surface fleet was so inferior in strength and numbers to the British Fleet that it could do little more than show that it knew how to die valiantly.[6]

Nevertheless, forty-nine of the available U-boats dutifully took up waiting positions at the end of August, many lurking in or near British coastal waters, while the British formed up convoys, called up reservists to elderly destroyers, and started to assemble their 'building blocks'. By the end of October U-boats had sunk forty merchant ships, as well as claiming two notable warship scalps: the aircraft carrier HMS *Courageous* on 17 September and the battleship *Royal Oak*, torpedoed on 14 October by Günther Prien's *U47* when supposedly safe at anchor in the Royal Navy's principal base at Scapa Flow.

Among the mercantile victims was the SS *Sea Venture,* a 2,327 coaster making for Norway on 20 October 1939. For several miles she had been following a Danish steamer across the North Sea, and at 1100 hours was passing Unst, most northerly of the Shetland Islands. Her radio operator, A. Spickett, was on duty in the wireless office when he heard a 'frightful commotion' on the deck above and realized the ship was altering course violently: 'I walked quickly . . . up on to the bridge to where the Captain and Mate were standing. Looking back at the sweeping wash from the stern, I said to the Old Man, "What! Are we turning back?" "Look there Sparks," he said.'[7]

A surfaced U-boat (*U34*) was breaking concealment from behind the Danish steamer. Spickett ran below and sent out the recognized signal for U-boat attack, repeating the letter S twelve times in Morse code, broken into groups of four. Just as the guard ship back at Lerwick answered, the U-boat started to shell the *Sea Venture*.

> I can tell you that once I had received this acknowledgement . . . I was out of the radio office and on to the deck outside in next to no time at all. There I found the Captain and the Mate leaning up against the bulkhead . . . sheltering from the shells still hitting the ship on the other side . . . it was then that I noticed that most of the crew were already in the lifeboat.[8]

The ship's DEMS gun crew, a solitary Royal Marine assisted by the *Sea Venture*'s galley boy, tried to retaliate but their enthusiasm was tempered by desperate lack of experience:

> The Galley Boy had previously been shown how to place the shell in the breech of the gun, and then place behind it a cordite cartridge. Apparently, after they had fired the first round, and the breech was re-opened and the cordite cartridge fell out, the galley boy hesitated. The Marine asked why he wasn't reloading. 'I'm waiting for the other bit to fall out first' he had replied. He had loaded two parts so expected the two pieces back![9]

Spickett ran for his lifejacket, while incoming German shells pounded the *Sea Venture*: 'I jumped back when one hit the galley door. I remember another hitting the Bosun's cabin. A shell then completely destroyed one of the lifeboats on the starboard side.'[10]

He followed the Captain and the Mate into the port side boat, climbing as fast as he could down a rope which hung over the ship's side. As they began to row away the U-boat maneuvered closer to the *Sea Venture*. The reason became clear when 'a gigantic water spout' rose up from the starboard side and the ship rolled over and slowly sank. Two small flying boats arrived belatedly from Lerwick but the U-boat submerged and escaped. Without Asdic or effective depth charges, the aircraft could only circle impotently above.

The crew of the *Sea Venture* began to row painfully slowly towards Unst, one of the flying boats circling protectively above until dusk. Eventually reaching land, they spent a night with local crofters before being taken to Lerwick and thence to the company offices in Newcastle, where they each received £47 to buy replacement clothing and equipment.

However, in this war the U-boats were not going to get everything their own way. The first to be sunk, *U39*, met her end on 14 September after an unsuccessful attack on the aircraft carrier HMS *Ark Royal*. Three more were sunk in the Dover Straits in swift succession following the completion of the Dover Barrage, after which the Straits were closed to U-boats.

Elsewhere in coastal waters, Germany's submariners were also facing difficulties. On 29 November, the Type VIIb *U35* was on patrol in the North Sea, covering a sortie by the battlecruisers *Scharnhorst* and *Gneisenau*, when the destroyer HMS *Icarus* caught her. *U35* crash-dived and *Icarus*, her Asdic malfunctioning, called for help. This duly arrived in the shape of the destroyers *Kashmir* and *Kingston*, of Lord Louis Mountbatten's 5th Destroyer Flotilla. The British warships obtained an Asdic contact more than 2 miles away from the frantically manoeuvring U-boat, and raced into the attack. *Kingston* dropped two patterns of depth charges, the second of which forced the U-boat to the surface. Gerhard Stamer was her Chief Engineer:

> There were no direct hits but leaks developed which made it increasingly difficult to hold the boat down and when the last salvo jammed the hydroplanes in the 'hard up' position the boat could no longer be held. The attempt to force the boat back below the surface through quick flooding of the ballast tanks failed as a main vent jammed . . . as the last person below deck I succeeded in clearing the jam and as I reached the bridge the boat sank beneath the Captain's feet and mine.[11]

U35's crew rushed on deck and attempted to man their deck gun. Commander Henry King of HMS *Kashmir* reported that:

> On a shot being fired across the bows of the submarine by the *Kashmir*, they left their gun, held up their hands and started to abandon the submarine whose engines were then stopped . . . the *Kashmir* then approached the submarine from aft and picked up 4 officers and 27 ratings while the *Kingston* carried out a circular sweep. On completion of the latter, the *Kingston* closed and rescued the remaining survivors including the Captain.[12]

The Captain – *Kapitänleutnant* Werner Lott – was in a bad way:

> My lifesaver had been damaged when the U-boat sank under my feet. I was already completely exhausted and stiff from the cold water . . . they threw me a rope which I could not hold in my stiff hands. To my amazement they lowered a boat, hauled me into it and threw me like a bag on to the destroyer's deck because I had become too weak to jump on my own in the heavy sea. Under a doctor's supervision I was put into a hot bath and a bottle of Scotch held to my mouth which altogether gave all of us a quick recovery.[13]

Both officers were impressed by the treatment they received in this early, arguably more innocent, part of the war, as Gerhard Stamer recalled: 'Our treatment was excellent, just like shipwrecked people . . . before we were turned over to the Army in Birkenhead he told me to sign the visitors book.'[14]

Chivalry aside, British coastal waters were not safe for U-boats. The lessons of 1914–1918 had been learned well, and by the end of October seven boats had been sunk. Five were valuable ocean-going boats, of which Dönitz had just twenty-six on the outbreak of war, and although the U-boats never disappeared entirely, they avoided coastal waters for much of the rest of the war.

In this theatre, Germany had other weapons that would prove far more effective, and by the time *U35* was sunk one of the most lethal had already been deployed. Early in the morning on 10 September 1939, the 2,796-ton collier SS *Goodwood* was on her way from the Tyne to Bayonne in France. Off Flamborough Head on the Yorkshire Coast at 0710 she was rocked by a violent explosion. Robert Black was her Second Officer: 'I came out of my room and I noticed the Master lying on the deck of the lower bridge. He had a lifebelt on. I went to his assistance but he would not allow me to remove him. His words were 'look after yourself. Never mind me.'[15]

Leaving his Captain as ordered, with both knees shattered and apparently set on going down with his ship, Robert went aft and supervised the lowering of the starboard lifeboat, in which the rest of the crew were able to get away. Seeing the ship still making way through the water and his wounded Captain alone on the bridge, Robert relented and began a desperate struggle to save his recalcitrant senior officer:

> I dived off the lifeboat in an attempt to get aboard by the falls. I lost my lifebelt and my pajamas were around my knees, and I got back to the lifeboat. On getting back the Chief Officer asked for volunteers to go with me to get the Master. Thomas Broderick and W Gill (ABs) volunteered. We got on board by grabbing the bulwarks of the ship as she was then sinking by the stern. We carried the Master to the lower deck. I ordered a lifebuoy to be thrown over the side and with the help of the others I dropped the Captain overboard (distance about 4 feet) and swam away with him to the lifeboat.[16]

Fifteen minutes later the survivors were rescued by a fishing boat and taken into Bridlington, where the Master was taken immediately to hospital. He later wrote to his courageous Second Officer, thanking him in a rather roundabout way for saving his life in defiance of instructions: 'I have to thank you and the others who came back (although against my orders as I had waved the boat to get loose and get away before all hands got dragged under when she sank) for the fact that I am here today.'[17]

Indiscriminate offensive minelaying had arrived in coastal waters. Most of those laid were conventional tethered mines, laid by submarines and also by the destroyers of the *Kriegsmarine*, venturing deeper into British waters than they ever would later in the war. But the Germans added a new twist by introducing magnetic mines, which responded to the distortion of the earth's magnetic field caused by a passing ship. These had been invented by the British at the end of the First World War, and the German Navy had continued to develop them in the inter-war period.[18]

Magnetic mines rested on the seabed, causing damage by their shock wave rather than by direct contact with a ship. As such, they had no cable to be cut by conventional Oropesa sweeping gear. At the start of the war only a few magnetic mines were available to the Germans and it is hard to establish from the historical record which ships actually fell victim to them, as it was not generally known that they were in use. The liner *City of Paris* was certainly one of the first victims, on 16 September. Northbound off Aldeburgh on the Suffolk coast her Captain reported a 'terrific explosion':

> The sandbags which were round the wheelhouse collapsed and we shipped a sea over the bridge, and I felt the deck move . . . At the same time the violence of this explosion released the brake of the starboard chain on the wheelhouse and the anchor dropped and the cable paid right out . . . the crew had made a rush for the boats. The quarters where they slept were fitted with beds in iron sockets, and these all collapsed causing [them] . . . to lose their heads completely [in panic].[19]

Within ten minutes the *City of Paris* had 16 feet of water in her Number 2 hold. One Lascar sailor had been drowned after falling into the boat from a great height and then rolling into the sea. The survivors were taken to Harwich although some, ultimately, were taken back to their badly damaged ship and managed to salvage her. In dry dock, the nature of the damage revealed the presence of magnetic mines for the first time.

The story was repeated all around the coast:

> 'The ship was lifted bodily out of the water, fell back, and broke her back' – Vital Delgoffe, master of the Dutch freighter *Alex van Opstal*, off Weymouth on 14 September.[20]
>
> 'There was a violent explosion and smoke was seen going up above her funnel and bridge. She was hit on the starboard side and the concussion lifted up the stern about three feet' – Mr W.H. Dugdale of the SS *Bramhill*, witnessing the end of the Swedish freighter *Albania* off the Humber on 23 October.[21]
>
> 'We . . . were 2 miles S.E. of the Shambles light vessel and all of a sudden we felt a terrific explosion' – Captain W. Moree of the Dutch freighter *Bennendijk*, off the Shambles Light Vessel, October 1939.[22]
>
> 'A terrific explosion took place . . . both compasses blew right out and the

> Fourth Officer landed on the bridge from the monkey island' – Captain T. Richardson, SS *Marwarri*, off the Scarweather Light Vessel, 4 October 1939.[23]

British minesweeping was stepped up and RNPS trawlers were rushed into action as fast as their crews could be trained. Fourteen trawlers and drifters were lost in 1939, and the strain on the crews was immense. Montague Hollinshed was a signalman aboard the minesweeping trawler *Lochalsh*, operating out of Grimsby, and recalled the collapse of one officer after weeks of risking his life to keep the war channel clear: 'After one day's sweeping the group anchored off the coast of Norfolk, the CO . . . later that night ordered away his rowing boat, in his pyjamas, rowing around the fleet shouting "abandon ship, abandon ship", he was then gently removed ashore and the group disbanded.'[24]

Tragically one man on Hollinshed's own ship was not identified soon enough to help him:

> After one particular day the ship's company reported that [one sailor] felt a little harassed, and was sitting alone in a corner with a knife. He was calmed down, I saw him later that evening, he was quite calm, but during the night whilst we were on passage he jumped overboard and was not seen again . . . I think this was purely the strain of minesweeping.[25]

Sometimes the coaster men had to take responsibility for their own protection. DEMS Gunner William Merryweather sank a mine four hours after joining his ship:

> [The Captain] came running from the bridge to the back of the boat and asked me if I could pop a mine off. He'd been steering for it thinking it was a buoy marking the edge of one of our own mine fields . . . I fired forty-eight shots, forty-three of which we heard the clang as the round hit but we didn't explode it. The skipper called up a destroyer which was doing a convoy duty fairly close, and they came over and searched for the mine but they said obviously the thing had sunk because of the punctures.[26]

Coastal shipping was also assaulted from the air, almost from the outbreak of war, although the start of the campaign was not auspicious for the *Luftwaffe*. The first attack, on 29 September, brought no success and on 21 October four Heinkel 115 seaplanes, outdated aircraft described by one *Luftwaffe* commentator as 'fat, tired birds', were brought down attacking an east coast convoy.[27]

Success was more forthcoming against warships. The minesweepers steaming up the war channel in nice straight lines were particularly vulnerable, and on 7 October HM ships *Niger* and *Selkirk* were attacked by

Dornier 18 flying boats. A few days later the Home Fleet destroyer *Mohawk* was bombed by Junkers 88 bombers whilst escorting a convoy and her 43-year-old Commander, Richard Jolly, was mortally wounded. He was later awarded a posthumous George Cross. Two Ju88s were lost in this raid, which also inflicted minor damage on the cruisers *Southampton* and *Edinburgh*.

More effective *Luftwaffe* operations began in November, when aircraft were employed to drop magnetic mines in the Thames Estuary and elsewhere in increasing numbers. By the Führer's regular naval staff conference on 22 November, *Großadmiral* Raeder was able to report to Hitler that destroyers had laid 540 mines off the Thames and the Humber, submarines had laid 150 mines on the east and west coasts, and aircraft had laid nearly eighty more over the course of three consecutive nights of operations.[28] What Hitler had decided to christen 'the siege of England' was well under way.[29]

Captain G. Girling's tanker *James J. Maguire* was a victim off Harwich on 18 November. Captain Girling was on the bridge when an explosion rocked his ship: 'The effect . . . was to raise the ship a considerable distance up from the water . . . every compass . . . was shattered and the aerial of our wireless came down.' *James J. Maguire* took on a starboard list and started to go down by the head. As he fought to save her, Captain Girling observed another victim slowly sinking, the Dutch passenger liner *Simon Bolivar*:

> I realised that she was in distress . . . I had my binoculars on her when suddenly I saw another explosion which was not extremely loud, but I am quite definite that she was struck just forward of the bridge . . . a huge column of water rose into the air . . . she sank and disappeared from sight quite rapidly.[30]

Although *James J. Maguire* was successfully salvaged, 130 people died on the *Simon Bolivar*. Over the next six days another six ships were sunk off Harwich, including the Japanese liner *Terukani Maru*, the wreck of which was to become a marker for east coast shipping over the next six years.

Sixty-eight more magnetic mines were dropped by air in shallow water during five operations between 20 November and 7 December.[31] J.A.J. Dennis was First Lieutenant of the Harwich destroyer HMS *Griffin*, which returned from the Mediterranean at the height of the offensive:

> There were wrecks of ships with only their upperworks standing above the muddy water. It was now early November, time enough to realise that the mines were magnetic, laid in shallow water under fifteen fathoms. But no effective protection yet existed and there seemed to be no safe way of

> sweeping them. As all our operations from Harwich were in mineable waters, one never knew, day or night, whether one might be blown up at any moment, so one tended to walk about with knees slightly bent.[32]

On 21 November Dennis witnessed one *Luftwaffe* minelaying foray first hand: 'We all entered harbour that evening. As we arrived there was quite a lot of activity. Some aircraft were being shot at and after we had passed the harbour mouth a Heinkel seaplane was seen to drop a mine on a parachute right in the channel.' [33]

Despite this, the entire 1st Destroyer Flotilla was ordered to sea a few hours later, to respond to a report of German destroyers at sea off the Dutch coast. The British destroyers were ordered to stay close to the edge of the channel, as far from the mine as possible:

> So off we went with ourselves leading the line . . . my lifebelt was fully inflated and my knees very bent. As we reached the spot I held my breath but nothing happened. Only a minute later our next astern, the *Gipsy*, blew up with an almighty bang and a flash of light. She broke in two right between the funnels. The Captain, Nigel Crossley . . . was catapulted on to the forecastle and never regained consciousness. Robert Franks, also on the bridge, landed on B Gun Deck in company with the magnetic compass binnacle on which he had been leaning at the time. He was quite unscathed.

Fifty men were killed; the remainder were left fighting for their lives in the gloom of the night and the fast-flowing water:

> We spent a dismal few hours trying to pick up survivors in the dark with the brown foamy current flowing by and the pervasive smell of oil fuel – later so familiar that it still strikes a chord of memory whenever I smell it. Mingled with the cries of the drowning men was the mournful tolling of the channel bell buoy. A fitting requiem for the first of our flotilla to go.[34]

Felixstowe Police recorded that bodies continued to be washed ashore for the next four months.[35] Magnetic mines also claimed the minelayer *Adventure* (damaged on 13 November) and the destroyer *Blanche*, sunk in the same incident, the brand-new cruiser *Belfast*, damaged on 21 November, and the battleship *Nelson*, damaged on 4 December. Fourteen merchant ships were sunk around the Knock Lightship during November.

However, by introducing air drops and using magnetic mines before they had sufficient stock to sustain a large-scale offensive the Germans had brought about their own downfall. On 23 November, a mine drop over the Thames Estuary was witnessed and a team led by Lieutenant Commander John Ouvry went on to the mud flats off Shoeburyness to recover an undamaged example. Ouvry dissected the mine on 24 November 'at great personal risk', for which he was awarded the Royal Navy's first gallantry award of the Second World War, a Distinguished Service Order. As a result the Achilles' heel of the magnetic mine was discovered: 'The German detonators responded to the North-South (or so-called "blue") magnetic fields of ships built in the Northern Hemisphere, where such is the natural polarity, and not to the South-North (or "red") polarity of ships built south of the Equator.'[36] The mines could thus be countered by reversing the magnetism of the ships using a powerful electric current passed around cables encircling the hulls just above the waterline, a process known as 'degaussing'.[37] In the meantime the dismantled mine was passed to the Royal Navy's Mine Warfare School, HMS *Vernon*, where an experimental flotilla of converted fishing drifters was formed to try to establish a means of sweeping them. Brooks Richards was a young RNVR officer on a minesweeping course at *Vernon* at the time:

> Somebody pointed out to us a diver walking across the lawn approaching an object in the middle of it. They said 'well that object . . . is something we've just discovered, which is the mechanism of a magnetic mine, dropped on a mud bank in the Thames estuary . . . we're just trying to find out whether we can remove these darned things by sending divers down to attach ropes to them to pull them up, but of course we've got to find out whether the diver is magnetic because of his helmet, to the point out where it would blow him up.[38]

Richards went away for a weekend's leave. When he returned the following Monday, he discovered that not only had a great deal of weekend working been put in on the subject of magnetic mines, but also that they were about to loom large in his service career. He was ordered to Glasgow to take over a herring drifter, hardly his ideal posting when he asked for 'small ships':

> Equipment had been assembled and prepared in the yard to equip them in such a way that four of the drifters would have searchlight generators in the hold, two in each of the fish holds, whereas the other four would have large electromagnetic coils mounted on their decks . . . they hoped therefore that when these drifters were paired off, one towing with the generators on board and the other evacuated but with the coil energised you'd have something that would blow up a mine on the sea bed. Everything was in a great state of hurry.[39]

Once again the crews came from the hard-pressed RNPS. Within a few days Richards was in Loch Ewe on the west coast of Scotland, sweeping around the damaged battleship *Nelson* to allow her to be towed to safety.

> We arrived there in December 1939 in these very dirty little ships . . . and tied up alongside this impeccable even though partly incapacitated battleship . . .

> We managed in the ensuing days to sweep the first magnetic mine ever swept and therefore to clear a channel out of which the *Nelson* could go to sea and be repaired in dockyard. Funnily enough the mine was swept just outside the buoyed channel and blew up the drifter which was destroyed and the chap in charge of that pair of drifters got . . . a right royal blowing up for having not switched off the current at the right point. Anyhow it did demonstrate even if at the cost of a drifter that the gear functioned.[40]

The system was later improved, with the drifters towing a cheap, easy to produce wooden raft known as a 'skid' to carry the coil, 'the idea being that you were going destroy this rather than destroy a ship every time you swept a mine.'[41] Wellington aircraft were also fitted with an outlandish magnetic loop, entirely encircling the aircraft from nose to tail and wingtip to wingtip, and by flying low over the water were also able to set off the mines. In desperation, the old freighter *Borde* was fitted as a mine-clearance vessel by equipping her with a huge electro-magnet; she performed sterling work around the coast although the first mine she cleared wrecked every instrument on board.

Developing these new techniques took time, as did degaussing merchant ships, either permanently by fitting them with cables or, because there were many ships and not much cable, the temporary expedient of passing them through a magnetic field, a technique known as 'wiping'. Joseph Wharton was serving on the SS *Clan Stuart* at the time: 'It took about six weeks to degauss a ship . . . because the only way of doing it was to haul heavy copper wire around the ship and they'd weld brackets on to the hull and it all had to be pulled by hand and it took time.'[42]

As midwinter neared, more and more RNPS men found themselves minesweeping. Sixty-eight converted wooden fishing boats were based at Harwich, and another fifty at Yarmouth and Lowestoft. More effective support was provided by naval fleet minesweepers, including the archaic-looking, First World War vintage, paddle minesweepers of the newly formed 12th Minesweeping Flotilla.[43] Those who manned them reached new levels of exhaustion. Anthony Nicholls was a young Lieutenant serving in the fleet minesweeper HMS *Sphinx*. On 20 November he wrote optimistically to his parents about his work on the east coast:

> There has been a good deal of mining activity off this part as the papers will reveal, and I expect we shall be kept pretty busy. But the war hasn't really touched us yet, we have only got as far as firing at the odd German aircraft, one of which dropped a couple of bombs, they however falling about a mile away. Personally I must confess that I do not mind the war at all. It gives me an aim and an object in life, even if only a limited one – though I suppose this is rather a terrible confession. The sight of blood would probably alter it.[44]

By 21 December all he could manage was: 'The last few days have been very hectic and I have had no time to write.' In a subsequent undated letter he confessed: 'It has been rather a black time for letters . . . I really don't know what the date is.'[45]

As the dreadful attrition from both magnetic and conventional mines mounted through the winter, the coasters kept on steadfastly ploughing along the coast, inspiring reluctant admiration even from their enemies. At the Führer's naval conference on 30 December, Raeder reported that: 'British and neutral merchant shipping are suffering severe losses . . . on the other hand, the British are constantly able to create gaps in the mine fields by taking advantage of the removal of individual mines by ships which had been sunk. Traffic is continuing by day at least, although at great risk.'[46] What this bland statement meant for the coaster men had been amply illustrated the day before. On 29 December, the collier *Stanholm* was laboriously making her way from Cardiff to London with 4,000 tons of coal when she was mined 4 miles south of Nash Point. Her master was the improbably named Captain Hook:

> Heavy explosion occurred amidships on the port side, about 130 feet from the bow. It was like a dull thud with no splash or flame. The bridge and wheelhouse were carried away, the second officer was blown off the bridge on to the lower bridge and all the lookouts and officers on the bridge were killed.[47]

All the boats were smashed and seven men had been killed. The surviving crew were too few in number to launch the heavy rafts, so they were forced to jump into the freezing Channel, relying on their lifejackets to save their lives. *Stanholm* sank in three minutes, leaving the survivors clinging to wreckage until a boat from the Norwegian ship *Liv* eventually rescued them.

Two days later, on New Year's Eve, the ocean-going freighter *Box Hill* was in the North Sea laden with 8,340 tons of wheat. She had fallen behind her convoy days before in the middle of the Atlantic but had struggled on alone as far as the Humber Light Vessel. Able Seaman H.E. Hailes was on watch on the bridge:

> Suddenly there was a loud explosion which threw the Captain, the Second Mate, and myself, on our backs . . . I did not see any splash or flame, only steam and ashes. I think the mine hit us under the engine room . . . I think the Number 2 ballast oil tank was blown up, as we were all covered in oil . . . the ship shuddered and broke in half right away, the stern broke off and sank in about two minutes. I was left on the fore end of the ship, the bows being lifted into the air and the after end dipping in to the sea. I tried to get to the boat deck but I was washed over the side.[48]

Out of thirty-four men on board, twenty-two died. The survivors, some injured, were picked up by the destroyer HMS *Ivanhoe*. These hard-pressed naval escorts were feeling the strain as much as the merchant skippers. Lieutenant Commander W.J. Phipps started the war in command of the 1918-vintage V&W class destroyer HMS *Woolston*, and spent most of it on the east coast. His unpublished diary is an illuminating testament to just how overstretched these small, often elderly, ships and their inexperienced crews were during those early months.

On 17 and 18 October 1939 *Woolston* was sent to hunt a submarine contact, possibly imaginary, off St Abb's Head: 'very little sleep both nights, about one and a half hours on my sea cabin settee'. After oiling at Harwich and getting only his second night in bed in ten days, Phipps took convoy FN24 up to Methil, rescuing survivors from the sunken SS *Orsa* on the way and coming under air attack throughout the afternoon of 21 October, although as was often the case at this stage of the war 'the scale of the attack did not warrant any drastic orders to the convoy.'[49] The attack only ended when the convoy was fogbound, leading to further strain.

On 22 October, *Woolston* was ordered south again, with yet another convoy. The sheer volume of traffic on the coast and the inexperience of naval personnel made for difficult conditions and a brush with the destroyer *Jupiter* at 0340:

> Expected to pass *Jupiter* about 0330 and listened out ahead on Asdic, heard her at 0340 about five miles ahead, counted revolutions, 218. Altered slightly to starboard to give her room and switched on dimmed navigation lights; she had tons of room to port of us but just at the wrong moment he put his helm to port and shot right across our bows and those of the starboard wing column giving them all a fright. Damned stupid thing to do.[50]

On the night of 13 November came a close shave with the sloop HMS *Pelican*. This time the fault lay with *Woolston*'s own exhausted and desperately raw watchkeeping officers:

> Apparently every ship in the world was running up or rather down the coast that night and passed sixty or more ships on the stretch between Hartlepool and Whitby . . . in the middle Grinham made a complete balls of it and draped ourselves across the bows of *Pelican*, partly her fault for running around unnecessarily to find the convoy but mainly Grinham in a panic to get on the searched channel, quite unnecessarily altering course thirty [degrees] to starboard and running across the line of traffic. Can't trust these chaps yet though I realise they are inexperienced.[51]

As if he had insufficient work to do, Phipps was briefly detached to the Thames for anti-aircraft defence duties, then on 26 November he was sent all the way back up to Methil to pick up a southbound convoy, FS43. Uncharacteristically, his frustration showed:

> Got a signal telling us to go to Tyne ready for FS43 sailing . . . I think it is absolutely wrong for Admiralty to butt in . . . we have few enough to do the job as it is and when some are taken away to do extraneous jobs like the defence of the Thames I think it is the limit. Got under weigh as quick as I could.[52]

On 27 November, Phipps went ashore for the first time in ten days. He got as far as the jetty. By 0100 on the 28th he was heading south with FS43. The convoys ran every two or three days throughout the winter without a break. Phipps and his men were subjected to endless false alarms, navigational hazards caused by fog, convoy indiscipline, the growing numbers of wrecks, aircraft sightings and the ever-present hazard of drifting mines: '18 December . . . sank five by rifle fire in the course of the day.'[53] Christmas was spent anchored in the Thames Estuary in thick fog. The *Woolston*'s crew got no leave until 26 January 1940, after five months at war.

Lieutenant Dennis of the Harwich destroyer *Griffin* also went on leave at this time. In London he found a complete lack of awareness about the exhausting, bloody war being fought around the coast: 'London still seemed to be on a peacetime footing . . . nightclubs full of people and blue smoke. It was irritating to hear them talking about the "phoney war". I wished some of them would . . . get blown up and go for a swim.'[54] The dreadful irony of his words was brought home after his return to Harwich, where 'large ice flows had begun to form [in] . . . the worst winter for many years'.[55] The 1st Destroyer Flotilla suffered another casualty on 19 January:

> We were steaming in line abreast when *Grenville* blew up amidships and sank rapidly. The water being shallow her forward and after parts remained for a while above water as the broken sections rested on the bottom. The first thing was to pick up survivors in the water, as they couldn't last long in those temperatures. There were the usual harrowing scenes and sounds with which we were to become so familiar. We rescued them all including George Creasy [*Grenville*'s Captain] himself. Cold and wet as he was, he insisted on coming onto the bridge and was only quietened by a shot given him by John Walley [*Griffin*'s Medical Officer], which assuredly saved him from death by pneumonia. But only about a hundred could be picked up. There was one man who somehow found himself outside the forecastle hull, clinging to the bars of the Naval Store scuttle. For a long time he refused to jump for *Grenade*'s boat as he couldn't swim.'[56]

The *Luftwaffe* was still maintaining a steady, wearing trickle of attacks. In the broad sweep of the history of the Second World War these would be lucky to get more than a line in most books, and would probably be described as 'nuisance' raids, but they were more than a 'nuisance' for the men who had to endure them. In December and January the Germans raided the Trinity House lightships, claiming they were legitimate targets as they marked the convoy routes. On 9 January, the tender THV *Reculver* was bombed and strafed, and at the end of the month the crew of the East Dudgeon light vessel were forced to abandon their ship and row ashore in the face of relentless air attack. Their boat capsized and six of the seven crew were drowned.[57] The British responded with outrage, calling it 'ungentlemanly' and *Punch* cartoons depicted it as a war crime. But the bluster was accompanied, more practically, by fighter patrols for the lightships.[58]

On the same day as the attack on *Reculver* the small coaster *Gowrie* was attacked for thirty-five minutes by two German aircraft off Stonehaven, 'so low we could see the men laughing at us . . . every bomb which fell anywhere near the ship seemed to lift us right out of the water.'[59] She sank after two direct hits. And on the 29th the SS *Stanburn* was sunk with the loss of all but three of her crew of twenty-eight. Able Seaman Edwin Dotchin was one of the lucky ones:

> We started to rush up on deck but before we got there the first bomb hit us amidships in the engine room killing ten people. Having arrived on deck I observed four men lowering the port lifeboat. That was the only lifeboat we had as the other was damaged in bad weather the previous night. We lowered the boat into the water and three men managed to climb into her. She then drifted away. While we were standing watching . . . the second bomb was dropped and it struck Number 3 hatch amidships. This blew the hatch to pieces and killed the men who were throwing over the forward raft. Eight of us including the Master threw over the after raft and seven of us managed to jump on to it. We left one man standing on deck. He refused to jump, and that was the last we saw of him. The waves soon took charge of our raft and we drifted away . . . we were unable to see much owing to the bad weather but occasionally caught a glimpse of what was going on when we rose to the top of the waves.[60]

Edwin was adrift with several other men for two hours in a raft that had been riddled with machine-gun fire. The tug *Gripfast* eventually appeared, but even the rescue was characterized by tragedy for the *Stanburn* men:

> *Gripfast* came alongside of us and threw us a rope. I took a turn with it round one of the spars of the raft and as it taughtened [sic] it jammed the Captain's foot which caused him to hit his head against the ship's side. He fell into the water and we never saw him again. The raft then capsized and we were all thrown into [the] water and were drifting along the ship's side grabbing at

> lines and falls which had been lowered for us. Five of us managed to catch hold of lines and after a few minutes I managed to catch hold of a ladder that had been lowered and scrambled on board. Two others managed to follow my example. The others unfortunately fell back into the water and I presume they were drowned.[61]

The deteriorating weather and the increasing volume of traffic on the east coast made navigation a nightmarish experience, with little room for error. William Donald was First Lieutenant of the anti-aircraft sloop *Black Swan*:

> Escorting these huge convoys – sometimes of fifty ships or more – who sailed in two lines at a depressing slow speed, was no child's play. Collisions were just as great a menace as was damage by the enemy. This was a thousand times more so at nighttime when two convoys, one southbound and the other northbound, had to pass. This invariably occurred with clockwork precision at a corner on the route, when there would be sometimes nearly a hundred ships, all without lights and in darkness, barging past each other in confined waters, with a minefield on one side and sandbanks on the other.[62]

Some mishaps were inevitable and it was perhaps something of a minor miracle that there were not more. Some were even amusing, once they were safely over. Edward Walker was serving on the V&W HMS *Wolsey*:

> We were escorting a convoy down the east coast, a dreadful fog developed. We lost contact with the convoy and the other escort vessels, since Aldis lamps were of no use and we had to maintain radio silence, so we proceeded southwards very slowly. The following morning brought no relief, with visibility still down to a few yards. The Captain decided to turn landwards and an Able Seaman was detached to carry out soundings so that we did not run aground. After some time, the end of a pier loomed out of the mist and the vague shape of a man could be seen. The Able called out 'What place is this?' Came the reply, 'Bridlington.' It is easy to imagine how the chap on the pier would relate this tale in his local public house that day.[63]

John Chrisp and his Admiralty trawler, *Jasper*, were transferred to convoy escort work in that long winter, and also had a narrow escape:

> It was very rough weather, the convoy was stretched out in single line with a destroyer ahead, trawler on either side and we were the junior ship right astern. I remember saying 'all right I'll have a little nap now . . . don't forget we'll turn down when we get in line with the Long Sands [buoy] and then alter course down for the Tyne.'[64]

When he returned from his 'nap' four hours later, John received a nasty shock:

> I looked at the chart and I found we'd actually gone about two hours towards the [East Coast] minefield. I said 'Good lord why haven't we altered course?' And he said 'well sir I'm following the next ahead!' I said 'something's wrong. Let's creep up the convoy.' (It was eight knots and we could only do ten) . . . we passed the first, then we passed the second, then we passed the third, then we got to the fourth and there was nothing in sight! The convoy had altered course and in the mist the merchantmen hadn't seen them.[65]

Altering course, the *Jasper* and her three strays finally caught up with the convoy just before it reached the Tyne.

All through the winter, the huge, lumbering coaster convoys continued to pay a heavy toll to mines. On 21 January the collier *Ferry Hill* was making her way from Blyth to Aberdeen. On her way to pick up her northbound convoy she was rocked by an explosion at 1415. J.M. Ovenston was her Chief Officer:

> I was blown right across Number 3 Hatch, and I had [sic] my forehead hit against the derricks. I knew that it was no good trying to go up to the boat deck so I looked aft. There was a door floating about on the after end and I told the Chief Engineer to come with me but he just stood there, dazed. I knew that it was a case of everybody for themselves, and I lost a grip on the door . . . I saw some more wreckage and I tried to get my sea boots off but my hands were so numb that I could not do so.[66]

Ovenston was luckier than most. The Steward and Second Mate were both killed, the latter last seen with a 'big split across his forehead'. The Second Engineer, Grassie, was saved by sheer luck. Off watch, he should have drowned below decks when the ship went down, but he had come on deck to inspect a repair and was blown into the water, seriously hurt. Ovenston spotted him:

> I swam out to Grassie who was also in the water. The ship went down in about four minutes. I saw that Grassie was badly hurt so I caught hold of him. We both held on to the hatch together until a minesweeper came along and picked us up . . . [they] . . . threw out some lines but they were not good enough so they threw some lifebelts. By this time I caught a turn round Grassie and kept him out of the water . . . They put a ladder overboard and I got up and helped Grassie up with me.[67]

It seemed as if the Captain of the *Ferry Hill* might have survived, as he was spotted in the water: 'The Captain of the minesweeper jumped into the water in his full clothing . . . he turned him over and when he found that he was dead he came back on board.'[68]

The survivors were landed at North Shields.

Oddly enough, the start of the war did not bring about an immediate national coal crisis. Lack of shipping capacity meant that domestic supply was maintained at the expense of exports, particularly to France.[69] Unfortunately this abundant supply was only available at source. With severe winter weather disrupting the railways, the inevitable slowdown caused by the introduction of regulated convoys, and the attrition of the German mining offensive, by January 1940 'there was severe pressure on all available coasters' and only two or three weeks' supply was being held by the big electricity and gas works in London and the South.[70]

As the winter wore on the *Luftwaffe* became more adventurous, and more effective. On 3 February, German aircraft caught up with Anthony Nicholls and his minesweeper, *Sphinx*. At 0912 a bomb struck forward of her bridge, destroying it completely and killing the Commanding Officer, Commander J.R.N. Taylor, before passing through the deck and exploding in the mess deck below. The catastrophic explosion folded the entire forecastle back over the bridge, breaking the sweeper open at the bow and letting in the sea. She was taken in tow stern first with her engines running astern until 2000 hours, when the engines gave up. The gallant little *Sphinx* capsized and the remaining men were forced to abandon her.

As Navigating Officer, or 'Pilot', Anthony Nicholls was the senior officer following the death of the Captain, and took over command during the desperate fight to save *Sphinx*. Comrades testified afterwards to his courage and good humour: 'The Pilot did everything humanly possible to save the ship and those on board: the efficiency and high morale of the ship's company was largely due to his cool bearing and very cheerful and encouraging disposition . . . he never left the Upper Deck, from whence he commanded the ship, for seventeen hours.'[71]

Tragically there were to be no more letters from Anthony. The remaining brief note in the short, moving collection of material held by the Imperial War Museum was added by his father, the Reverend Reginald Nicholls, who was living in Malta at the time: 'About six o'clock on February 5th I returned from an afternoon's visiting. A note for me, said Herself [his wife, Phyllis], brought by a Maltese messenger. I opened it casually and the cruel words seemed to burn my eyes. "It has come," I said. "What has come?" "Anthony."'[72]

Fifty-three men died from HMS *Sphinx*, roughly half the ship's company. The body of Anthony Nicholls, who was twenty-six, was never found, and his name is recorded on the Chatham Naval Memorial. For his actions on that day he was Mentioned in Despatches.

As the young naval reservists laid down their lives, more arrived to take their place during the long, bitter winter of the 'not so phoney war'.

Twenty-year-old RNVR midshipman Hugh Irwin had worked in the shipping industry before the war. In February 1940, he arrived to join the sloop HMS *Lowestoft*, and was subjected to a rude introduction to life as a very junior officer, and one who was the only RNVR man, commissioned or not, on board the ship:

> [The commanding officer] invited me down to the wardroom . . . and asked me 'would I have a drink?', and suggested a gimlet which was a gin and lime, which I thoroughly enjoyed, it was threepence, and at the end of the month . . . he called me into his cabin and he said 'Your wine bill is stopped, Midshipmen are not allowed to drink gin,' but he'd suggested it and I was the only Midshipman in the ship, it was bloody stupid, quite absurd . . . he was a tough character.[73]

Snobbery, prejudice and 'bullshit' had not, it would seem, always been set aside for the war years.

The east coast was a small world, and with one convoy every two days or so the vagaries of merchant skippers and commodores became familiar to the men of the escorts, who encountered them week after week. Some individuals became well known 'characters' – not always for the right reasons. Hugh Irwin remembered one particular Commodore with some amusement:

> I never forget one ship called the *Ice Maid*, Commodore Newman, he was a Lieutenant Commander RNR, and he liked to get into the Tyne quick on a Saturday night, so he could get his beer and go home. And on this occasion he was Commodore and he was way ahead of the convoy and in the afternoon watch I reported to the Captain that it was impossible, that this ship was going too fast, so he sent a signal to the *Ice Maid* reprimanding him, and he replied to say that he was sorry, the *Ice Maid* had been milking revolutions whilst he was asleep.[74]

Lieutenant Commander Phipps of *Woolston* also crossed swords with Newman, christening him 'non-stop Newman'.[75] But for Phipps, over-enthusiastic commodores were not good news. Taking FS88 down to Southend in filthy weather on 6 February he found that his charges had spread themselves all over the North Sea:

> Went up the line at twenty [knots] for an hour by which time I had counted twenty-six [ships] and a large gap and no signs of [HMS] *Grimsby*. Thought a position would be a good egg then, so ran in and made Flamborough then out to *Pilsudski* [a well-known wreck]. Made the head of the convoy . . . and I reckoned convoy was spread over 19 miles. Commodore had obviously battled on at full speed and as usual I'm all right and damn all the rest. About twelve with him.[76]

As winter turned to spring the tempo of the *Luftwaffe* assault on shipping increased. On 13 February, the 371-ton coaster *Boston Trader* was making her way from King's Lynn to Yarmouth in ballast. She was just 6 miles from land when at 0730 her lookouts sighted an aircraft approaching from straight ahead. *Boston Trader*'s Captain, H. Brown, ran on deck and ordered his crew to take cover as the aircraft flew over the ship, raking her decks with machine-gun fire. As the German pilot manoeuvred for a second pass, Brown took desperate evasive action:

> He made a circle of about a quarter of a mile and I put the helm hard over so that when he returned he was forced to fly athwartships instead of from bow to stern. This time he dropped four bombs which followed each other closely . . . none of these hit the ship, but the concussion blew the port lifeboat out of the davits and we lost it.[77]

Boston Trader was attacked eight times: 'He would approach us at a height of about six hundred feet, dive down to about seventy feet, then flatten out and drop his bombs. He dropped twelve bombs altogether.'[78] Each time Brown desperately carried out the same manoeuvre, putting his helm over and forcing the German pilot to approach the ship beam on. This cool display of ship handling meant that instead of having the entire length of the ship on which to plant his bombs, the German airman had only her narrow width, a far more difficult target. But on the fifth pass *Boston Trader*'s luck finally ran out: 'One bomb . . . exploded immediately alongside the ship, causing damage to the hull . . . the main engine stopped dead . . . the vessel was now making water in the engine room [and] the accommodation was burning fiercely, so I decided to abandon ship.'[79] *Boston Trader*'s assailant circled her while the remaining boat was lowered but made no attempt to interfere. Leaving the little coaster on fire he made off to the east. The Sheringham lifeboat picked up the survivors.

Lieutenant Dennis's destroyer, *Griffin*, was attacked by German aircraft on 9 March:

> A Heinkel III came suddenly out of the clouds and ran a stream of machine gun bullets right along our decks from aft to forwards. I was on the bridge and was rather narrowly missed by a bullet, which made a nice hole in the Deck Log. Sadly we did suffer our first casualty – Cook Shirtleff who was in the galley, cooking, was hit and died later.[80]

Soon afterwards Dennis was sent on leave. On the long journey south on the night train he became aware of how badly the relentless strain of the war on the coast had affected his nerves: 'Three of us . . . were asleep on the benches when for some reason the train rumbled over a rough set of points. There was a shake and a roar. Within seconds all three of us found ourselves out in the corridor, blowing up imaginary lifebelts.'[81]

Six month of relentless tension had affected some merchant sailors just as badly. Joseph Wharton's luck ran out in the Channel on 10 March when the *Clan Stuart* collided with a coaster in thick fog some 50 miles west of Start Point.

> We heard this siren very close at hand and we jumped up and ran for the port rail, we knew that something was going to hit us any minute and sure enough this fairly large coaster came out of the fog there and it struck us by Number Two hold. It kind of grazed its way all down the side of the ship taking the railings and everything else with it and in no time the ship was down by the head. The old man got Chippie [the carpenter] to go around and take soundings and it was found that her plates couldn't stand up to a blow like that and she was going down. The order came to abandon ship . . . we got in to the lifeboats and there were four boats pulled away. It was very flat sea, very calm, no wind, thick fog. The boats were tied to each other to keep together.[82]

In the boats the unremitting strain manifested itself in the actions of one crew member:

> We eventually saw very low down on the water these port and starboard navigation lights and a masthead coming for us. The Chief Steward started screaming and screaming that it was a U-boat, and we should pull and get the hell out for it. Anyway I think someone forcibly calmed him down and it was a French trawler, the *Notre Dame*, she had found our SOS and with her direction finder she'd come to our assistance and she picked us up.[83]

By now the effort put into beating the magnetic mine was beginning to bear fruit, and the minesweeper crews were starting to experience the satisfaction of actually clearing them. On 7 March, the Commanding Officer of a group of minesweepers based at Harwich reported with satisfaction the clearing of another magnetic mine, 'the third exploded in this area', 350 yards from the old wreck of the *Terukani Maru*:

> The explosion blew a column of water in the air, the central pinnacle of which reached about 300 feet and the outer ring about 180–200 feet. Mixed with this were pieces of debris and timber and also pebbles and shingle which landed on the deck of the *Slogan* which was in station forty yards on the port beam of the *Colne*.[84]

Colne was the triumphant sweeper, whose victory was probably slightly marred by the page-long list of damage to her hull, fixtures and fittings included in the official report. Chief Skipper Grace of the sweeper *Berberis* was in no doubt about the improving morale of his ship's company: 'Effect on ship's company generally was pleasure . . . that at last after eight months service we had justified our existence as a mine-sweeper during the last two days. Ship's company hope to have the honour of blowing up the next mine.'[85]

March had actually seen a decline in the number of airdropped magnetic mines, mainly due to the inter-service squabbling and political points scoring which characterized the Nazi regime. At the Führer's naval conference on 29 March, *Großadmiral* Raeder's anger at his *Luftwaffe* counterpart, Hermann Göring, was plain:

> Operations with aerial mines . . . agreed upon with the Commander-in-Chief, Air [Göring], were planned for 28 March, however on the evening of 27 March they were cancelled by the Commander-in-Chief, Air, without any reason being given, and any further operations prohibited.[86]

Hitler and the Commander-in-Chief of the Armed Forces, General Keitel, apparently agreed to take the matter up with Göring, and minelaying operations were swiftly resumed. German technicians also changed the rule-book of this relentless, cerebral game. In April 1940, suspecting the reason for the declining effectiveness of magnetic mines, they reversed their polarity, rendering degaussing ineffective. On 17 April, the now co-operative *Luftwaffe* scattered large numbers of these new 'red' mines along the East Anglian coast and the attrition rate in coastal waters began to rise once more.

This time, however, the advantage was to be rather more short-lived. Less than two weeks later, on the night of 30 April, a Heinkel III bomber on a minelaying mission strayed over land and crashed at Clacton-on-Sea. The aircraft exploded, destroying fifty houses, killing two people and injuring another 156. Incredibly, one of the 'red' mines being carried by the aircraft somehow survived intact to be picked apart by the experts at *Vernon*. The heyday of the magnetic mine was over, but it had exacted an appalling cost: between September 1939 and May 1940 mines claimed 114 ships in British coastal waters, mostly amongst ships sailing independently, and therefore not following dedicated minesweepers.[87]

Notes

1. IWM Sound 13242 Wharton, Joseph.
2. *Führer Conferences on Naval Affairs: 1939*, Admiralty, London, 1947, p. 5. Minutes from these staff meetings held between Hitler and his senior commanders were captured by Allied Intelligence towards the end of the war. Translated and annotated editions were published by the Admiralty for internal use.

3. Lund, Paul and Ludlam, Harry, *Trawlers Go To War*, New English Library, London, 1972, p. 19.
4. IWM Sound 9377 Maggs, Charles.
5. *Führer Conferences on Naval Affairs: 1939*, p. 12.
6. Raeder, Grand Admiral Erich, *My Life*, United States Naval Institute, Annapolis, Maryland, 1960, p. 281.
7. IWM Docs 87/2/1 Spickett, A., p. 45.
8. Ibid., pp. 47–8.
9. Ibid., p. 52.
10. Ibid., p. 48.
11. IWM Docs 90/23/1 King, Captain H.A.
12. Ibid.
13. Ibid.
14. Ibid.
15. NA ADM 199/2130 Survivors' Reports: Merchant Vessels 3 September to 30 November 1939.
16. Ibid.
17. Ibid.
18. In the interests of balance it should be recorded that the British also mined German coastal waters and rivers, with conventional and influence mines, in a campaign which eventually accounted for 645 enemy or enemy controlled merchant vessels in the waters between Archangel and Gibraltar. (Roskill, *War at Sea*, vol. III, Part 2, p. 476).
19. NA ADM 199/2130 Survivors' Reports: Merchant Vessels 3 September to 30 November 1939.
20. Ibid.
21. Ibid.
22. Ibid.
23. Ibid, p. 104a.
24. IWM Sound 16794 Hollinshed, Montague.
25. Ibid.
26. IWM Sound 12550 Merryweather, William.
27. Bekker, Cajus, *The Luftwaffe War Diaries*, Corgi, London, 1972, p. 332.
28. *Führer Conferences on Naval Affairs: 1939*, p. 42.
29. Ibid, p. 19.
30. NA ADM 199/2130 Survivors' Reports: Merchant Vessels 3 September to 30 November 1939.
31. Research Institute for Military History (eds), *Germany and the Second World War: Volume II Germany's Initial Conquests in Europe*, Clarendon Press, Oxford, 2003, p. 174.
32. IWM Docs 95/5/1 Dennis, Commander J.A.J., p. 18.
33. Ibid., p. 23.
34. Ibid., p. 23.
35. Foynes, *Battle of the East Coast*, pp. 18–19.

36. Ibid., p. 25.
37. Named after Johann Carl Friedrich Gauss (1777–1855), an early researcher in the field of magnetism.
38. IWM Sound 9970 Richards, Sir Brooks.
39. Ibid.
40. Ibid.
41. Ibid.
42. IWM Sound 13242 Wharton, Joseph.
43. Foynes, *Battle of the East Coast*, p. 28.
44. IWM Docs 05/80/1 Nicholls, Lieutenant A.
45. Ibid.
46. *Führer Conferences on Naval Affairs: 1939*, p. 65.
47. NA ADM 199/2131 Survivors' Reports: Merchant Vessels 1 December 1939 to 28 February 1940, p. 72.
48. Ibid., p. 74.
49. IWM Docs 75/105/1 Phipps, Commander W.J., p.80.
50. Ibid.
51. Ibid., p. 7.
52. Ibid., p. 11.
53 Ibid., p. 17.
54. IWM Docs 95/5/1 Dennis, Commander J.A.J., p. 24.
55. Ibid., p. 27.
56. Ibid., p. 29.
57. Woodman, *Keepers of the Sea*, p. 139.
58. Foynes, *Battle of the East Coast*, p. 12.
59. NA ADM 199/2131 Survivors' Reports: Merchant Vessels 1 December 1939 to 28 February 1940, p. 90.
60. Ibid., p. 117.
61. Ibid., p. 117.
62. Donald, Commander William, *Stand by for Action*, New English Library, London, 1975, p. 12.
63. BBC PW A2913068 Walker, Edward.
64. IWM Sound 16843 Chrisp, John.
65. Ibid.
66. NA ADM 199/2131 Survivors' Reports: Merchant Vessels 1 December 1939 to 28 February 1940, p. 111.
67. Ibid.
68. Ibid.
69. Hancock, W.K. (ed.), *History of the Second World War: UK Civil Series – Coal*, HMSO, 1951, p. 59.
70. Ibid., pp. 62-3.
71. IWM Docs 05/80/1 Nicholls, Lieutenant A.
72. Ibid.
73. IWM Sound 9956 Irwin, Hugh.

74. Ibid.
75. IWM Docs 75/105/1 Phipps, Commander W.J., p. 80.
76. Ibid, p. 26.
77. NA ADM 199/2131 Survivors' Reports: Merchant Vessels 1 December 1939 to 28 February 1940, p. 139a.
78. Ibid.
79. Ibid.
80. IWM Docs 95/5/1 Dennis, Commander J.A.J., p. 34.
81. Ibid., p. 35.
82. IWM Sound 13242 Wharton, Joseph.
83. Ibid.
84. IWM Docs 85/44/1 Dobson, Commodore J.P.
85. Ibid.
86. *Führer Conferences on Naval Affairs: 1940*, p. 24.
87. Grove, *The Defeat of the Enemy Attack on Shipping 1939–1945*, Table 26 'British Allied and Neutral Merchant Vessels of all Tonnages Sunk by Mines in all Areas 1939–1945'. Seventeen ships were lost in convoy, the remainder were independents.

Chapter 4

Enemy at the Gates

1 May 1940 to 5 July 1940

By now, of course, the 'Phoney War' was no longer very phoney for anyone. On 9 April, Germany had invaded Norway and Denmark and the tempo of the war on the coast had increased once more. The day after the invasion Lieutenant Commander Phipps of the *Woolston* found himself escorting convoys to Norway instead of Southend when he got involved in his first full-scale battle:

> At 1720 sighted a long trail of smoke left by two machines. Thought they must be friendly though prepared to engage. When they turned I still thought they were Blenheims though rather big. Then saw the black cross on one of them. One shot but the other came on and dropped two bombs very near big Swedish tanker. Very soon three Spitfires put in an appearance and we ceased fire at once, sat in the stalls and watched a real thrilling battle. Spitfires simply flew rings round the Heinkel who still continued to blow out lots of smoke from his exhaust. Within a few minutes two chaps left the machine by parachute and the machine gradually lost height fired at by the Spitfires all the way down, his tail and wing flapping in the breeze, and eventually he came down in the sea about a mile ahead with a lovely bang.[1]

Phipps picked up the badly wounded pilot, *Oberleutnant* Albert Vogel: 'The pilot had been shot through the right shoulder, the bullet remaining in his right arm, a head wound, and two bullet wounds on the right side of his body and right leg.'[2]

Phipps was attacked again on 22 April by a Heinkel 115 seaplane, which initially passed over, apparently 'off to lay more bloody mines' before he 'had the effrontery to come and have another look at me'.

> Fired 0.5s at him like hell as he banked across the stern and close up the starboard side at 500ft. As he banked over both 0.5s let fly about 300 rounds at him and why he didn't come down I cannot think. Rear gunner machine-gunned us on the way up and I was standing by to duck as he got to the bridge when he stopped so we may have killed him. No casualties and only a few holes in the after funnel.[3]

On 10 May, German forces swept into northern France, Belgium and Holland, changing the dynamic of the war on the coast for good. The Allied armies collapsed and fell back, and by the end of the month most of the soldiers of the British Expeditionary Force (BEF) were surrounded in the northern French port of Dunkirk.

As the military situation on the Continent deteriorated beyond salvation, the Admiralty put into motion last-ditch plans to evacuate the BEF. These plans had been drawn up by Vice Admiral Bertram Ramsay, the Flag Officer, Dover, working out of a tiny room buried deep within the White Cliffs that had once housed a dynamo. The resulting operation was thus codenamed 'Dynamo'. Dover Command's War Diary records its commencement on 26 May in matter-of-fact style:

> This operation, which had been in preparation for some time, consisted of the evacuation from such ports as might be available, and from suitable beaches of the Allied Armies from Belgium and northern France, by means of light draught vessels such as drifters, Thames Barges, paddlers, and small coasters, including Dutch 'scoots' manned by service crews.[4]

The German armoured divisions that had thrust like a dagger though the heart of Belgium and France had been halted on Hitler's direct orders, and responsibility for preventing the evacuation lay with the *Luftwaffe*, which reduced Dunkirk to rubble and sank 137 ships and boats, out of 647 taking part.[5] But thanks to the efforts of French troops and the heavily outnumbered Royal Air Force, the defensive perimeter held for nine precious days.

This book will not attempt to tell the story of 'Dynamo' in detail, although it involved many of the men who had already spent the grim winter of 1939/40 fighting their largely unrecognized war against mines, *Luftwaffe* and weather in coastal waters. Both the coasters and their Royal Navy escorts went to Dunkirk to bring back their priceless cargoes of khaki-clad refugees. The nightmare return journeys, truly day trips from hell, were too chaotic and vulnerable to be dignified by the name of convoys.

Commander Brian Dean took HMS *Sabre*, the Royal Navy's oldest destroyer, to Dunkirk a remarkable ten times. His ship was repeatedly attacked by enemy aircraft and when she returned to Dover for the third time on 29 May, with 500 rescued soldiers aboard, *Sabre* had fired off most of her anti-aircraft ammunition. The following day, restocked with ammunition, Dean took his antique ship back into the breach, and managed to retaliate against one of the Ju87 Stuka dive-bombers which were wreaking havoc over the beaches:

> We held our fire until we could almost 'see the whites of his eyes' and then let him have it from everything we had got. I think we must have shot the pilot: anyway, he did not release his bombs. The machine missed our mast head by

> a few feet, zoomed up until it was climbing almost vertically, stalled, slipped backwards a few yards, and crashed into the sand dunes – the bombs going off with a shattering explosion. There was nothing to be seen except a big hole and little bits of twisted metal.[6]

Alongside the warships were coasters, some taking stores in to the perimeter as well as taking troops out – the thousands of men waiting on the beaches and those who were gallantly holding the perimeter still needed food, water and ammunition. William Lind went across with the Everard's coaster *Sodality*:

> When we arrived there the harbour was in flames, the oil tanks were blazing away and every now and then one of them would explode, in between enemy planes roared over the harbour dropping their bombs, but we were very lucky, none of the bombs hit us. The French stevedores abandoned the job of discharging the ship. We had a consignment of foodstuff in her hold for the troops. The British officers there managed to get the soldiers that were wandering about aimlessly together, and with our ship's winches we discharged the cargo.[7]

Captain W.A. Young took the 803-ton coaster *Levenwood* into the maelstrom on 31 May, armed only with an antique 12-pounder, a Lewis gun and a salvaged army Bren light machine gun. He arrived at Dunkirk at 1130, anchored offshore, and sent in his boats to bring off the troops.[8]

At noon German dive-bombers found the *Levenwood* but she escaped unscathed and apparently succeeded in downing one aircraft, which crashed in the dunes. Shortly afterwards a naval launch came alongside and the occupants asked Captain Young if he would be prepared to beach his ship, to make unloading quicker and easier. Young took the potentially suicidal request in his stride: 'I answered "yes" and immediately did so. I ran up on the bridge, blew the fore-peak tank and got in as far as I could, about a quarter mile from the dry beach, the depth of water at our bows being about eight feet.'[9] *Levenwood* remained in this exposed position all afternoon, while the Chief Officer and four men ferried exhausted soldiers out from the beaches.

'Dynamo' even drew grudging praise from the enemy. The German Naval Staff War Diary entry for 1 June concluded:

> The embarkation of troops on the Franco-Belgian coasts between Nieuport and Dunkirk continues its progress under strong attacks by aircraft, and artillery fire from the land. The steady laying of mines from the air, and the nightly successful appearance of German speedboats, heighten the extremely great difficulties of this retreat. The impression remains, nevertheless, that the Western Powers, under a ruthless use of naval forces and transport vessels, will

> succeed in getting a considerable part of their troops over to England, even though in complete disorder and without heavy arms or equipment. The losses, however, must be enormous.[10]

And so it proved to be. On the night of 3 June, Ramsay's destroyers slipped in to Dunkirk one last time and brought off 27,000 French soldiers. This was the last act of 'Dynamo'. Although many soldiers of the gallant French rearguard had to be abandoned to captivity, the Admiralty estimated that 338,226 Allied soldiers were successfully evacuated.[11] On the other side of the Channel, Dover Command's War Diary concluded: 'The work of all vessels engaged whether H.M. ships, auxiliary vessels or ships of the Merchant Navy was worthy of the greatest praise.'[12]

In coastal waters there was no breathing space between the end of the Battle of France and what Churchill was to term the Battle of Britain. As French forces gave ground, the *Luftwaffe* moved closer to Britain, relocating to improvised bases along the French coast. Air attacks on coastal shipping grew more frequent and ferocious.

Even the fishing fleet was not immune from this unwelcome attention. On 2 June, off Spurn Head at the mouth of the Humber, the crew of the trawler *Greynight* were repeatedly bombed and strafed by two German aircraft in a brutal attack which continued long after their tiny ship had slipped beneath the waves. The crew took to their only boat, among them Chief Engineer James Cowie:

> We had all managed to get into the small boat with the exception of the mate and one of the deck hands, who were left aboard. The deck hand jumped for it and the mate went down with the ship and when he came up he found a plank, and in spite of a wounded arm and being over seventy years of age he managed to hang on to it. The planes now were machine-gunning us in the boat . . . we all then laid down in the boat and pretended to be dead. A bullet from the machine gun now hit the Skipper and killed him. Later we found that he had actually had four bullet wounds. While the planes were machine gunning us they waved to us at the same time.[13]

The attack only ended after the *Greynight*'s tormentors apparently ran out of ammunition. The survivors were rescued four hours later. The following day the equally diminutive drifter *Katreen*, launched in 1916, was subjected to a similarly venomous attack in the same area, but despite being continually attacked with machine guns and near missed by bombs twelve times over a period of an hour and a half she stubbornly refused to sink. She returned to port with her holes plugged with tallow and oakum and most of her crew bailing her out with buckets.[14]

The mining offensive was also renewed with vigour as the *Luftwaffe* and *Kriegsmarine* drew nearer. On 6 June 1940, Cook Jim Stanworth was steaming up the Channel on the SS *Harcalo* to pick up a FN convoy in the Thames Estuary, listening uneasily to the sounds of gunfire coming from the French coast and watching drifting bodies in the water:

> I returned to the galley to prepare the lunch for serving and was standing with one foot on the oven door (all ships ovens come down and rest on a leg on the kitchen floor) when a terrific explosion occurred. The ship seemed to lift up several feet and fall down again and, being off balance, I fell on the floor and everything on the stove followed me. There were two kettles of boiling water, boiler of soup, pans containing vegetables, rice puddings, all sorts of containers ready for serving lunch for the different mess rooms.[15]

Jim ran for the door but, blinded by the steam, he tripped and fell, catching his eye against the corner of a table. Panicked, he scrambled to his feet and crashed into the steel door, smashing his nose. Eventually he managed to climb first the stove and then the pan rack above it, and scrambled out through the skylight onto the open boat deck. By now the ship was resting on the seabed, and the rest of the crew were scrambling into the lifeboats. As the adrenaline wore off Jim realized he was badly hurt:

> I was in terrible pain, my face, neck, all my left arm, my chest and right shoulder and down my left leg to just below the knee was scalded. I was helped into the lifeboat and it moved away from the stricken ship. One chap said humorously, 'What are you moaning about Jim? You are the only one who had any dinner today.' I must have looked a wretched sight, my left eye was closed where I had hit the corner of the table, my nose was bleeding where I had run into a closed door and the blood had run all down my singlet. My left arm was one huge blister and my hair was full of barley . . . from the soup.[16]

The *Harcalo*'s Second Officer treated Jim with the only medicine he had available: brandy. As he sipped gratefully, a cry was heard from the ship and a badly wounded survivor was spotted on the deck, Joe Muscat, a Maltese engine room hand:

> [He] was in the engine room when the mine exploded. He had a broken femur and his head, shoulders and all down his back was scalded from boiling water and steam escaping from broken pipes in the engine room. He told us that as the water rose in the engine room, he held onto the steps and let the rising water lift his body until the ship rested on the sea bed, he then pulled himself up a rope fastened to the engine room sky lights and dragged himself with a broken femur along the boat deck, shouting to us to go back for him.[17]

Another freighter stopped and Jim was helped aboard, where he was immediately given a tumbler full of neat rum. Thanks to the combination of rum, brandy, pain and exhaustion, he immediately passed out on the deck where he lay:

> I barely recollect being lifted onto the Ramsgate Lifeboat with Muscat, they must have thought I was unconscious. I suppose I was really, but it was brandy and rum unconscious. The next thing I remember was waking up at about 3.00 am in Ramsgate General Hospital. I didn't know which was worse, my burns or my bad head, because I was never a drinking man and I kept being sick but the nurse said it was caused through the anaesthetic. I had been in the theatre and my burns had been scrubbed, sprayed with tannic acid and gentian violet, drying it with a hairdryer every four hours for a few days. They told me that this stuff would stay on, making an airtight seal, for about twenty-one days. When it peeled off they hoped that a new skin would be formed. This was quite true as long as it didn't turn septic. Some parts of my body did turn septic and left ugly scars which I still have, but I'm lucky to still be here and everybody was unbelievably kind.[18]

The hospital was full of badly wounded Dunkirk survivors, 'men with arms off and some with legs amputated. You felt terrible asking the nurses for anything as they were busy attending to dying men.'

After two weeks Jim was transferred by bus to Orpington, along with several other patients from Ramsgate, and it was here that he gained a shocking insight into the severity of his injuries:

> A man from Ramsgate . . . was about four [beds] to my right in Orpington. The ward at Ramsgate [had been] dimly lit, the windows all sandbagged. The old gent asked me if I was in the Ramsgate Hospital to which I replied, 'Yes'. He said 'I wonder what happened to that dark chap in the end bed by the door?' I said, 'That was me, I was nearest the door.' 'Don't talk silly,' he said, 'I meant that black fellow that nobody would go near because he stank, everybody said that he smelled putrid.'[19]

In Ramsgate, Jim's neighbour had only been able to see his left side, burned, covered in gentian violet and smelling septic: 'I turned around in bed so he could see my left side and he laughed . . . at his mistake.' Jim Stanworth was discharged after ten weeks. His suffering was not untypical for shipwrecked mariners in wartime, in coastal waters and elsewhere.

On 9 June, the freighter *Empire Commerce* was making her way slowly from Portland to Sheerness carrying 5,400 tons of pulpwood. Ironically, after waiting more than two weeks to be wiped against magnetic mines she ran into one of the old-fashioned contact types west of the Spit Buoy, near Margate. It broke her back and in the ensuing chaos one member of her crew distinguished himself, as Captain H.B. Miller later reported:

> The lower engine room ladder was torn away and the Engineer on watch, Carrington, was caught by the inrush of water and was floundering about with the water rising. Maurice Holden had left the engine room but he turned around, saw Carrington below, and went down to his aid. He swam to him, and dragged him out at the risk of his own life. The engine room was a shambles, the engines now being at an angle of 45 degrees.[20]

Maurice Holden, *Empire Commerce*'s Greaser, was sixty-two years old, a not uncommon phenomenon in the Merchant Navy in general and in coasters in particular.

Hot on the heels of the *Luftwaffe* minelayers came a new enemy which would eventually define the war on the coast: the *Kriegsmarine*'s motor torpedo boats, known to the Germans as *Schnellbooten*, or 'fast boats', and rather obscurely to the British as E-boats – 'enemy boats'. They were a formidable weapon, capable of speeds of over 40 knots – almost 80 kilometres per hour – and armed with torpedoes and an array of automatic weapons. They had a sinister beauty, like a hunting cat, although for Petty Officer Sydney Barnes of the Harwich-based corvette HMS *Widgeon,* who encountered his first E-boats off Dunkirk, they conjured up a different animal altogether: 'Those E-boats . . . always reminded me of rabbits, when you see a rabbit running away and you see the white of his tail, and all you could see with these very fast E-boats was the plume of white water that they put up through speed.'[21]

Many British veterans of light coastal forces agree that, boat for boat, the E-boats were far better than their Allied equivalents, although British superiority in numbers eventually made up for this later in the war. Fred Coombs 'test drove' a captured E-boat at the end of the war, and compared it to a British Fairmile 'D' Motor Gun Boat:

> Testing the sea going qualities of an E-boat in the same conditions as a 'D', seemed to prove that Gerry could go faster into a heavy head sea but [the E-boats] were a lot dirtier and [they] would not see a lot if they did . . . In a more favourable sea, their cruising speed was nearly their top speed which, considering that we could maintain our top speed for no more than 20 minutes, was a big advantage . . . Being a lot heavier and more solid construction, they could sit lower in the water giving a much smaller target . . . the lower, streamlined and armour plated bridge, giving more cover to the bridge crew and with the smaller open cockpit, less opened up to the elements, seemed more comfortable than the open bridge of a 'D'.[22]

E-boats were formidable adversaries for the unwary. One group had already caught and crippled Captain Lord Louis Mountbatten's destroyer, HMS *Kelly,* on 9 May, when operating off the German coast. The fall of Holland had brought them south, to new, closer bases at Ijmuiden, The

Hook and Den Helder. They had been a menace at Dunkirk, and, like the *Luftwaffe*, as France collapsed they moved further south, to bases at Boulogne and Cherbourg approved by Hitler himself.[23]

On 10 June, SS *Baron Elphinstone*, bound from Southend to Middlesbrough carrying iron ore, encountered the new predator in the Thames Estuary while she groped through the night in search of her north-bound convoy. Shortly before midnight her Captain heard the sinister growl of high-powered engines in the dark: 'Thinking she was probably one of the convoy, perhaps a small Dutch motor vessel, I switched on my masthead and starboard lights at half power, to avoid a collision. Immediately the reply was a torpedo direct for my starboard light, fired about fifty yards away.'[24]

The torpedo passed under the ship and Captain Muir commenced frantic evasive action, 'steaming all out . . . but zigzagging continually, turning each time about eighty degrees,' whilst his DEMS gun crew engaged the enemy with their antiquated 4-inch. Periodically silence would fall as the E-boats stopped their engines to listen, then they would roar into life once more as they maneuvered for their shot.

This menacing game of cat and mouse lasted for two hours, during which time the *Baron Elphinstone* miraculously evaded another seven torpedoes. Finally, at 0230, the enemy made off. The E-boats had arrived in coastal waters. On 12 June, Coastal Command aircraft spotted them in their new lairs, and on 17 June they fought an inconclusive battle with the British destroyers *Vesper* and *Vivacious*.[25] Two days later they attacked the freighter *Roseburn*: 'Shortly after midnight a signal was received from SS *Roseburn* . . . that she was being attacked by two U-boats. Actually four E-boats were concerned and four torpedoes were seen, of which three passed alongside and the fourth hit her stern when she was three miles east of Dungeness.'[26]

On 22 June, France signed an armistice with Germany – for the first time in over a hundred years, Britain faced a hostile power across the Straits of Dover. But despite these dreadfully changed circumstances in coastal waters, throughout June and well into the beginning of July the large OA series convoys from the Thames Estuary, with their tempting mix of coasters and big ocean-going ships, continued to make their way slowly through the Channel and out to their Atlantic dispersal points. Their days were numbered.

On 2 July, German aircraft bombed and strafed the SS *Baron Ruthven*, which had departed Southend the day before as part of OA177G:

> At 7:50 am one aircraft dived over vessel, from west to east, dropping one bomb. The bomb exploded about thirty feet from starboard side of ship on contact with the sea, and spraying the vessel with bomb splinters. 5 casualties were incurred, namely the Master, Captain Richmond, Chief Officer Williamson, Carpenter Birrell, Apprentice Blackie and Cabin Boy Elliot.'[27]

Richmond and Williamson were seriously hurt. Although a medical officer was transferred across from an escorting destroyer both men died before *Baron Ruthven* reached Portsmouth. Later in the day the 10,000-ton freighter *Aeanas* was also bombed; hit amidships she was eventually abandoned.

The schedule for OA177G was typical of the complex arrangements that characterized the OA convoys, and helped make them so vulnerable. Twenty ships left Southend on 1 July. Ten ocean-going ships 'buttoned on' from Falmouth and Plymouth, by which time most of the coasters had departed, and a further eighteen joined when the convoy merged with its twin OB series convoy out of Liverpool late on 2 July. Crawling along at an average speed of less than 8 knots, groups of ships left for Bilbao, Lisbon and Casablanca. When OA177G finally reached its Atlantic dispersal point only two ships were left to scatter.

With enemy sea and air forces increasing in strength almost daily, the end of the honeymoon in the Channel was inevitable, and when it came it was swift and bloody. On 3 July 1940, OA178 left Southend, fifty-three ponderous freighters passing through the Channel escorted by nothing more formidable than the Flower Class corvette HMS *Clarkia*, a 940-ton anti-submarine escort armed with just one 4-inch gun and four anti-aircraft machine guns. Captain W.J. Rogerson of the 5,500-ton freighter *Hartlepool* remembered leaving the Downs on 3 July 'in single line ahead . . . looking back I could not see the tail end of the convoy'.[28] Hindsight makes the risks clear but British complacency was perhaps forgivable: 3,404 ships had taken this route since the beginning of the war, but with the U-boats wary of coastal waters, only eight had been lost to date.[29]

Throughout 3 July, sightings were made of German aircraft, ominous heralds flying high over the convoy on their way to inland targets, prompting those on the bridge of the SS *Deucalion* to speculate whether it would be their turn the next day. The night passed uneventfully, but the following morning German aircraft appeared again. They were noted by Captain Norman Shalton of the big ocean-going freighter *Dallas City*: 'During the morning of the 4th, right from earliest daylight, we saw single planes flying around at odd intervals. I thought they were Germans as they were coming from the east, and I think they were getting details of our position.'[30]

Captain Rogerson of the *Hartlepool* recalled that the convoy was passing dangerously near to the French Coast, 'parading' to use his own phrase:

> I went on the bridge at roughly 6:45 am on the 4th July and the mate pointed out to me the Isle of Wight, which appeared to me to be rather far away. I commented that we must be south of our course. After breakfast I took double altitude positions with the 2nd Officer and after obtaining the result I remarked to him 'Good Heavens! We should be able to see Cap La Hague and Alderney.' With that I went out of the Chart Room door and without the need for

> binoculars I saw the whole of Cap La Hague, the French coast and also the Channel Islands. It was exceedingly clear, visibility being about fourteen miles.[31]

Undoubtedly the Germans had been watching the passage of the OA convoys for some time. The poorly escorted mass of OA178, straggling past within sight of the French coast with no air cover visible, was too great a temptation for the élite dive-bomber pilots of the newly victorious *Luftwaffe*. Junkers 87 Stukas led by Major Oskar Dinort of *Stukageschwader* 2 pounced at about 1300, giving no warning except for the banshee shrieking of the wind-powered sirens mounted under their engines to terrify their targets. Off Portland they fell on their first target, Captain Jenkins' SS *Flimston*:

> They attacked one after the other, diving almost vertically with a frightful whistling noise. They appeared to come down as low as 250-300 feet, then straight up again. The bombs . . . fell astern of us shaking the ship considerably . . . One ship was on fire fore and aft, this was the *Irene Maria*, another one was in a sinking condition, an Estonian vessel was hit and the *Eastmore* was also badly damaged.'[32]

The Stukas attacked in waves of six aircraft for well over two hours. The corvette *Clarkia* valiantly tried to defend her charges but her solitary 4-inch gun made little impact on the gull-winged dive-bombers. *Deucalion* was amongst the first to be overwhelmed. Her Chief Officer was J.D. Holm:

> Suddenly the sky seemed to be full of them . . . they dived down very low and started attacking the convoy from a height of about 100 feet. The first bomb hit us while the Captain and I were on the bridge and there were about eight direct hits after that . . . when the fifth or sixth bomb hit us the whole deck was opened right up and the winches were blown away.[33]

Deucalion rapidly began to founder, her Captain and her carpenter both badly injured by high-explosive bullets. As soon as the attack had eased off the crew took to the boats.

Norman Shalton's *Dallas City* did her best to die hard: 'The . . . Merchant Navy Gunlayer behaved marvelously. Although he was being machine-gunned continuously he continued firing. When they were at their lowest altitude he let them have round after round and placed his shells right in front of them.'[34]

Despite these heroics three bombs struck *Dallas City* simultaneously. With the worst of luck, one went down through the engine room skylight and another through the funnel, both exploding deep inside the ship and starting fires. Another exploded inside Number 3 hold, tearing away a large section of deck, lifting the ship out of the water, and stopping her dead. *Dallas City* was doomed, although miraculously only two men had been injured. Behind her, Captain Jenkins' *Flimston*, herself damaged by a series of near misses, had no chance to avoid *Dallas City's* stationary hulk: 'I increased my speed to the utmost, putting my helm hard a starboard, but could not get away from her. I was going eleven knots but I was afraid to turn to port in case she rammed me. She followed me and smashed the port lifeboat, carrying away the davits.'[35]

The two ships were locked together for an agonizing fifteen minutes, *Dallas City* ablaze, until *Flimston* finally managed to pull free and limp into Portland. For *Dallas City* there was to be no such happy ending. Norman Shalton:

> By this time the fire was spreading rapidly and the engine room was a mass of flame. Having already lost my starboard boats I thought it best to get the remainder of my lifeboats in the water before they were burned. I got all the crew into the two port boats and got them away. I stayed on deck until about 1700. During this time there were a number of terrifying explosions from the engine and boiler room. The fumes from the cargo [of ammonium sulphate] were getting very bad and flames were starting to come through Number 3 Hatch.[36]

Norman eventually joined his crew and waited for rescue, which arrived three hours later in the unlikely form of the damaged tanker *Antonio*, already laden with the *Deucalion* survivors. *Antonio* had been near-missed so many times many witnesses thought she had been sunk. Peter Webster was her Third Officer:

> SS *Antonio* was damaged by nine or ten near misses, which affected the rudder and stanchions supporting the propeller shaft, causing us to reduce our speed drastically and steer a very erratic course. At the same time we were subjected to machine-gun fire but, by good fortune, no one was hit. It was a time of great fear and tension. I personally suffered damage to my ear from the sound of explosions and noise of the Ack Ack [anti-aircraft] gun, which I was in charge of. As the attack subsided, we were able to rescue sixty-seven survivors, two of whom were seriously injured, from the sunken ships. We slowly made our way towards Portland and eventually dropped anchor in Weymouth at about 11pm.[37]

Four ships had been sunk and many more damaged. As the battle continued to rage around OA178 the Commodore signalled that the surviving ships should proceed into Portland and the protection of the harbour defences.[38]

Unfortunately Portland was anything but a safe haven. The naval base suffered from a chronic shortage of anti-aircraft guns, which had plagued the British since the beginning of the war. This deficiency had in part been rectified by the arrival of HMS *Foylebank* on 9 June as anti-aircraft guardship. *Foylebank* was an odd kind of warship. A 5,500-ton Bank Line freighter, she had been requisitioned by the Admiralty and armed with four twin 4-inch high-angle gun mounts, multiple 2-pounder quick-firing pom-poms and 0.5-inch machine guns.

Ron Walsh was a range setter on one of her 4-inch guns. Brought up in Ipswich, Ron had joined the Royal Navy in 1936 as a Boy Seaman, aged just sixteen. A run-in with his Captain on board the cruiser HMS *Glasgow* had caused him to desert in 1938 but he had returned when war broke out, and his misbehaviour had been quietly expunged from his record. *Foylebank* had already been bombed several times since arriving in Portland but at 0815 it became clear she was to be singled out for special attention as part of the well co-ordinated assault on OA178. Twenty-six Stukas appeared over the horizon and bombs struck the ship repeatedly before many of her crew even had time to reach their action stations. Ron Walsh was one of them:

> All of a sudden they sounded action stations . . . I looked at my mate and I said 'Well I suppose we'd better bloody get up there hadn't we?' He said, 'Well what else, let's go.' He went out first and . . . I got half way out and there was an almighty bang and I found myself flying across the canteen flat on my face! I got up, went back to the mess and looked in and there was all the hammock netting burning, the double ladders that go up and down were all twisted with blokes in them all twisted round . . . it was a terrible sight.[39]

Ron and his messmate started to make their way along the port side of the ship, heading aft to their action station at 'X' gun:

> We got halfway down and they dropped one down the funnel and blew the side of the ship out, and we could see the docks just out there so we had to turn around and come back. We went right round the other side, down the port side alley, and we're below decks and there's this bright sunshine shining down through a hatch, and opposite the hatch at the bottom is the Master at Arms' office . . . All of a sudden . . . they all rushed out of the office and up the stairs to go up on the deck; [the Germans] machine gunned down it and they all went.[40]

Reaching the aft end of the ship, Ron passed through the crowded Sick Bay. From here a ladder led to the upper deck. As Ron started to climb, a bomb drove through the deck and exploded in the Sick Bay below him, killing everyone inside and his messmate who had been frantically climbing the ladder behind him. Ron eventually struggled out into the blinding sunshine, only to find his gun wrecked and the crew dead or wounded. Others aboard *Foylebank* were still able to fight:

> I heard someone shouting about and I went to the back and looked over and there's old Badger Otley, a Leading Seaman, he was on the *Glasgow* with me actually, and he was going to town, he had his gun going . . . and it was a sight. He had two crew there, and the coconut matting around the gun was on fire and he was saying 'give us some ammo, give us some ammo', and they were saying 'we can't we've only got that practice shell', and he said 'well give us that then' . . . and rammed it up. There was a plane coming down and he wanted to get a crack at it. And he poked this practice shell in and hammered that up.[41]

The deck 15 feet below Ron was a nightmare vision of twisted metal and bodies. *Foylebank*'s First Lieutenant spotted him and told him to get down and head forward as the ship was going to be abandoned. The ladder broken, Ron was forced to jump the last 10 feet, permanently damaging his spine as he did so, although adrenaline shielded him from the pain until much later. Slowly he picked his way forward:

> I got to the passage leading forward and it was about eight or ten feet wide. I got nearly along to the starboard pom poms and there was a body of men all piled up there you know. I looked at them and the PO [Petty Officer] was stood beside the pom poms. 'Go on, push your way through, walk over them they're all dead', he said 'get up here . . . Mantle's still firing and when he's finished we'll have to get him down.'[42]

Jack Mantle was a 23-year-old Leading Seaman. A bomb had shattered his left leg but he was still desperately trying to hit back at *Foylebank*'s tormentors:

> He'd pulled himself up on the gun and he was having difficulty getting the change-over lever on the top from electric to hand, it was slightly bent and he was getting it bit by bit, at the same time cursing and swearing at the plane that had gone out over the bay, turned round and was coming back in over the mole. And he got the lever back at the same time as the plane opened up – they opened up together, him with four barrels of pom pom and the plane with machine gun. What happened to the plane I don't know, it just seemed as if it all blew apart and Mantle flaked out over his gun, he'd been hit across the chest with machine gun [fire].[43]

As others helped Jack Mantle down from his gun, Ron helped to scour the ship for survivors in the last few minutes before she sank. By now *Foylebank* was a vision from hell:

> Our Surgeon Lieutenant was sat on a bollard with his guts in his hands . . . I went down below with the First Lieutenant, and we had a look round where we could, a lot of places were flooded, there was a couple sort of sat against

> the bulkhead, the First Lieutenant went over and said 'come on', shook their shoulders and they fell apart.[44]

Foylebank's survivors climbed down ropes from the forecastle into a mass of civilian craft that had come to their rescue, despite the continued bombing. Taken ashore, they mustered in Boscawen and the role was called. Sixty men had died. More would later perish as a result of wounds sustained in this terrible action, among them Jack Mantle who died in Portland Hospital. For his actions on 4 July 1940 he was awarded the Victoria Cross, Britain's highest award for gallantry. The Commander-in-Chief at Portsmouth, Admiral Sir William James, wrote later that he had 'behaved too magnificently for words.'[45]

Without question *Foylebank* had done her best. But Portland was defenceless by the time the ships of OA178 hove into view, seeking sanctuary from the relentless air attacks. Three freighters sheltering in the harbour had already been damaged and a difficult decision had to be made. Trapped in such confined waters without protection from air attack or room to maneuvre was no place for more than forty priceless merchant ships. To the bewilderment of many skippers the convoy was turned around once more, within sight of apparent safety.

As the day drew to a close the dive-bombers left, but the torment of OA178 was not yet over. In Boulogne, E-boats of the newly arrived *1.* and *2. Schnellbootflottillen* were putting to sea into the gathering twilight. Without any effective escort, the scattered ships of the convoy provided what must have seemed like an unlimited supply of targets. Just before midnight William Clibborn's *Elmcrest* was unlucky enough to meet them:

> I was on the bridge and saw the track of a torpedo on my port quarter. I put the helm over and managed to clear this torpedo. We were zigzagging at the time . . . at a speed of five and a half knots, our maximum . . . Five minutes later, at midnight, we were hit on the port side.[46]

Elmcrest was hit in one of her coal bunkers, which may have helped to soften the blow. Certainly there was no fire or explosion and the ship developed no list, but she was now a sitting target and Captain Clibborn ordered his crew to abandon ship. All thirty-eight men successfully boarded the boats and rafts. The German commander, *Leutnant-zur-See* Götz Freiherr von Mirbach in *S20*, clearly in no great hurry, circled and tried again:

> In less than a quarter of an hour from being hit, I was just going down on to one of the rafts on the port side, when a second torpedo hit the ship on the starboard side in the engine room. His torpedo had passed under the starboard lifeboat, which was just pulling away from the ship, and this caused the boat to capsize. Sixteen of these men were drowned.[47]

This second blow was all the battered *Elmcrest* could take, and she broke in two and sank in a matter of seconds. Von Mirbach departed, leaving the survivors alone in the dark. Six hours later a Dutch coaster rescued them.

R.R. Williamson, Master of the big freighter *British Corporal,* witnessed *Elmcrest*'s end. Soon afterwards his own ship became the target of *Oberleutnant-zur-See* 'Bobby' Fimmen in *S26*:

> Without any warning at all a torpedo struck us on the starboard side in way of the after peak. There was a dull explosion, no flame, but a great column of water shot up and covered everyone with soot and oil. There were pieces of metal flying all over the for'ard deck. It went right through the after end, took away the rudder and had blown a hole through the counter exposing a number of steam pipes. The after boat had completely disappeared and various ventilators and the accommodation were damaged. The 4.7-inch [gun] had gone over the side . . . there was no list in the ship but she seemed to settle aft. The Chief Engineer reported that the engine room was flooding.[48]

When the crew mustered to abandon ship, the Second Engineer and the Second Cook were missing. As they started to lower the boats at 0020 a second torpedo hit the ship, bursting her boiler in a second catastrophic explosion.

The *British Corporal* survivors took to the boats and headed for Portland, but on the way they were rescued by a patrol boat that took them back past their derelict ship, giving them an opportunity to inspect the damage. Although badly damaged, *British Corporal* remained afloat and was eventually towed in to harbour where the bodies of the two missing men were found, buried beneath piles of debris deep inside the ship.

It is hard to imagine the fear and tension of that dreadful night, as ship after ship was methodically stalked and torpedoed by an enemy that remained invisible to most of their victims. *Hartlepool* was next in line, her assailant once again Fimmen in *S26*. Captain Rogerson had clearly seen the attacks on first *Elmcrest* and then *British Corporal*, but frantic maneuvring was not enough to save his ship: 'We were torpedoed aft, right by the propeller, which was blown off . . . there was fire aft and the cordite locker blew up, which probably set off the magazine at the same time.'[49]

Rogerson ordered abandon ship, *Hartlepool* was not sinking but she was dead in the water and a sitting target for *S26*, which announced its continued presence by raking the ship with bursts of machine-gun fire. Fortunately this did not cause any casualties, apart from the Chief Officer, whose nose was cut by a passing bullet.

Rogerson only abandoned his ship reluctantly after repeatedly being told to do so by successive naval escorts. His assessment of *Hartlepool*'s condition seems to have been accurate, as she was towed into Weymouth and beached the following day.

At dawn on 5 July, OA178 was joined by a replacement escort, the veteran destroyer HMS *Broke*, commanded by Commander B.G. Scurfield. Unsurprisingly Scurfield later reported that the convoy was 'in some confusion having been bombed and attacked by E-boats on the previous day' but continued that it soon closed up and proceeded to its dispersal point in the Atlantic.[50] So ended the nightmare of OA178.

The consequences of the massacre were felt almost immediately. Later on 5 July, Winston Churchill sent one of his legendary 'Action this Day' memos to the Admiralty:

> Could you let me know on one sheet of paper what arrangements you are making about the Channel convoys now that the Germans are all along the French coast? The attacks on the convoy yesterday, both from the air and by E-boats, were very serious, and I should like to be assured this morning that the situation is in hand and that the Air is contributing effectively.[51]

The inevitable conclusion drawn was that the Channel was now too dangerous for the valuable ocean-going freighters, and the OA series of oceanic convoys from the Thames Estuary were abandoned. In future OA convoys from the east coast would assemble in the Scottish port of Methil and proceed around the north of Scotland to their dispersal points. The Port of London and the enormous commercial port of Southampton were effectively 'emasculated' as one author has written,[52] and the slack resulting from their near closure had to be taken up by west coast ports, notably Liverpool.

Nowhere near enough surplus capacity existed to take the great ports of the north-east out of service as well. Some ocean-going freighters made the reverse trip around the north of Scotland to terminate on the east coast, but in other cases coasters had to step into the breech. In so called 'Emergency Ports' set up in sheltered west coast anchorages, ocean-going ships discharged directly into their holds, allowing their vital cargoes to be taken to the east coast without exposing their valuable hulls to the dangers.[53]

Before this story leaves OA178, a little double-edged perspective might be helpful. In the end, only five ships were actually sunk, out of fifty-three which originally set out; eleven more were damaged. Considering the weak escort and how close the convoy passed to enemy bases on the French coast, this was not a particularly outstanding success rate on the Germans' part. The Stuka pilots had been trained as 'flying artillery' whose primary role was to provide close support ahead of the Army, bombing largely immobile military targets. Even during the Norwegian and Dunkirk campaigns, successes had often been scored against ships that were either stopped or operating in very confined waters. Hitting a small, moving ship in open water was an entirely new skill, one which the dive-bomber pilots had to learn from scratch, and whilst they later became very good at it – in the Mediterranean in 1941, for instance[54] – at this early stage in the war after-action reports

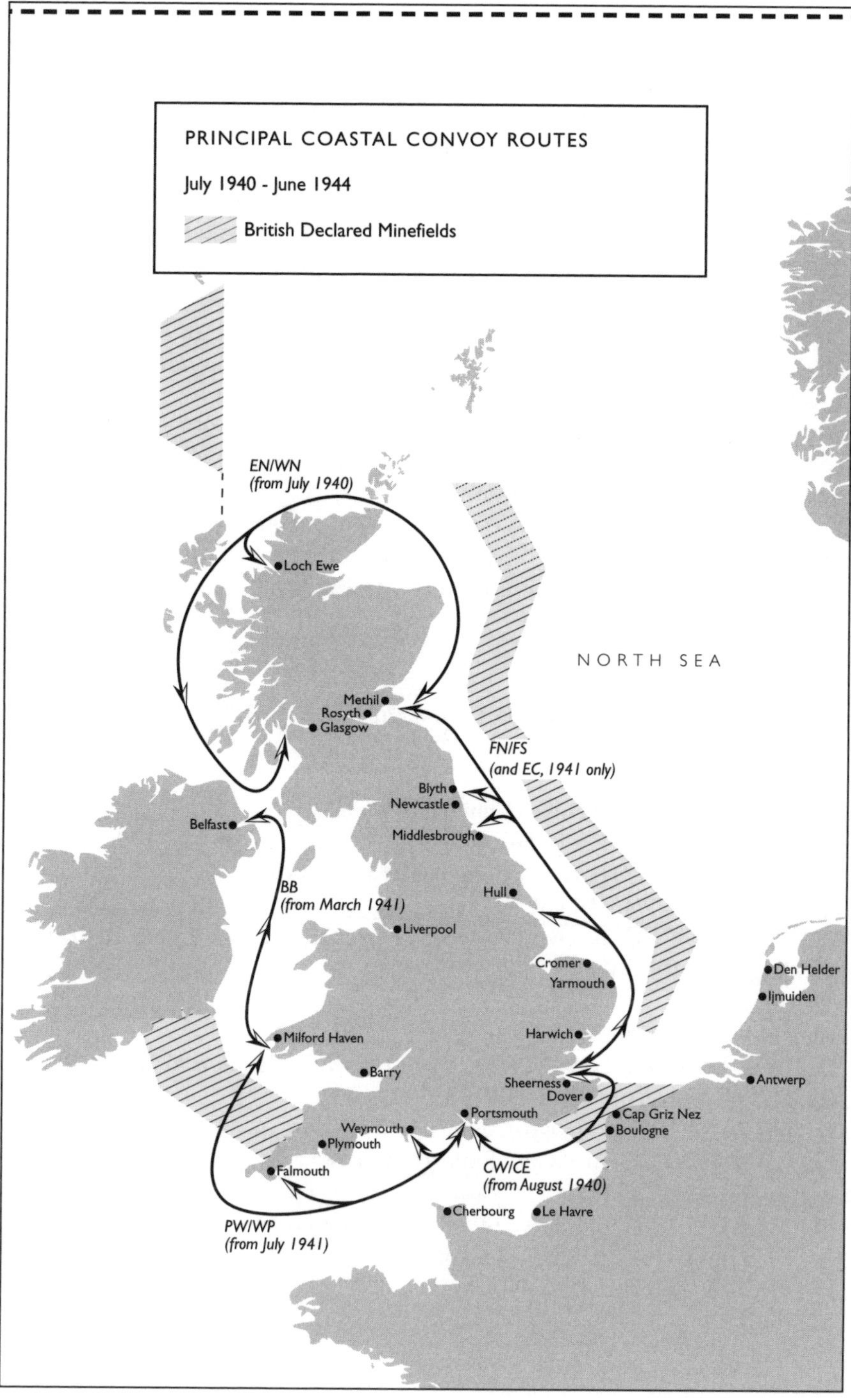
PRINCIPAL COASTAL CONVOY ROUTES
July 1940 - June 1944
British Declared Minefields
EN/WN
(from July 1940)
Loch Ewe
NORTH SEA
Methil
Rosyth
Glasgow
FN/FS
(and EC, 1941 only)
Blyth
Newcastle
Belfast
Middlesbrough
BB
(from March 1941)
Hull
Liverpool
Cromer
Yarmouth
Den Helder
Ijmuiden
Milford Haven
Harwich
Barry
Sheerness
Antwerp
Dover
Portsmouth
Cap Griz Nez
Boulogne
Weymouth
Plymouth
Falmouth
CW/CE
(from August 1940)
Cherbourg
Le Havre
PW/WP
(from July 1941)

from attacks in open water tend to be peppered by references to near misses rather than sinkings.

On the other hand, five ships was five too many. At the beginning of the war some 3,000 deep-sea dry cargo ships and around 1,000 coasters were registered in Britain, and the country desperately needed them all in order to ensure both a constant flow of war materiél *and* the continuation of trade.[54] The shipbuilding industry had been badly run down during the Great Depression, and those yards that survived were mostly still lumbering along wedded to pre-war attitudes and technology. In 1940, it still took years rather than months to build a freighter, and the era of the 'Liberty' ship was far in the future. Three OA178s a week could put a sixth of Britain's available merchant shipping to the bottom in a year – which was why the Channel had to close to ocean-going freighters.

Unfortunately for the coaster men, the south coast still urgently needed coal. Whilst the big ocean-going freighters were routed north, the colliers had to keep on coming. Channel convoys, codenamed CE (Channel Eastbound) or CW (Channel Westbound) were introduced for coastal traffic, initially from the Downs to the Isle of Wight, after which the coasters sailed independently to Bristol, lying up in ports by day.[55] Their great trial was about to begin.

Notes

1. IWM Docs 75/105/1 Phipps, Commander W.J., p. 37.
2. Ibid., 38.
3. Ibid., 42.
4. NA ADM 199/360 Dover Command War Diary, p. 166.
5. Atkin, Ronald, *Pillar of Fire*, Sidgwick & Jackson, London, 1990, p. 234.
6. IWM Docs 97/31/1 Dean, Commander B., p. 149.
7. IWM Docs 99/43/1 Lind, William, p. 6.
8. ADM 199/2133 Survivors' Reports: Merchant Vessels 1 June 1940 to 31 August 1940, p. 6.
9. Ibid.
10. *Führer Conferences on Naval Affairs: 1940*, p. 52-3.
11. Dear, I.C.B. and Foot, M.R.D., *The Oxford Companion to World War II*, Oxford University Press, 2001, p. 327.
12. NA ADM 199/360 Dover Command War Diary, p. 170.
13. ADM 199/2133 Survivors' Reports: Merchant Vessels 1 June 1940 to 31 August 1940, p. 17.
14. NA ADM 199/2133 Survivors' Reports: Merchant Vessels 1 June 1940 to 31 August 1940, p. 18.
15. BBC PW A6021154 Stanworth, James.
16. Ibid.
17. Ibid.
18. Ibid.

19. Ibid.
20. NA ADM 199/2133 Merchant Navy Survivors' Reports 1 June 1940 to 31 August 1940, p. 31.
21. IWM Sound 15429 Barnes, S.
22. IWM Docs 91/7/1 Coombs, F.B.
23. *Führer Conferences on Naval Affairs: 1940*, p. 58
24. ADM 199/2133 Survivors' Reports: Merchant Vessels 1 June 1940 to 31 August 1940, p. 35.
25. NA ADM 199/360 Dover Command War Diary, p. 199.
26. NA ADM 199/360 Dover Command War Diary, p. 211.
27. ADM 199/2133 Survivors' Reports: Merchant Vessels 1 June 1940 to 31 August 1940.
28. Ibid., p. 111.
29. Statistics from Grove, *The Defeat of the Enemy Attack on Shipping 1939–1945*, Table 10 'Numbers of British, Allied and Neutral Ships Sailed in North Atlantic Trade Convoys and N. Russia Convoys to and from the United Kingdom September 1939-May 1943', and Hague, Arnold, *The Allied Convoy System 1939–1945: Its Organisation, Defence and* Operation, Vanwell, 2000, pp. 147–9.
30. ADM 199/2133 Survivors' Reports: Merchant Vessels 1 June 1940 to 31 August 1940, p. 103.
31. Ibid., p. 111.
32. ADM 199/2133 Survivors' Reports: Merchant Vessels 1 June 1940 to 31 August 1940, p. 107.
33. Ibid., p. 105.
34. Ibid., p. 111.
35. Ibid., p. 107.
36. Ibid., p. 111.
37. BBC PW A6178070 Webster, Peter.
38. In addition to *Dallas City* and *Deucalion*, other losses were the *Kolga* (3,526 tons) and the big Dutch freighter *Britsum* (5,255 tons), which went down with the loss of nine men.
39. IWM Sound 27308 Walsh, Ronald.
40. Ibid.
41. Ibid.
42. Ibid.
43. Ibid.
44. Ibid.
45. James, Admiral Sir William, *Portsmouth Letters*, Macmillan, London, 1946, p. 71.
46. ADM 199/2133 Survivors' Reports: Merchant Vessels 1 June 1940 to 31 August 1940, p. 102.
47. Ibid., 102.
48. Ibid.

49. Ibid., p. 111.
50. NA ADM 199/212 Reports of Proceedings of Convoys May 1940 to July 1940.
51. Churchill, Winston S, *The Second World War*, vol. II: 'Their Finest Hour', Cassell, London, 1949, p. 566.
52. Woodman, *The Real Cruel Sea*, p. 57.
53. Ibid.
54. The elite *Fliegerkorps X*, which specialized in anti-shipping strikes, hit almost every ship in the Mediterranean Fleet during the battles off Greece and Crete between March and June 1941. Three cruisers and eight destroyers were sunk.
55. Roskill, Captain S.W., *The War at Sea*, vol. I, HMSO, London, 1954, p. 42.
56. Hague, *The Allied Convoy System 1939–1945*.

Chapter 5

Battle for the Channel

6 July 1940 to 30 September 1940

It is tempting to see the slaughter of OA178 as the start of the German offensive against coastal shipping which formed the first round of the Battle of Britain, although at this stage the *Luftwaffe* was still drawing breath after the Battle of France. Plans were being drawn up for the forthcoming offensive, but this particular attack may well have been a local initiative to keep the Stuka pilots sharp, providing training and combat experience, and an opportunity to test the British defences. The newly promoted *Reichsmarschall* Hermann Göring did not directly order strikes against coastal shipping until some days later, in a directive issued on 11 July. The object of this so-called '*kanalkampf*' (Channel Battle) was to 'secure a permanent weakening of morale, matériel and personnel in the British fighter force' prior to taking the air offensive over British soil itself. Ultimately the aim was to neutralize British air and sea power to facilitate the planned invasion of Britain, Operation *Seelowe* (Sealion).[1]

For the British, the new Channel coaster convoys were too important to be stopped, but not important enough to risk a significant proportion of the available fighter aircraft in their defence in conditions that greatly favoured the enemy, for all Churchill's demands for 'the air' to 'contribute effectively'. In effect, the vulnerable coal convoys were about to become a tethered goat which neither the German tiger nor the British farmer saw as the main meal, although this was small consolation to the men who took them through the Straits and cared little for matters of grand strategy. Throughout July German attacks on coastal shipping increased in scale and intensity.

At 1300 on 10 July, officially the first day of the Battle of Britain, a German force of Dornier 17 bombers attacked CW3, twenty-five little ships stretched out between Folkestone Gate and Dungeness. They were intercepted by RAF fighters, which forced the Germans to bomb at high altitude causing little damage to the convoy.[2]

Many excellent books have been written about the Battle of Britain, and this has no pretensions to become another. It is, however, worth remembering that when the ships escaped almost unscathed, as in this case, it was usually thanks to the furious efforts of the small number of RAF pilots assigned to convoy patrol duty. Amongst the defenders of CW3 was Pilot

Officer Henry Ferris:

> When we got to the scene there were twenty-four Dorniers altogether in three bunches. The first bunch had already dropped their bombs and the second lot was about to go in. The third wave never delivered an attack at all. It was a really thrilling sight as I looked down on the tiny ships below and saw two long lines of broken water where the first bombs fell. Our Squadron Leader gave the order to attack. We went screaming down and pumped lead into our targets. It shook them up quite a bit. When I broke away and looked around for a prospective victim I saw a Dornier some distance away lagging behind. Three of us went after him. He went into a gentle dive but we overtook him and started firing at home. He was obviously in a bad way when we left him and went back to the main battle.[3]

Turning from the Dornier Henry engaged and shot down a Messerschmitt 109 fighter, before his luck took a turn for the worse:

> At the precise moment [the Messerschmitt] disappeared from my gun sights I felt a sting in my leg. Just as I had been firing at him three of his friends were firing at me. I did a quick turn again and made for home but it wasn't going to be quite as easy as all that. My attacker had put my port aileron [flap] out of action, so that I could hardly turn to the left at all. The control column went heavy too and then I realised that my engine was beginning to run quite rough. There were no clouds to hide in except those up at 10,000 feet and they seemed miles away. Practically all my ammunition had gone so it would have been suicide to stay and fight. I watched my pursuers carefully. When they got near me I made a sudden turn and saw their tracer bullets go past my tail. I gained a bit on them and then they overtook me again and once more I turned quickly when I thought they had me within range. I did that about a dozen times but they didn't get me again.[4]

Henry Ferris managed to nurse his battered Hurricane home. He collected a fresh aircraft, rejoined his squadron and set off almost immediately on another patrol, a remarkable testament to the efforts made by the outnumbered pilots of the token convoy patrols to protect their charges.

On 11 July, the Stukas returned to Portland, which was still reeling from the attack on *Foylebank* a week before. This was followed by a brief lull and a series of largely ineffective raids, followed by concerted strike on CW6, lumbering along between Dover and Eastbourne on 14 July. Tactically the dive-bomber pilots were already starting to hone their anti-shipping skills. The first wave crippled the convoy's sole escort, the 1918-vintage destroyer HMS *Vanessa*. Other aircraft pounced on the coasters, before they were themselves intercepted by the RAF convoy patrol in an action witnessed and broadcast by the BBC correspondent Charles Gardener. Gardner, a pre-war sports reporter, had an unusual approach to war reporting, which left the world with a broadcast of undoubted drama, albeit of slightly questionable taste when heard or read nearly seventy years later:

> There are about ten German machines dive-bombing the British convoy, which is just out to sea in the Channel . . . there's one going down in flames. Somebody's hit a German and he's coming down with a long streak – coming down completely out of control – a long streak of smoke – and now a man's baled out by parachute. The pilot's baled out by parachute. He's a Junkers 87, and he's going slap into the sea – and there he goes. SMASH! A terrific column of water and there was a Junkers 87. Only one man got out by parachute, so presumably there was only a crew of one in it.[5]

The jingoistic savagery of Gardner's presentational style may well have been necessary given the circumstances of the time, but it is perhaps ironic that the unfortunate man he describes seems to have in fact been British, Pilot Officer Mudie, a Hurricane pilot who died the following day of his injuries.[6] The next 'kill' he witnessed was apparently less debatable:

> Oh, we have just hit a Messerschmitt. Oh, that was beautiful! He's coming right down. I think it was definitely that burst got him. Yes, he's come down. You hear those crowds? He's finished! Oh, he's coming down like a rocket now. An absolutely steep dive. Let us move round so we can watch him a bit more. Here he comes, down in a steep dive — the Messerschmitt. [Here Gardner looks for a parachute] No, no, the pilot's not getting out of that one.[7]

Despite the gallant defence, and Gardner's claims that 'not one single ship' was hit, some Stukas did reach CW6. Two ships were damaged and the coaster *Island Queen* was sunk. A scratch escort was assembled to shepherd the battered convoy onwards to Portsmouth.

On 20 July the next westbound Channel convoy, CW7, was also singled out for the attention of the Stukas, this time accompanied by heavy fighter cover. Several concentrated on one of the escorting destroyers, HMS *Brazen*, which was rapidly enveloped in waterspouts. During a two-hour battle for survival, *Brazen*'s gunners shot down three Stukas but eventually a bomb exploded underneath her, breaking her back. She sank at 2000, although remarkably only one man was killed.

Amongst the merchant ships the collier *Pulborough* seemed to be singled out for special attention, her Master, J.A. Stark, counting twenty bomb splashes within twenty feet of the hull 'in a space of two seconds'. *Pulborough*'s DEMS gunner managed to fire twelve rounds from his antique naval gun, and the ship's Chief Officer four magazines from a First World War Lewis machine gun, but claims of hits were probably fanciful. Eventually one bomb dropped just a little too close:

> One dropped within three feet of our starboard side and shook the ship badly. The vessel seemed to lift up bodily about six inches and came down with a thud . . . I think she must have opened out aft which forced up the bottom. The deck foundations must have given way causing the gun to collapse.[8]

Her engines disabled, *Pulborough* began to lose way and Stark gave the order to abandon ship, although he remained on board himself until the decks were awash, when he 'thought it was time to move'. Carrying out one last check of his sinking ship before leaving her for the last time, he found one of his firemen, 'about four foot nothing tall, and well over sixty years of age'. They jumped together into the heavy sea and were eventually hauled into the lifeboat, the fireman with a clay pipe still clamped firmly between his teeth.[9] Rescued by the escort trawler *Lady Philomena*, Captain Stark and his men witnessed the end of their ship: 'By this time she was under water to the extent of the centre of the after hatch. After about five or ten minutes there was a sudden rush of water and I saw the bulkhead disappear . . . the sudden rush made her list at an angle of 45 degrees, then she took another dive.'[10]

Although the attack on CW7 was an ordeal, the coaster men had stood up to the assault admirably and in his report the Commodore, Commander B.B. Grant RNR, wrote that their conduct had been excellent throughout the action. More was to come the following day, however, when CW7 was caught again off the Isle of Wight, the SS *Terlings* being sunk and the Norwegian *Kollskeg* badly damaged and set on fire. Commander Grant reported that the convoy 'became somewhat disorganized after the attack', although he stoically put this down to ships joining from Portsmouth not having been provided with pendant numbers, rather than the relentless bombing.[11]

Worse was to come as the *kanalkampf* increased in intensity. Night bombing began, as witnessed by Commander Phipps of the *Woolston* when he brought a convoy through the Straits on the night of 22/23 July: 'Just as I got on the bridge a stick of bombs fell at the head of the convoy. No hits but not far off, the Commodore and a lot of them pooped off . . . shots going off all over the place and they told me afterwards they were firing at the sound. Bloody fools!'[12]

Phipp's scathing criticism of the trigger-happy coaster men under his protection is understandable but rather unfair. No merchant seamen had been subjected to such intensive air attack before, and it would seem to be a very instinctive reaction to 'shoot first and ask questions afterwards'. Further vicious air fighting took place on the 24th. Joining in for the first time was the *Luftwaffe* fighter ace Adolf Galland, who took his squadron over the Thames Estuary to provide top cover for bombers:

> We got involved in a heavy scrap with the Spitfires which were screening the convoy . . . I glued myself to the tail of the plane flying outside on the left flank.

> During a right-handed turn I managed to get in a long burst. The Spitfire went down almost vertically. I followed it until the cockpit cover came flying toward me and the pilot bailed out. I followed him down until he crashed into the water. His parachute had failed to open.[13]

No ships were damaged in this action, which later became known as 'The Battle of the Thames Estuary'. But it was really only the overture for the 25th, the darkest day of the Channel convoys, later christened 'Black Thursday'.

Channel convoy CW8 consisted of twenty-one ships, assembled as usual in the Thames Estuary. The smallest, the SS *Jolly Nights* of Devonport, was a mere 351 tons. The largest, the *Tamworth* of Southampton, was only 1,332 tons.

By 1500, CW8 was trudging past Dover. The SS *Gronland* was a refugee from occupied Denmark, now operating out of Plymouth under the command of Captain H.C.A. Fischer. She was the leading ship in the line, and carried the convoy's Commodore, the experienced Commander A.C. I'Anson RNR. At 1500, Captain Fischer was waiting to depart when around a hundred German aircraft appeared in the sky to the east. The small RAF convoy patrol was completely overwhelmed and unable to prevent four separate dive-bombing attacks being made by Stuka formations led by *Hauptmann* Paul Hozzel.

In theory, dive-bombing was a simple business, as in effect the aircrew 'sat on the bomb' and guided it almost onto the target before pulling up out of the dive at the last moment. In practice there is no doubt that it took great courage and skill to carry it out effectively. Hozzel recalled the experience long after the war:

> We turned the plane down at a dive angle of seventy degrees. With the gas shut off the plane quickly gained speed by its own weight, whilst the diving brakes kept it at a steady pace of 450 kmh. We aimed through a reflector sight keeping the whole plane in the centre of the target and allowing for velocity and direction of the wind, with the aid of the right lead angles. A continuously adjustable red marking arrow was mounted on the altimeter, set to local altitude above mean sea level, whereby the required bomb releasing altitude could be set. When passing that altitude in the dive, a loud and clear horn signal was sounded, warning the pilot to press the bomb releasing button on the control stick and to pull out the plane . . . the normal bomb releasing altitude was close to 700 metres. Experienced pilots would also venture down to 500 metres in order to increase the bombing accuracy.[14]

Captain H.S. Lawton's ship, the SS *Henry Moon*, was at the back of the convoy as Hozzel's experienced pilots lined up methodically: 'The planes dived vertically, in single line ahead, each plane diving at one ship, with the following plane diving on the next ship, in that formation.'[15]

Without fighter cover, the ships could only rely on their own inadequate armament. In the collier *Tamworth*, Merchant Navy gunner John Gallagher ran to his antiquated 12-pounder as the action stations klaxon blared and the Stukas scored their first success, against the Hull collier *Leo*, whose Captain later recalled that the bombs 'split her right open'.[16] By the time John Gallagher reached his gun on the *Tamworth*, *Leo* was wallowing upside down, two survivors clinging to the propeller shaft.[17]

The convoy scattered, although in the confined waters of the Straits there were few places to hide. Several Stukas singled out the *Henry Moon* for attention as she fled, Captain Lawton's men doing their best to fight back:

> We opened fire with both the Lewis gun and the 12-pounder, getting off twelve rounds from this latter gun . . . the gunner in charge was a Seaman RNR who had joined us in May, and he put up a very good show indeed . . . The Lewis gun was worked by the 2nd Mate and the Steward who also did well. The whole convoy was firing and put up a terrific barrage.[18]

Their desperate efforts brought relief to the beleaguered *Henry Moon*, as her tormentors sheered away, leaving the coaster riddled with shrapnel. Other ships were less fortunate. John Gallagher's *Tamworth* was left helpless as a stick of bombs exploded beneath her keel, putting her engines out of action as another wave of dive-bombers approached. Gallagher desperately tried to hit back, targeting a Stuka as it pulled out of its dive, temporarily vulnerable. Later he recalled the moment: 'There was neither emotion nor calculation – no time for theory of gunnery, for estimating the amount of deflection to give, for aiming off . . . it was the time for instinctive firing, like a shot-gun swung from the shoulder at a flock of partridges.'[19]

John Gallagher claimed a hit on a Stuka, which seemed to break up and fall into the sea. His efforts may well have been enough to spare his ship. Tugs were sent from Dover as the Stukas made for home and she was hauled painfully into the safety of the harbour, eventually tying up to the long western arm of the Dover breakwater.

On board the Commodore ship, *Gronland*, Captain Fischer was beginning to think he had escaped the carnage when:

> Suddenly, two bombers dived over our ship, to a height of about 150 feet. The first plane released a salvo of three bombs, one of which was a direct hit which blew off the stern, and the other two fell near, lifting the ship out of the water and denting the sides . . . both aircraft machine-gunned us as they dived.[20]

For Fischer, like Gallagher, the battle was over. With *Gronland* wallowing helplessly in the water there was little more he could do. An Admiralty tug came out from Dover and his ship was towed into the harbour to lie alongside the *Tamworth*.

One of the convoy's smallest ships, the SS *Summity* of Devonport, only 554 tons and carrying cement, had also been singled out for special attention. She was hit three times almost simultaneously:

> The first bomb, on the port side abaft the bridge, blew a naval signalman off the bridge; the second, on the starboard side of the main hold, blew the second naval signalman off the bridge; the third landed right in the main hold. That last one made a mess of the ship and the master [Captain E. Milton MBE], although he and the helmsman had been severely wounded in the wreck of the wheelhouse, decided to beach her. The engines were still running, but the *Summity* could not be steered with her rudder. By manoeuvring the engines ahead and astern, dropping an anchor and sheering with the tide, she was put upon the beach.[21]

The *Summity* ended the battle high and dry on the beach under Shakespeare Cliff near Dover. Despite the battering she had suffered she was salvaged and survived the war, taking part in the Normandy Landings in June 1944.

At 1615, with the convoy off Sandgate, the Germans returned. Captain Lawton's *Henry Moon* was again the subject of their attention, but this time the valiant efforts of her gunners were not enough to save her. Almost immediately she was hit by a salvo of four bombs, with another salvo of four dropping close alongside: 'I was down in my cabin; I heard the klaxon once and then the cabin collapsed around me. The enemy must have appeared very suddenly as there was no sound of engines to warn us. When I reached the deck the aircraft had disappeared.'[22]

The side of the ship was ripped open and she immediately began to take on water and list to port. Staying on board was not an option and the order was given to abandon ship. *Henry Moon*'s boats had been badly holed during the earlier attack off Dover and when they were launched, one immediately capsized and the other filled with water. This left only two small rafts in which to cram sixteen men. *Henry Moon* sank within ten minutes. The SS *Broadhurst* rescued the crew but fortunately as it later turned out, they were transferred to a motor torpedo boat and taken to Dover. One man died in hospital as a result of his injuries.

By the time the air attacks finally ended five ships had been sunk. Five more had been so badly damaged that they were forced to put in to Dover. At Dover, Vice Admiral Ramsay commented phlegmatically that 25 July was 'a good full day!'[23] What the coaster men would have made of such comments would probably be unprintable.

The Germans had not finished with CW8. When the dive-bombers left, the E-boats of *Kapitänleutnant* Birnbacher's *1. Schnellbooteflottille* arrived to pick off stragglers. Dover Command's War Diary records that as early as 1330, ten or eleven E-boats were reported off Cap Griz Nez, steering west. They were tracked heading westwards until 1645 when it was assumed that they were heading to join the attack on CW8. If the E-boats reached the colliers it would be, in the words of one account, 'like a professional pug [boxer] slamming an innocent bystander,' and so two destroyers from the 1st Flotilla at Dover were sent out to drive them off.[24]

These ships, HMS *Boreas* and HMS *Brilliant*, were in fact the only remaining units from the 1st Destroyer Flotilla which were still operational, the remainder having been sunk or damaged over the course of the summer's hard fighting. They engaged the E-boats, which duly turned away but in the course of the action both destroyers inadvertently steamed dangerously near the French coast. On their way back to Dover they were attacked twice by dive-bombers. At 1800 a direct hit was scored on HMS *Boreas*, which penetrated deep inside the ship and exploded in her galley flat, killing fifteen men and injuring twenty-nine.[25] John Bartholomew was serving on board her at the time:

> My position on board was Gun Layer on Y Gun, which is positioned on the quarter deck (a position that saved my life) . . . The report on the front page of the *Daily Mirror* on 27th July 1940 was that the two Destroyers were damaged and on the *Boreas* there were casualties . . . That was putting it very mildly . . . half the crew were killed and all our guns were knocked out of action, except Y Gun but we were of little use as we had no engines, no steering, no power and we had to wait like a cork for a tug coming out of Dover. As the *Boreas* was so badly damaged the crew were eventually returned to the Barracks.[26]

Brilliant was also damaged, two bombs passing through her stern but miraculously causing no casualties. By the end of the attack she was also immobilized and both ships had to be brought into Dover by tugs. Their valiant efforts had driven off the E-boats for a while but they soon returned once safely cloaked in darkness.

William Anderson, a Sunderland man, was Master of the collier *Broadhurst*, recent saviour of the crew of the *Henry Moon*. At 2110 the *Broadhurst* and three other ships detached from the convoy and made their way into Shoreham as per instructions. This was a perfect opportunity for E-boats, and soon after detaching William heard the sinister growl of their engines on the *Broadhurst*'s port bow. He started to turn the ship to head towards the sound, to present a smaller target to the enemy, when he heard the sound of compressed air being released and saw a torpedo approaching his starboard bow, apparently from a second boat.

There was no time for evasive action. The torpedo struck the starboard bow, collapsing the forecastle completely and killing the four men asleep there instantly. The lamp trimmer, who was also asleep forward, was injured and only escaped after struggling through neck-deep water. *Broadhurst* sank in five minutes, the successful E-boat Captain once again *Leutnant-zur-See* von Mirbach in *S20*. Twelve men escaped in a lifeboat and another, James

Taylor, was rescued from the water afterwards. They set out for Shoreham and were picked up some 3½ miles offshore.[27]

Later in the night it was the turn of the SS *Sanfry*, which had already been bombed repeatedly during the day. Captain H. Lawson:

> At about 0230 I heard the sound of a motor boat's engines ahead of me . . . I quickly gave the order to put the wheel hard to starboard and increased my speed to ten knots which is the highest attainable by my vessel. I then saw an object on my port quarter, which looked like a large edition of a cabin cruiser. I saw the outline of a conning tower.[28]

Lawson was luckier than most. The E-boat fired two torpedoes, both of which passed under the *Sanfry*. The collier's gunners exchanged fire with the German warship, and although splinters injured Marine Gunner Jewell, they succeeded in driving it away to search for easier prey. Gratefully, Captain Lawson took the *Sanfry* into harbour. The E-boats took another three ships during the night, and only eight ships of the convoy made it safely through the Channel.[29]

Two days after CW8, on 27 July, the *Luftwaffe* followed up on its success by launching a saturation dive-bombing attack on Dover. One destroyer, HMS *Walpole*, was damaged and another, HMS *Codrington*, was sunk in the harbour after her back was broken. On 29 July the dive-bombers came again, sinking the destroyer depot ship *Sandhurst* and the unfortunate SS *Gronland*, previously Commodore ship of CW8, which was hit by three bombs and sank in the harbour, watched by Captain Fischer. Ironically he was ashore waiting to meet his superintendent, who had come down from Leith to inspect the damage sustained on 25 July.[30]

On the same day off Portland, fifteen German aircraft pounced on the destroyer HMS *Delight*, on her way from Portland to Liverpool after a refit. Several hits immobilized her and by the time rescue ships arrived she was ablaze from stem to stern. Eighteen men were killed and another fifty-nine were badly hurt, mostly burned. Once the survivors had been taken off, *Delight* was left to burn herself out. Later in the night she exploded and sank. By day at least the Channel belonged to the Germans.

The aftermath of the July 1940 carnage has sometimes been misrepresented, with authors writing of 'the abandonment of the coastal convoys'[31] or that 'the English Channel was closed.'[32] In part this stems from a misunderstanding of why the convoys were being run in the first place, which in turn comes from viewing the air element of the Battle of Britain as standing alone in splendid isolation.

For instance, it has been argued on occasion that the convoys were being run 'as bait that would bring the *Luftwaffe* to battle'.[33] Nothing could have been further from the truth. The convoys were being run, as we have already seen, because the south coast needed some 40,000 tons of coal a week to keep its power stations going, and thus avoid great civilian hardship and the paralysis of essential war work. Quite apart from anything else, there were nowhere near enough ships available in 1940, merchant or naval, for them to be squandered in such a grandiose gesture.

There was simply no alternative: 'Coal in particular could not be carried in adequate quantities to the south coast ports . . . it was essential to keep those little ships sailing.'[34] Alone, the road and rail networks could not supply this volume of coal, and even if they had been able to do so, it would have resulted in the dislodging of other vital traffic, notably the movement of troops. To claim, as one author has, that 'the coastal convoys, carrying domestic cargoes, were still being sent through the dangerous waters of the Channel instead of the goods going by railway, as they did later'[35] is quite frankly ludicrous and a grave injustice to the decision makers of the day. Official sources confirm that the maintenance of the coal convoys by the Ministry of Shipping during this difficult period formed 'a precarious but quite invaluable stream of supplies'.[36]

Those charged with protection of the convoys were in no doubt as to their importance. John Ellacombe was a Hurricane pilot with 151 Squadron, and flew many dreary convoy patrols during the summer of 1940: '[We] flew up and down, up and down, one end to the other, watching these poor wretched ships ploughing along. We were told that a convoy of ships was the equivalent of about 1,000 trains so they were absolutely essential to get the goods from one part of the country to the other.'[37]

As far as 'bait' was concerned, quite the reverse was true; the Germans were hitting the convoys in an attempt to draw out Fighter Command into costly engagements over the Channel, nearer to *Luftwaffe* bases. This would have 'levelled the playing field' as far as combat time and the ability to retrieve downed aircrew was concerned. However, aside from very limited convoy patrols of no more than six aircraft, the RAF refused to be so drawn: the convoys were essential, but it was still impossible to justify squandering desperately needed fighter aircraft and pilots in a battle which would have been fought entirely on the enemy's terms. Furthermore, the *Luftwaffe* held the initiative: whilst the RAF would have to escort every convoy, the Germans could concentrate their strength where and when they chose, thus they would almost always outnumber any escort.

There was, however, little doubt that by the end of July the morale of the coaster men was fast being eroded by the relentless air attacks by day and the threat of E-boats by night. G.W. Thompson, Master of the SS *Hodder*, took his ship though the Straits with CW8, and his fury at the apparent inability of the Admiralty to protect his men is clear:

> The master wishes to bring to the notice of the Authorities that there is great dissatisfaction amongst the crews owing to the very slight protection which is given to convoys and he foresees the time arriving when the crew will just refuse to take the ships to sea. In the present case there were only two trawlers to

escort a convoy of twenty-one ships stretching for about six or seven miles.[38]

If round the clock air cover was not an option, alternative means of protecting the convoys thus had to be considered, and while plans were made and decisions taken, the convoys were briefly suspended. New 'building blocks' were going to be necessary for the changed situation in the Channel.

One of the first to be introduced was the 'extemporized and possibly unique' Channel Mobile Balloon Barrage Flotilla.[39] Barrage balloons were a proven means of deterring low-flying aircraft, in particular dive-bombers, although their effectiveness was arguably offset by their erratic nature: the first victims of British barrage balloons during the Second World War were RAF aircraft. The Mobile Balloon Barrage would allow this protection to be extended over the Channel convoys. A number of small 'warships' were improvised from transports and ships taken up from trade – HMS *Haslemere* was fairly typical, a 726-ton horse and car ferry built in 1925.[40] The flotilla was under the command of C-in-C Nore and based at Sheerness. As many as seven of these ships would accompany each convoy and in addition many of the coasters would also be equipped with their own small kite balloons.

Perhaps the most extraordinary feature of the balloon ships was that, although as far as ship handling was concerned they were under the command of Royal Navy (or actually more often, Royal Naval Reserve) officers, operational decisions relating to the use of the balloons were made by often quite junior officers from the RAF's Balloon Command. The lack of obvious signs of friction in the detailed reports compiled by both RAF and RN officers seems to indicate that this potentially tricky arrangement worked very well.

A second new building block was the creation of specially trained teams of anti-aircraft gunners to supplement the coasters' regular DEMS crews. Normal DEMS training was not considered adequate for the very intense air attacks being experienced in the Channel, as one confidential report makes clear:

> Channel convoys were a special case because their defence called for an efficiency among the DEMS guns crews considerably above the standard acceptable for ships sailing in areas where the gunners would get in only an occasional shot at a passing FW200 [German long-range patrol aircraft] or a surfaced submarine. Therefore a special corps of DEMS Naval ratings with their own officers was formed, to supplement and strengthen the existing naval anti-aircraft personnel on the ships. It was suggested . . . that the corps should be known as the AA Guard.[41]

Carrying their own Lewis guns, as there were not enough available to leave them on the ships, the men of the Channel AA Guard would be sent to join a westbound (CW) convoy assembling in the Thames Estuary, whereupon they would 'ride shotgun' until it reached its destination. One officer would command two ships' gun crews, with a Leading Seaman as his second-in-command in charge of the men on board the second ship. At the end of the journey, they would either immediately run the gauntlet again with an eastbound convoy, or if none were available, they returned by train to Southend and picked up another westbound one. It is hard to imagine the strain that these often very young reservists lived under. Harold Watkinson was one of their officers: 'It was, however one looked at it, a strange assignment. Periods of extremely high tension were followed by long meandering train journeys to the port where we would pick up the convoy. Then the inevitable pre-convoy party when we worked off the "twitch" with too much alcohol.'[42]

Even the brief periods ashore provided no respite. If the gunners were not bouncing across the country in drafty, unheated trains, they were 'stowed away in garages and gun turrets' or taking cover in air-raid shelters and slit trenches.[43]

At the beginning the Channel Guard consisted of twenty-six officers and 200 gunnery ratings. They were almost certainly sustained in part by the sense of being an élite. According to one account, Channel Guard gunners carried a card bearing the following (probably paraphrased) exhortation: 'When you go aboard this vessel, you will say to yourself "I am the Navy." Throw out your chest, go immediately to your gun and make ready. Never leave your gun at any time.'[44]

Interestingly, at the beginning, many of the AA Guard were recruited from the Royal Canadian Navy Volunteer Reserve, including all but three of the twenty-six officers – Harold Watkinson was one of the Britons. Thousands of Canadians had volunteered at the beginning of the war, and by the summer of 1940 there were far more Canadian reservists than there were ships. However, this was by no means the only reason for their recruitment: the informal approach to 'spit and polish' that characterised the Royal Canadian Navy was also, for once, seen as an advantage:

> The deliberate choice of Canadian officers for the AA Guard is very interesting. As may be readily imagined, the DEMS ratings were not always handled by the merchant ship Masters in the way to which they had become accustomed in the Navy and grievances multiplied. This friction was the main reason for the decision to place a naval officer in charge of each ship's AA Guard party . . . the officer was on his own, but his status called for tact and a personality which would not be irksome to the Merchant captains. Canadians were chosen because it was thought they would best meet the requirements.[45]

Life in the Channel Guard was hard, and although the experience of CW8 and OA178 meant that the new gunners were generally welcomed by the coaster skippers, the 'combat-readiness' of the older colliers left much to be desired:

> There were four of them, carrying their kit, their bedding, their Lewis guns and their ammunition. They were Cockneys, cheery, quick-witted, at home anywhere. They dumped their kit on the deck, clamped their guns to the rail with a special gadget made for the purpose; they looked around the deck, saw that the cargo of coke was higher than the hatchways, and borrowed shovels from the crew. Then they began to dig. In a few minutes they had dug themselves foxholes in the coke, curled themselves up on the deck by their guns – and fallen asleep.' [46]

The AA Guard and the Mobile Balloon Barrage Flotilla went some way towards reassuring the coaster skippers with regard to air attack, or at the very least, gave them the satisfaction of being able to 'hit back'. The other principle threat was posed by E-boats.

Destroyers were the only truly effective deterrent against E-boats, but losses at Dunkirk and Norway, and Mediterranean commitments following Italy's entry into the war on 10 June meant that there were simply not enough available. The new Hunt-class escort destroyers were perfect ships for coastal waters, and were introduced as fast as possible – the first, HMS *Fernie,* joined the 1st Destroyer Flotilla at Dover on 31 July[47] – but it was still not possible to allocate more than two to Channel convoys. As compensation, they were instead provided with anti-submarine trawlers and, in an attempt to play the E-boats at their own game, a number of Motor Launches (MLs) or Motor Anti-Submarine Boats (MASBs), the forerunners of the Royal Navy's Motor Gun Boats.

Unfortunately these stopgap escorts were inferior to the E-boats in terms of armament and speed, as well as being indescribably uncomfortable in anything approaching a heavy sea. Thomas O'Leary served in one Falmouth-based ML:

> It was 110 foot long, 17 foot beam, 4 foot draught. We had a 7-pounder forward and a couple of twin Lewis and a [projector] which was for throwing depth charges . . . In harbour, lovely, at sea, terrible . . . it's indescribable. I thought I'd never get used to it. When we first started at Falmouth our patrols used to be down to the Scilly Islands. Once you passed Land's End it could get awful. Sick, sick, sick, when you get back you'd say 'I'm getting off these!' . . . You'd think it was someone with an enormous sledge hammer hitting you underneath and you'd think the boat was going to fall to pieces.[48]

The feelings of those who were expected to take MLs into action against the big, seaworthy and heavily armed E-boats can only be imagined. However, the MASBs were, if anything, even less adequate. Their top speed was only some 25 knots and their armament limited to .303-inch machine guns, giving them a reputation for being 'E-boat fodder' if they were ever unfortunate enough to engage one, as William Harrison found out when he volunteered to join *MASB 54* towards the end of the summer:

> I saw the Chief Stoker who was the man in charge of the regulating office there, told him what had happened and he nearly went ballistic. Called me a bloody young fool, told me I'd be dead in a week, that they were hauling people out of the turrets every night, been shot up by E-boats, and quite frankly I began to think maybe I hadn't done the right thing.[49]

Although the attraction of 'fighting fire with fire' by including MASBs in convoy escorts is easy to understand, their deployment was not a success. They were too loud, which reduced the effectiveness of the escorting destroyers' Asdic, and their white wakes were visible for miles. But by far the greatest concern for naval and merchant skippers alike was their close resemblance to the very threat they were supposed to be countering. One irritated SOE submitted the following report later in the year, no doubt after several white-knuckle encounters with motorboats in the blackness of a Channel night:

> It is the considered opinion of Commanding Officers that the Motor A/S boats are a menace both to the convoy and themselves. This opinion is heartily endorsed by the Masters of the Merchant vessels . . . their frequent appearance amongst the convoy stretches taut nerves to the limit and there is no doubt that there will be a regrettable incident sooner or later, probably sooner.[50]

The new building blocks, some of clearly debatable utility, were assembled in record time. Less than a week after the debacle of CW8, the eastbound Channel convoy CE8 slipped through from Falmouth without loss, other than the coaster *Audacity* whose boiler inconveniently blew up. In line with another new policy, the Straits were passed at night, a source of vexation to some coaster skippers who failed to understand why they were being instructed to wait or slow down.

CE8 numbered twenty-five ships, carrying wool, stone, wheat and of course, coal. With an escort of two destroyers, three anti-submarine trawlers and no less than seven balloon vessels, as well as minesweeping trawlers, MLs and MASBs, the coasters were close to being outnumbered by their attendant warships, which represent a staggering commitment of manpower and resources relative to the ships and cargoes being protected. It is hard to imagine any more eloquent testimony to the importance attached to maintaining coal supplies.

The successful passage of CE8 brought renewed confidence and on 6 August the westbound convoy CW9 began to assemble at Southend. The regular shuttle service was back in action and it seemed that the Channel was open for business again. According to one account, the coaster masters were given a particularly aggressive pep talk at the regular conference held before sailing. 'We don't give a damn for your coal,' the Commodore is reputed to have said. 'We'd send you through empty, if we had to. It's a matter of prestige. Field Marshal Göring has told the world "The Channel is in German hands." We're going to prove him wrong, even if we have to give you battleships to get you through.'[51]

Possibly this ill-conceived but well-meant exhortation by a retired RNR officer explains the enduring myth that the coal convoys were nothing but a propaganda exercise. Unfortunately the Germans were also assembling 'building blocks', and darkness was no longer a guaranteed shield. Newly installed Freya radar tracked CW9 carefully as the convoy passed through the Straits of Dover late on 7 August. On the other side of the Channel the four available E-boats of *Kapitänleutnant* Heinz Birnbacher's *1. Schnellbootflottille* deployed to wait for their prey in the swept channel.[52]

At 0200 they struck. Joseph Cowper, Chief Engineer of the Commodore ship, the 1,042-ton coaster *Empire Crusader*, recalled how a torpedo missed his ship by about six feet, slamming into the vessel following. Realizing that the convoy had run into 'a nest of E-boats', *Empire Crusader* put on all available speed and began to zigzag, as the night erupted in fury: 'Then followed a series of engagements – Very lights were falling all round the ship almost continuously . . . in the light from these I could see shots crossing and recrossing. Our gunners were in action and we got shots back in return.'[53]

The *Fife Coast* was torpedoed at 0220 by *Leutnant-zur-See* Bernd Klug's *S27*. The explosion ripped open the little coaster's flimsy plates, killing one of her DEMS gunners and four of her crew instantaneously. She sank in five minutes, giving the six remaining crew no time to lower the boats. They were left clinging to wreckage and a solitary raft as the battle raged around them. H.E. Philpott was the Master of the *Fife Coast*:

> We were in the water about three hours before being picked up. The 2nd Officer, the wounded naval gunner, Collins, and myself, swam round the [raft] most of the time, as we did not want to overcrowd it. As it was this raft was continually capsizing as it was only a small one and the swell, combined with the wash made by the E-boats as they swung close, upset it very easily. Each time it capsized the three of us had to put the injured men and a young AB, who could not swim, back onto the raft. The other men on the raft were less strong than we were, and we thought it only fair to give them what chance we could.[54]

At one point the *Fife Coast* survivors were actually caught in the crossfire as the E-boats engaged the rapidly scattering convoy. Second Officer A. Davis vividly recalled what must have been a terrifying experience: 'When I was swimming in the water . . . I saw both red and white tracers in the darkness and the sound of the E-boats was like that of a fast sports car, they stopped, then accelerated, then stopped again.'[55]

Behind the *Fife Coast* was the collier *Polly M*, accelerating hard as she came under concentrated cannon and machine-gun fire. For Captain Guy, stopping would have been suicide:

> About three minutes after the first ship was torpedoed we were shelled and machine-gunned both from port and starboard . . . about ten minutes later the *Fife Coast* was blown to pieces. I steamed right through the wreckage and could see some of the crew in the water. I dared not stop to pick them up, but continued zigzagging.[56]

At 0315 the *Polly M* avoided two torpedoes: '[they] came on top of the water and made a rushing sound like a big charge of compressed air.' Shortly afterwards the ship came under gunfire once more. His small command riddled with shell holes, Captain Guy ordered his crew to take to the boats but as they were lowered, the night fell silent. Birnbacher's E-boats had gone. Behind them, after three hours of swimming in freezing cold water, a trawler picked up the exhausted, oil-covered survivors from the *Fife Coast*.

The coaster *Holme Force* was also torpedoed, and in the darkness and confusion the big collier *Rye* collided with the *Ouse*, sending the latter to the bottom. The convoy disintegrated into what one author has called a 'seething, scattering mass of individual craft, each trying to save itself'.[57] By the following morning the surviving ships were straggling over 10 miles, desperately vulnerable to the Stukas, which arrived, predictably enough, soon after daybreak.

Unfortunately CW9 was steaming straight into what some commentators have identified as the opening of the next phase of the Battle of Britain. On 1 August 1940, Adolf Hitler, through the German Armed Forces High Command (OKW), issued Directive No. 17, authorizing the *Luftwaffe* 'to use all the forces at its disposal to destroy the British air force as quickly as possible' from 5 August.[58]

Hermann Göring issued his own operational orders to the *Luftwaffe* the following day. *'Adlertag'* – the 'Day of the Eagle' – was set for 8 August, a mass attack using the full operational strength of the *Luftwaffe*. From the Channel coast to Norway, German airmen prepared for battle. Hans-Joachim Jabs was a fighter pilot flying Messerschmitt 109s with the *Luftwaffe*'s *Jagdgeschwader 27*. On 8 August, as CW9 straggled down through the Channel, his unit was placed on 24-hour standby: 'For some reason, all of us had a gut feeling that something was now about to break . . .

Many trucks were seen arriving at the base and we could only assume that they were bringing in fresh supplies of fuel and ammunition, everyone seemed to know that the planned invasion of England was near.'[59]

When *Adlertag* was repeatedly delayed by local weather problems, something had to be found for these battle-ready airmen to do, and those who could get into the air were deployed against targets of opportunity. Consequently, as the sun rose above the scattered ships of CW9, a strong force of Stukas took off to meet them, escorted by Hans Jabs and his fellow Me109 pilots.

Unlike CW8, CW9 had support from the RAF, who had codenamed the convoy 'Peewit'.[60] Four fighter squadrons intercepted the first wave of dive-bombers and drove them off before they could attack the vulnerable coasters.

Further down the coast and later in the morning the *Luftwaffe* came again, in greater strength, and once again the RAF was there to meet them. Out of sight of the ships, a brutal battle for control of the air began to unfold. Squadron Leader J.R.A. Peel of 145 Squadron was one of the first to intercept the enemy:

> We climbed to 16,000 feet, and looking down, saw a large formation of Ju87s approaching from the South with Me109s stepped up behind to 20,000 feet. We approached unobserved out of the sun and went in to attack the rear Ju87s before the enemy fighters could interfere. I gave a five-second burst to one bomber and broke off to engage two Me109s. There was a dogfight. The enemy fighters, which were painted silver, were half rolling, diving and zooming in climbing turns. I fired two five-second bursts at one and saw it dive into the sea. Then I followed another up in a zoom and got him as he stalled.[61]

Me109 pilot Werner Andres could well have been one of Peel's early victims:

> I was hit in the instrument panel and in the engine, thick white steam and plumes of black oil rushed past the canopy of my aircraft and much of it managed to enter the cockpit, maybe my controls had been shattered also as I had no control over the now fast descending aircraft. The waters of the Channel were fast coming towards me; I knew that the situation was hopeless. I managed to throw back the cockpit hood and took all the necessary precautions for a crash landing in the water. It was my good fortune that I was approaching the water at an angle so as to make a belly landing, had I been diving straight down, it would have not been possible to survive. I prepared myself for the impact, then suddenly I was pushed forwards and my arms cushioned the impact as a wall of white water engulfed my 109 and the icy waters seemed to cut me in half. I jumped from the aircraft almost before it had come to a standstill, and within one minute the tail of the aircraft rose dramatically and the Bf109 slid head first to the bottom.[62]

Not all the German aircraft were intercepted before they could reach the merchant ships. The coaster *Balmaha* was not even part of CW9; she was on her way to Falmouth in ballast, but by this stage the convoy was spread so widely that other ships passing through the Channel had become hopelessly mixed up with it. At 0915, Captain J.M. Forsyth spotted eight Stukas roaring in from his starboard quarter:

> The first machine dived steeply, flying diagonally across the ship and dropped a salvo of five bombs which fell very close to our port bow. As he pulled out of the dive he let go with his machine gun, wounding the gunner who was at the Lewis gun on the bridge. This man, H. Antrobus, who was one of the naval gunners, had a bullet right through his leg but refused to leave his post at the gun.[63]

Each near miss lifted the *Balmaha* bodily out of the water: 'Every wooden bulkhead was blown out, the wooden structure was blown off the bridge, the forecastle had perforated steel plates from the machine gunning, doors were blown off, beams fell off the hatches and No. 2 tank started to leak.'[64]

The attack only lasted around five minutes, although it must have seemed like an eternity to Captain Forsyth and his men, before RAF fighters appeared and drove off the German bombers. Picking up survivors who had prematurely abandoned the damaged coaster *Surte* and taking another disabled ship, the *Scheldt*, in tow, Forsyth nursed the *Balmaha* into port. It would have been hard to present the arrival of such a rag-tag refugee column as anything approaching a victory.

Out to sea the battle was still raging. At noon off the Isle of Wight, Chief Engineer Joseph Cowper was snatching some desperately needed food aboard the *Empire Crusader*. The coaster's lookouts, presumably exhausted from the previous night's life-and-death tag game with E-boats, gave no warning as the Stukas dropped out of the bright summer sky. 'I was having lunch in the saloon at the time with the 2nd Mate and a naval rating when there was a terrific explosion forward as a bomb struck the fore deck.'[65] A second bomb hit the ship on her port side, raising a column of water 60 feet high and lifting the ship upwards. When the smoke and spray cleared, *Empire Crusader* had lost her mast and the hatches that covered her holds had been blown off. In the middle of the coal that filled her exposed bunkers was a deep, burning crater.

In the saloon, the Second Mate had suffered a terrible wound. Cowper faced a nightmare struggle to get him across the deck to the relative safety of the lifeboats:

> The 2nd Mate was there, his hand had been shot off . . . I got a naval rating [William Robson] to assist me in getting [him] across the skylights to the boat. While he was assisting me he was hit by a machine-gun bullet and although

> wounded he did not complain until we had got the 2nd Mate on to a raft. Until the Naval Rating was hit I did not realise that we were being machine-gunned – I could not hear anything, because the noise from the aircraft and the bombs falling around us was so terrific.[66]

Cowper returned to the bridge in a fruitless search for his Captain, passing more nightmare scenes as he went. *Empire Crusader*'s naval gunners had been exposed to the full fury of the Stukas attack: 'As I came out of the chart room I saw two Naval ratings, one of them was dead and the other was so seriously injured that I knew I could do nothing for him.'[67] With the fire in the coal bunker spreading rapidly and the ship going down by the head, Cowper was forced to realize that it was time to go, and he made for the lifeboat. An escorting trawler picked up the survivors.

The Peewit Battle was one of the bloodiest days of the Battle of Britain. In the desperate struggle above the convoy, fourteen RAF and sixteen German aircraft were destroyed. When the *Luftwaffe* finally abandoned its attack, the convoy was hopelessly scattered, with most of its ships damaged and making for port. But only *Empire Crusader* and one other ship, *Coquetdale*, had actually been sunk. However bad it may have appeared to those who fought so desperately to defend it thousands of feet above, CW9 marked a turning point in the Channel.

The Channel convoys owed their salvation to Hermann Göring and the evolving strategy of the *Luftwaffe*. Bad weather still precluded *Adlertag*, and on 9 and 10 August there was no flying at all; 11 and 12 August saw more dispersed attacks wherever German formations could get into the air. But instead of shipping, these were focused on other glittering 'targets of opportunity': ports, RAF airfields and the coastal 'Chain Home' radar stations. Finally, on 13 August, came *Adlertag,* which heralded almost two months of intense air fighting over English soil.

The worst of the Battle of Britain was over for the men of the Channel convoys, who from now on would largely become spectators to the great drama being played out further inland by men like Spitfire pilot Thomas Neill:

> We crossed over . . . a convoy which had come out of the Thames Estuary and was going north, a convoy of our own ships, and we flew across the tops of the convoy at about . . . mast high and then I saw the Dornier was getting slower and slower and its nose was getting higher and higher . . . Suddenly about ten miles beyond the convoy the tail hit the water and it just plunged into the water, and the Spitfire and I flew round a couple of times and saw there was nobody getting out of it and then we turned round and flew back to England. As we crossed the convoy the second time, obviously we couldn't hear anything, all the ship's whistles had steam coming out of them . . . they were blowing their horns to say how pleased they were.

The *Luftwaffe* may have moved on to other things, but there was still one more surprise in store for the Channel convoys. On the morning of 22 August, CE9 was passing through the Straits of Dover. At precisely 0922, 'several heavy explosions occurred on either side of the convoy.'[68] Bewildered lookouts on board the escorting destroyers *Fernie* and *Garth* searched the sky in vain for German aircraft, although their commanding officers soon came to the correct conclusion: the convoy was being shelled by German coastal artillery. The 'Channel Guns' had arrived.

Back in July, as part of the preparations for the invasion of England, Adolf Hitler had issued OKW Directive No. 16, ordering the establishment of heavy coastal batteries to protect the flanks of the most likely invasion route, across the narrowest stretch of water, between Dover and Calais:

> The Navy will . . . supervise the establishment of coastal batteries, and will be responsible for the organisation of all coastal guns. The largest possible number of heavy guns must be installed as soon as possible to safeguard the crossing and to cover both flanks against enemy interference from the sea.[69]

His commanders were ordered to arrange a detailed survey of likely locations for the batteries and report back. By the regular Naval Conference held on 25 July 1940, the responsible officer (a Captain Voss) was able to confirm that the guns would be ready by early August. Ultimately five principle batteries were constructed near Calais by the forced labourers of the *Organization Todt*. *Batterie Lindemann* near Sangatte, the most powerful, was equipped with three 16-inch guns.

As CE9 crept along the Channel, the guns opened fire again. Lieutenant Commander Garth Owles was the senior officer of the Mobile Barrage Balloon Flotilla, who submitted this report after CE9 had arrived at its destination:

> At 1053 four explosions occurred about 1500 yards to the southward, and eight minutes more a further four also well to starboard. It was realised that these were shell splashes and then gun flashes were observed on the French Coast in the vicinity of Cap Gris Naz [sic]. Further salvoes of 4 fell short until 1120 when the leading ships of the convoy were straddled. By this time having been ordered to increase speed SS *Eddystone*, SS *Copeland*, HMS *Greenfly* and *Gatinais* had drawn well ahead of remaining ships. Enemy fire was concentrated on these ships throughout the action. From 1120 until 1207 they were straddled by every salvo, these being fired at approximately two to three minute intervals.[70]

The Channel convoys were shot at regularly between August 1940 and the final clearing of the battery sites towards the end of 1944. According to one contemporary account:

> During the following two years one out of every five of the convoys passing through the Straits was attacked, and each convoy attacked received on the average twenty-nine rounds from the German heavy guns ashore. Then there was a lull, and in 1943 no convoy was fired at from the shore. But shooting commenced again sporadically in 1944 and so continued until the German batteries were finally silenced.[71]

As far as this author has been able to establish, not one ship was ever directly hit by a shell fired by the Channel guns until the Normandy landings in 1944, although some damage and a few casualties were caused by near misses, including at least one fatality.[72] But fear of the guns became something of an obsession to those passing the Straits, with SOEs submitting increasingly unrealistic proposals for dealing with them, including the entirely impractical suggestion that the batteries be saturation-bombed by the RAF each time a convoy passed by.[73] British batteries were set up soon after the attack on CE9, the first being nicknamed 'Winnie', after Churchill. The second, almost inevitably, was christened 'Pooh'. From early 1941 the two sides would infrequently duel across the Straits.

With the cold clarity of hindsight, the Channel guns provide a fascinating illustration of how the perception of a threat can induce a disproportionate reaction relative to the reality. The guns may have never hit anything – or at least, no ships; parts of the town of Dover, being larger and immobile, were regularly reduced to rubble. But every sailor passing through the Straits during the Second World War was surely worried that his ship was going to enter the history books by becoming the first. And unlike the regular hazards of war, the Channel gunfire was predictable; like the soldier passing along a trench under the watchful eye of an enemy sniper, the men of the convoys knew, almost without doubt, that at a particular time and place, shells the size of small cars would be heading their way. To make matters even more unbearable, there was a thirty-two second delay between the flash of the guns and the arrival of the shell – thirty-two seconds to think of your hopes and fears and make your peace with God.

The Straits of Dover were christened 'Hellfire Corner', a sobriquet that remained in place for much of the war. The apparently uncontested existence of such an enormous threat to life and limb was initially a serious threat to morale. This was reflected not only by the restrained commentary of naval officers like Garth Owles, who wrote in one report that 'it is disheartening to all concerned to see the enemy being allowed a free shoot,'[74] but by more serious manifestations of discontent amongst the men of the coasters, for whom perhaps the economic realities which underlay their dangerous journeys had not been spelt out sufficiently clearly.

On 11 September, a man named C.W. Eakins accompanied convoy CW11 as it plodded down the Channel under the watchful eye of the redoubtable Commodore 'Non-Stop' Newman. Eakins was a representative of the

Ministry of Shipping, travelling on the coaster *Polgarth*. CW11 came under attack by a substantial force of Junkers 88 dive-bombers which overwhelmed and crippled the escorting destroyer *Atherstone*. This morale-sapping sight probably helps to explain Eakins' subsequent report, which tells a tale of men pushed close to the edge:

> The crew of the *Polgarth* was a scratch crew picked up at Blyth and I was told by the Master that the deck hands were very raw; indeed some of them had no experience on deck before. The regular crew of the ship refused to sail on the convoy and left the ship at Blyth. Every member of the crew to whom I spoke told me that he would not sail in the convoy again. Their general attitude was that they would be prepared to sail if the cargo carried by the ships of the convoy was of vital importance to the national effort, but they would not sail if the ships were merely carrying cargoes of household coal which can be sent by other routes. I found it very difficult to find an answer to this complaint, if, indeed, there is an answer.[75]

Eakins went on to conclude that 'the fear of the shelling from the French coast . . . seems to be the dominant factor in creating the crew's dislike for this convoy.'

At the beginning of 1941, Admiral Ramsay at Dover grimly reported that: 'The situation which now exists is both unsatisfactory and unacceptable . . . having lost our grip on the Straits it should be our endeavour to regain it to the greatest extent possible in the shortest time.'[76]

But as it turned out, the mayhem of the summer of 1940 was the worst that the Channel convoys would have to endure. A total of 234 ships were lost in coastal waters, mostly in the Channel and Thames Estuary.[77] It would never be so bad again, although the CW and CE series were to remain almost unique operations for most of the war, with their enormous naval escorts and their plethora of naval and military gunners. As the war went on their journeys would become almost routine, and after the first shock, even the malevolent shellfire from Cap Griz Nez was recorded in convoy reports in a reassuringly matter-of-fact style.

Notes

1. Ob.d.L. Füst Ia, No. 5841/40 g.Kdos (op 1) Chefs., of 11 July 1940. From Jacobsen, Dr Hans-Adolf and Rohwer, Dr Jürgen (eds), *Decisive Battles of World War II: The German View*, André Deutsch, London, 1965, pp. 80–1 and 423 note 7.
2. Smith, *Hold the Narrow Sea*, p. 89. According to Smith the sole casualty was the Dutch schuit *Bill S* which sank without loss to the crew.
3. IWM Sound 2466 Ferris, Henry.
4. Ibid.
5. IWM Sound 2254 Gardner, Charles.

6. http://www.battleofbritain.net
7. IWM Sound 2254 Gardner, Charles.
8. NA ADM 199/2133 Survivors' Reports: Merchant Vessels 1 June 1940 to 31 August 1940, p. 151.
9. *British Coaster 1939–1945*, p. 51.
10. NA ADM 199/2133 Survivors' Reports: Merchant Vessels 1 June 1940 to 31 August 1940, p. 151.
11. NA ADM 199/42 AN, ANF, AS, BN, CE, CW and WS Convoys: reports 1939–1941.
12. Smith, *Hold the Narrow Sea*, p. 94.
13. Galland, Adolf, *The First and the Last*, Fontana, London, 1975, p. 26.
14. Hozzel, Brigadier-General Paul-Werner, *Recollections and Experiences of a Stuka Pilot 1931–1945*, Ohio Battle Institute, 1978, p. 22.
15. NA ADM 199/2133 Survivors' Reports: Merchant Vessels 1 June 1940 to 31 August 1940.
16. NA ADM 199/2133 Survivors' Reports: Merchant Vessels 1 June 1940 to 31 August 1940, p. 160.
17. McKee, Alexander, *The Coal Scuttle Brigade*, New English Library, London, 1973, p. 11.
18. NA ADM 199/2133 Survivors' Reports: Merchant Vessels 1 June 1940 to 31 August 1940.
19. McKee, *The Coal Scuttle Brigade*, p. 11.
20. NA ADM 199/2133 Survivors' Reports: Merchant Vessels 1 June 1940 to 31 August 1940.
21. *British Coaster 1939–1945*, HMSO, 1947, p. 50.
22. NA ADM 199/2133 Survivors' Reports: Merchant Vessels 1 June 1940 to 31 August 1940, p. 161.
23. Woodward, David, *Ramsay at War*, William Kimber, London, 72. The other ships sunk were *Portslade, Polegrange* and *Corhaven.*
24. McKee, *The Coal Scuttle Brigade*, p. 13.
25. NA ADM 199/360 Dover Command War Diary.
26. BBC PW A4197125 Bartholomew, John.
27. NA ADM 199/2133 Survivors' Reports: Merchant Vessels 1 June 1940 to 31 August 1940, p. 168.
28. NA ADM 199/2133 Survivors' Reports: Merchant Vessels 1 June 1940 to 31 August 1940.
29. NA ADM 199/2133 Survivors' Reports: Merchant Vessels 1 June 1940 to 31 August 1940, p. 156. The other lost ships were *Lulonga* and *London Trader.*
30. NA ADM 199/2133 Survivors' Reports: Merchant Vessels 1 June 1940 to 31 August 1940, p. 179.
31. Slader, John, *The Fourth Service: Merchantmen at War 1939–1945*, Robert Hale, London, 1994, p. 32. See also Unwin, Peter, *The Narrow Sea*, Review, London, 2004, p. 262.

32. Burn, Alan, *The Fighting Commodores: Convoy Commanders in the Second World War*, Leo Cooper, Barnsley, 1999, p. 49.
33. Unwin, *The Narrow Sea*, p. 261.
34. Roskill, *War at Sea,* vol. I, pp. 323–4.
35. Deighton, Len, *Fighter*, Pluriform Publishing, 1977, p. 147.
36. Hancock, W.K. (ed.), *History of the Second World War: UK Civil Series – Coal*, HMSO, 1951, p. 95.
37. Air Commodore John Ellacombe DFC – Second World War Experience Centre.
38. NA ADM 199/2133 Merchant Navy Survivors' Reports 1 June 1940 – 31 August 1940, p. 165.
39. Roskill, *War at Sea*, vol. I, p. 324.
40. Other quirky 'warships' of the Mobile Barrage Balloon Flotilla were HMS *Gatinais* (an ex-French wine carrier), three First World War-vintage rescue tugs and HMS *Sambur*, a Channel Islands ferry, later gloriously renamed HMS *Toreador.*
41. IWM Docs 66/277/1 Watkinson, Viscount Harold: report.
42. IWM Docs 66/277/1 Watkinson, Viscount Harold. Viscount Watkinson went on to a post-war career in politics and business. His IWM records include the confidential report mentioned here (entitled 'Canadians on Loan'), his personal diary, notes for an interview given to the BBC and his memoir: *Turning Points: A Record of our Times*, Michael Russell, Salisbury, 1986, from which this quote is taken, pp. 9–10.
43. Ibid., report and notes.
44. Mckee, *The Coal Scuttle Brigade*, p. 48.
45. Ibid: report. The Canadians were given the opportunity to return to general service in the spring of 1941. As a reward for their services they were each apparently able to choose their next appointment.
46. Mckee, *The Coal Scuttle Brigade*, p. 48.
47. Smith, *Hold the Narrow Sea*, p. 102.
48. IWM Sound 11289 O'Leary, Thomas.
49. IWM Sound 22619 Harrison, William.
50. NA ADM 199/42 AN, ANF, AS, BN, CE, CW and WS Convoys: reports 1939–1941. The report was compiled by the Commanding Officer of HMS *Atherstone* on 1 September 1940.
51. McKee, *The Coal Scuttle Brigade*, p. 26.
52. Smith, *Hold the Narrow Sea*, p. 103. The available boats were *S20, S21, S25* and *S27.*
53. NA ADM 199/2133 Survivors' Reports: Merchant Vessels 1 June 1940 to 31 August 1940, p. 211.
54. NA ADM 199/2133 Survivors' Reports: Merchant Vessels 1 June 1940 to 31 August 1940, p. 207.
55. Ibid., p. 207.
56. Ibid., p. 213.

57. Smith, *Hold the Narrow Sea*, p. 103.
58. Jacobsen, Dr Hans-Adolf and Rohwer, Dr Jürgen (eds), *Decisive Battles of World War II: The German View*, André Deutsch, London, 1965, p. 83.
59. http://www.battleofbritain.net: chronology, p. 23.
60. As on the East Coast, Channel convoys were given simple operational code names which were reused. There would be many 'Peewit' convoys.
61. http://www.battleofbritain.net/0023.html
62. Ibid.
63. NA ADM 199/2133 Survivors' Reports: Merchant Vessels 1 June 1940 to 31 August 1940, p. 215.
64. Ibid, p. 215.
65. Ibid, p. 211.
66. Ibid, and McKee, *The Coal Scuttle Brigade*, p. 31.
67. Ibid.
68. NA ADM 199/42 AN, ANF, AS, BN, CE, CW and WS Convoys: reports 1939–1941.
69. *Führer Conferences on Naval Affairs: 1940*, p. 68.
70. NA ADM 199/42 AN, ANF, AS, BN, CE, CW and WS Convoys: reports 1939–1941.
71. *British Coaster 1939–1945*, p. 50.
72. Garth Owles' flagship *Haslemere* suffered splinter damage in November 1940, resulting in the death of Sub Lieutenant John Chambers. NA ADM 199/42 AN, ANF, AS, BN, CE, CW and WS Convoys: reports 1939–1941.
73. NA ADM 199/42 AN, ANF, AS, BN, CE, CW and WS Convoys: reports 1939–1941.
74. Ibid.
75. Ibid.
76. Woodward, *Ramsay at War*, p. 78.
77. Roskill, *War at Sea*, vol. I, p. 617.

Chapter 6
E-boat Alley

1 August 1940 to 28 February 1941

It should not be imagined that other parts of the coast were quiet during the summer of 1940, while the ships of the Channel convoys twisted and turned in German bombsights and their crews flinched at the sound of high-powered engines in the dark. The east coast did not generally experience mass air attacks, but the *Luftwaffe* was still a 'clear and present danger' to FN and FS convoys in the Thames Estuary, and E-boats were no respecters of naval command demarcation lines, alternately threatening Channel and North Sea traffic throughout the war. If this was not enough, there was always the constant, morale-sapping, threat of mining.

By the end of 1940, coasters were fighting back when they could, although their ability to do so was still very limited. One particularly spirited example was the coaster *Highlander*, attacked on 1 August off the north-east coast of Scotland by Heinkel 115 seaplanes. According to Captain W. Gifford, what happened next was possibly the only wartime success directly attributable to a much-maligned piece of equipment:

> This machine circled and . . . approached from port and when he was within range both our guns opened fire. The bomb from the Holman projector struck the machine head on, and this, together with the fire from the Lewis gun, caused the plane to sheer (probably having wounded the pilot) so that his tail caught our midships port boat. He was almost level with the deck then, the port wing fell on to the deck, the rest of the machine carried on, carrying away the after cranes and flattening the Holman gun, and then it fell into the sea just astern and caught fire . . . the two gunners were injured and we at once took them below where they were looked after by the Stewardess.[1]

One unlikely success was not enough for the men of the *Highlander*, and when another He115 swooped down ten minutes later it was swiftly despatched by the ship's Lewis gunners. One of them, George Anderson of Leith, who was actually the ship's Steward with a few days rudimentary DEMS training, was awarded the OBE, along with Captain Gifford. The anonymous Stewardess, although surely a rare presence in wartime, was not thought to require any further explanation in Gifford's report.

On 11 August, the fiercest air battle took place over an east coast convoy when around fifty Stukas and Messerschmitt 110 long-range fighters attacked FN249, a huge northbound convoy of more than fifty ships. In the air the outcome was roughly even, with two Spitfires and two Hurricanes being shot down in exchange for four Me110s and two Stukas. But at sea the much-improved fighter defence of the convoys was starting to show. Only two ships were hit and none were lost: the 3,829 coaster *Kirnwood* was set on fire and towed into Yarmouth, and the empty tanker *Oiltrader* was badly damaged when a bomb hit her magazine and wrecked her steering gear.[2] Captain McLeod's report serves as a useful reminder that after France fell, Britain was anything but 'alone'. Men and women from all over the Empire gave their support and often their lives in her defence and the Hong Kong Chinese personnel on board *Oiltrader* were no exception: 'Everyone behaved very well, including the Chinese crew who first of all put on their best clothes and then proceeded quietly to their boat stations. When the water supply failed they formed a human chain to pass buckets of water to fight the fire. I had told them to take cover during the attack.'[3]

It will be remembered that after the disaster of OA178, outward-bound ocean-going convoys had been routed from Methil out into the Atlantic, avoiding the hostile coastal waters as much as possible. This was not, however, enough to protect them from long-range bombers. On 23 August, OA203 fell victim to a mercifully rare attack by torpedo aircraft, almost certainly more He115s, which swiftly despatched the freighters *Llanishen* and *Macalla*. Roskill describes this as a 'new and potentially dangerous development' but goes on to point out that the number of torpedo-carrying aircraft available to the *Luftwaffe* at this stage was extremely low, and political tension with the *Kriegsmarine* ensured they would not become significant until the worst period of the war in coastal waters was long since past.[4]

Later on the same day, OA203 experienced the kind of attack that would typify the next phase of the air war in coastal waters. At 2100 the freighter *Beacon Grange* was attacked by a single aircraft, which dropped out of the greying twilight some 30 miles east of Clythness. The ship was straddled on the first attack, and then hit twice when the aircraft made its second run: '[The second bomb] struck the ship in Number 6 Hatch and passed through into the cargo which immediately caught fire. The ship itself had caught fire with the first direct hit and now ship, cargo and insulation were ablaze at the after end of the ship.'[5]

Captain A.B. Friend stopped his ship to fight the fire which was soon raging out of control. The sloop HMS *Leith* arrived at 0100 and tried to take her in tow but the 10,000-ton *Beacon Grange* was simply too large for her to make any headway. Finally salvage tugs arrived and brought her into

Kirkwall in Orkney at 2110 on 24 August. By now *Beacon Grange* had been on fire for almost twenty-four hours:

> The fire had spread from No. 6 to No. 7 by now, and it was almost impossible to get near the fire as it had spread right across the ship and the bulkhead had already become very hot . . . The pilot would not take us right into Kirkwall as he was afraid the fire would spread to the wharves.[6]

It was six days before the fire was extinguished. Increasingly, as the autumn of 1940 turned to winter, these 'tip-and-run' raids by single aircraft attacking by night would become the norm on the coast.

Of course not all *Luftwaffe* assets took part in this airborne *guerre de course.* Most were occupied with the bombardment of Britain's cities – the 'Blitz' – which began with a daylight raid on London on 7 September and continued throughout the winter.[7] Still more were used to reinvigorate the mining offensive, which had been given new impetus with the introduction of a sinister addition to the German underwater arsenal.

German scientists had worked hard to regain the initiative, and had come up with not one but two new approaches. The first was to produce new variants of the magnetic mine, both 'bipolar' versions which required new forms of degaussing to counter them, and delayed-action mines, which were only cocked by the passing of a sweeper, detonating some time later. These were short-term measures and relatively easy to counter once it was clear to the British what was going on. Far more serious was the threat posed by acoustic mines, which were detonated by the sound of a ship's propellers and which first appeared in August. Acting with greater caution this time, German aircraft carrying acoustic mines were banned from overflying mainland Britain, although the impact of the new weapon was once more limited by introducing it before sufficient stocks had been prepared. Roskill also quite rightly points out that 'new developments in the minelaying campaign were expected' and that Admiralty technical staff were already working on a solution.[8]

This dispassionate appraisal is of course only available with hindsight. For the coaster men, it meant a new wave of unexplained explosions and the resultant unbearable expectation of impending destruction with every mile steamed.

Edward Gueritz encountered his first acoustic mine as a junior officer on board the destroyer HMS *Jersey* at Sheerness, and learned that the new threat was anything but discriminating. *Jersey* was on her way to Plymouth to join her flotilla, and left Sheerness in common with a 'fine looking motor cruiser', pressed into service as a patrol boat:

> There was suddenly a very heavy explosion on our starboard side and we stopped and the Chief came up and said that there was water coming into the

1. 'Mostly, it was all about coal': miners at the face, 1942. (IWM D8265)

2. 'The Indestructible Highway': a typical East Coast collier convoy, viewed from the escorting trawler *Sapphire*. (IWM A17494)

3. 'Chance is a wonderful thing': the infamous Holman Projector, operator by Wren N.S. Hopkins on the DEMS ranges at Cardiff, 1943. (IWM A20405)

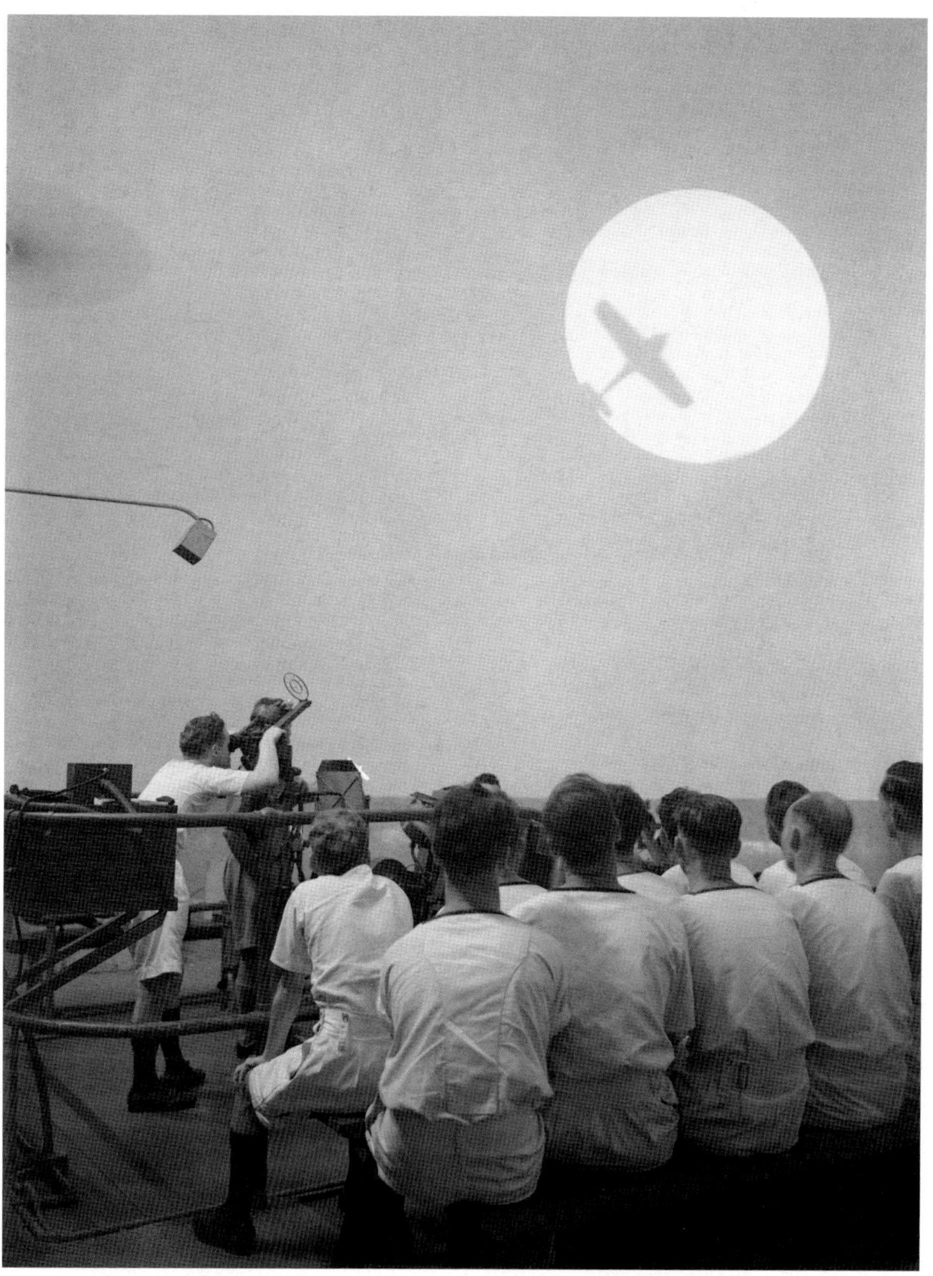

4. 'Remembered with varying degrees of affection and resentment': DEMS gunners use the Dome anti-aircraft trainer, 1944. (IWM A24965)

5. 'Limited training and no experience': Commodore's signalman at work on the freighter *Empire Kangeroo*, east coast, 1942. (IWM A7803)

6. 'Harry Tate's Navy': 'Skipper Bill' Stewart RNR (left) and Able Seaman Sam Gibbs (right) of the RNPS-manned trawler *John Stephen*. (Courtesy of IWM Department of Documents)

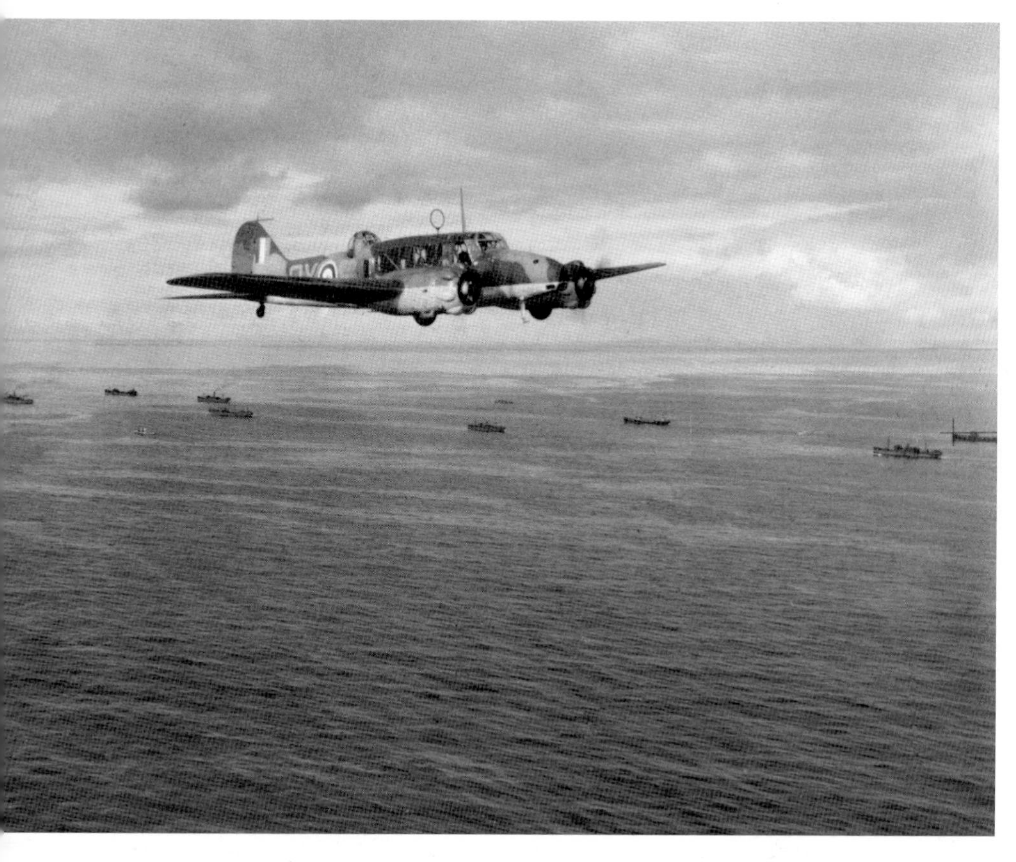

7. 'Inadequate to the efficient execution of its function': an Avro Anson Mk 1 of 48 Squadron RAF patrols above an east coast convoy, 1940. (IWM C3043)

8. 'A marker for east coast shipping over the next six years': survivors abandon the Japanese liner *Terukani Maru* after she detonates a magnetic mine off Harwich, November 1939. (Getty Images 267782)

9. 'Indiscriminate offensive minelaying': a defused German magnetic mine on an English beach. (IWM HU57325)

10. 'We have few enough to do the job as it is': veteran East Coast escort officers Lieutenant Commander W.J. Phipps of HMS *Woolston* (above) and Midshipman (later Lieutenant) A.G.F. Ditchman, the would-be captor of *S53* on the night of 19/20 February 1942 (right). (Courtesy of IWM Department of Documents)

11. 'Day trips from hell': the Isle of Man ferry *Mona's Queen*, mined and sinking off Dunkirk, 29 May 1940. (IWM HU1145)

12. 'I was appalled by the noise they made as they hurtled down out of the sky': the *Luftwaffe*'s Junkers Ju87 Stuka. (IWM GER18)

26. 'The largest and bleakest bridge on the coast': the veteran coastal tanker *San Roberto* underway. (Courtesy of Kees Helder)

27. 'Pretty basic': the V&W class destroyer HMS *Westminster*, launched in 1918. (Courtesy of Derek Tolfree)

28. The bridge of HMS *Westminster*, 1943. Midshipman Derek Tolfree is in the centre, smoking a cigarette. On the left is *Westminster*'s First Lieutenant, Alfred Tedford RNVR. (Courtesy of Derek Tolfree)

29. 'I was almost sorry for the U-boat': Robert Atkinson aged twenty-one, in 1938. By 1944 he was in command of the brand new corvette HMS *Tintagel Castle*. (Courtesy of the IWM Sound Archive)

30. 'Coasters triumphant': French children play in front of a typically battered coaster discharging directly on to the beach, Arromanches, Normandy, July 1944. (IWM A24674)

13. 'Attack on a Convoy seen from the Air': by Richard Eurich RA, 1941. (IWM ART LD1326)

14. 'Singled out for special attention': the collier *Summity*, aground on Shakespeare Cliff near Dover after the battle of CW8, July 1940. (From *British Coaster 1939-1945*, HMSO, 1947)

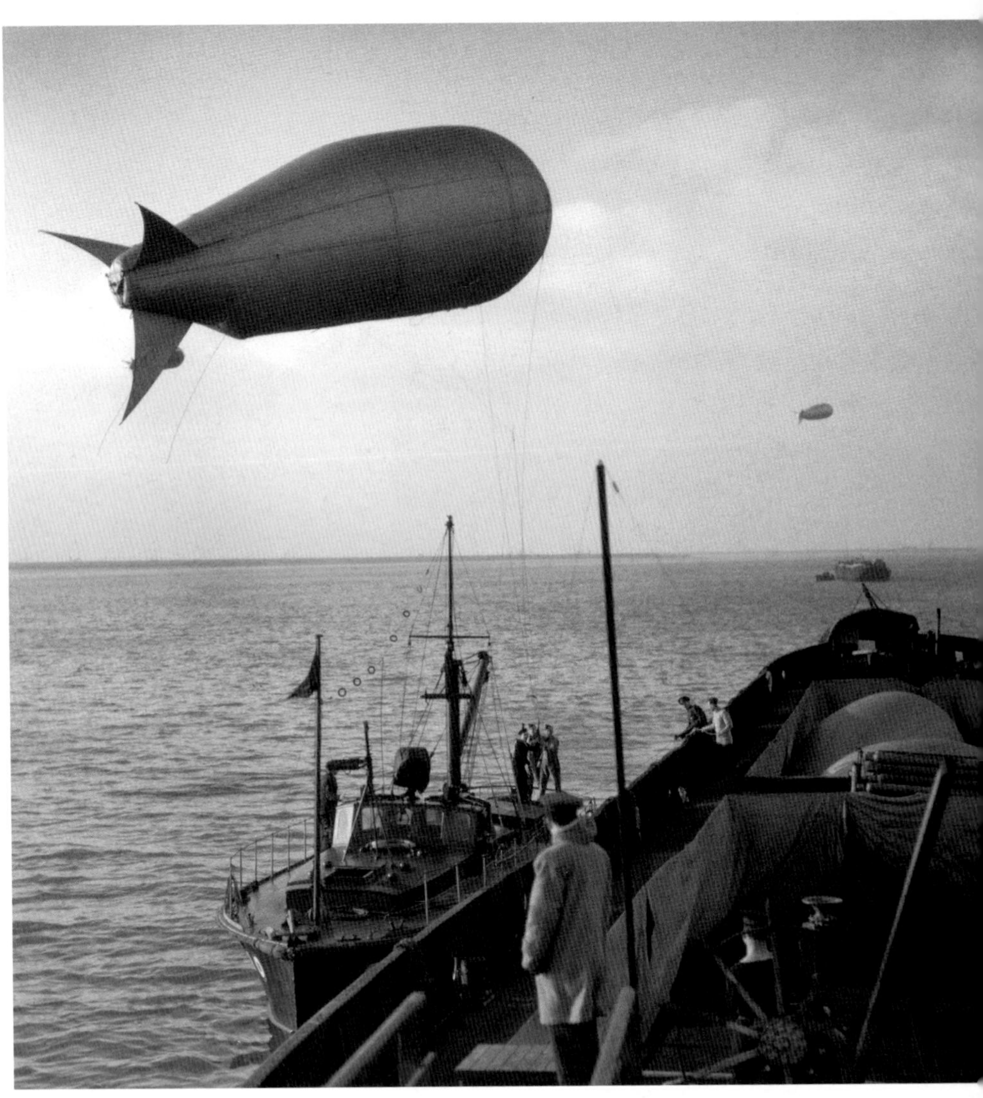

15. 'This potentially tricky arrangement worked very well': mixed Royal Navy and Royal Air Force personnel operating a barrage balloon ship. (IWM COL204)

16. 'Improvised warships': the 'gloriously renamed' ex-Channel Islands ferry HMS *Toreador*, of the Channel Mobile Balloon Barrage Flotilla. (IWM FL20132)

17. 'In harbour, lovely, at sea, terrible': *ML129*, a typical coastal patrol Motor Launch, underway. (IWM A7565)

18. 'It is disheartening . . . to see the enemy being allowed a free shoot': German coastal guns near Calais. (PA Photos EMP-4716756)

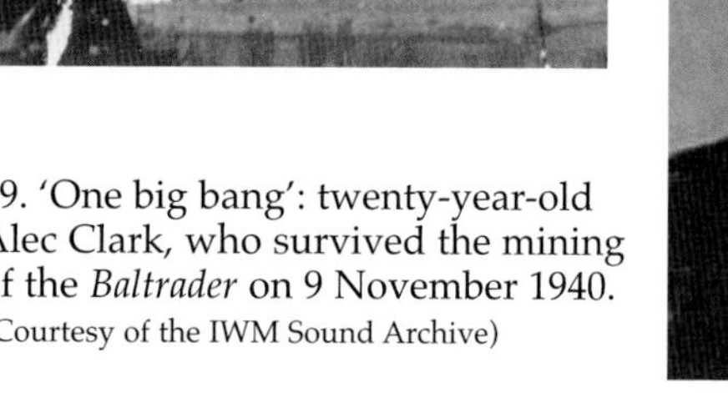

19. 'One big bang': twenty-year-old Alec Clark, who survived the mining of the *Baltrader* on 9 November 1940. (Courtesy of the IWM Sound Archive)

20. '32 seconds to think of your hopes and fears and make your peace with God': shellfire impacts near a Channel Convoy, August 1940. (Getty Images 3276538)

21. 'They had a sinister beauty, like a hunting cat': *Schnellboot* ('E-boat') at speed at the end of the war. (IWM A29320)

22. 'Established veterans': experienced *Schnellboot* officers Klaus Feldt (left) and Bernd Klug. (Courtesy of Bildarchiv der Bibliothek für Zeitgeschichte, Stuttgart)

23. 'Super little ships': the seasoned coastal Hunt-class destroyer HMS *Fernie* underway in January 1943. (IWM FL10250)

24. 'Monstrous triumphs of engineering': one of the Royal Navy's Maunsell Forts in the Thames Estuary. (IWM AX66a)

25. 'On fire and screaming for help': blindfolded prisoners from the sunken *S71* are led ashore from HMS *Garth* following the night action of 17/18 February 1943. (IWM A14449)

> boiler room, the compasses all seemed to have gone mad and there was obviously some damage to the ship, so the Captain reversed course to make our way back again towards Sheerness.[9]

The motor cruiser approached *Jersey*, signalling to offer assistance: 'Then there was another very heavy explosion and the motor cruiser disappeared! We were able to pick up her crew but by subsequent deliberation it appeared that we had encountered two of the first acoustic mines.'[10]

Jersey was sent straight to dry dock at the Isle of Dogs, which at the height of the Blitz was barely safer than the east coast: 'We unkindly suggested that there were more holes in the ship when we came out of dock than there had been when we went in.'[11]

A year of mining and air attacks had turned Britain's shores into a grim scrapyard of a place, which sent a chill through many of those who were sent to serve there. RNVR Lieutenant Derric Breen arrived on the east coast with the sloop HMS *Egret* towards the end of 1940:

> I've never forgotten that sight, it was appalling; wherever I looked, I could see the skeletons of dead ships; masts, stems, sterns and, here and there, a lonely bridge protruded from the water. It was like walking through a graveyard . . . in which a careless sexton had neglected to see that the dead were properly buried. This, then, was the war at sea, the war the Press insisted we were winning.[12]

But as the year drew to a close it was the E-boat threat which most occupied the minds of the men of the coastal convoys. Thanks to the endless squabbling between the *Kriegsmarine* and the *Luftwaffe,* their area of operations was initially restricted to the zone between Felixstowe and the South Foreland, on the White Cliffs of Dover. This was, however, more than enough space in which to wreak havoc and their hunting ground was soon christened 'E-boat Alley' by what one cynical naval officer dismissed as 'the more hysterical organs of the press'.[13] But for the coaster men life in the 'Alley' was not lightly dismissed. Second Officer Sam Williams described a typical attack:

> They used to lie in wait for us impudently tied up to our channel buoys. Then as the convoy approached, they would cast off from the buoy, roar at us at terrific speed, fire their torpedoes at us, and then scuttle off towards their bases in France. Guns were let loose, tracers lit up the night sky and the sea was churned up with projectiles . . . the convoys on the east coast were endless and when they were under night attack, it appeared like a gigantic fuse, the fire creeping closer and closer as ship after ship resorted to its own defence and repelled the enemy. A brilliant spectacle, though perhaps a little grim!'[14]

On 3 September, Heinz Birnbacher's *1. Schnellbootflottille* marked the anniversary of the start of the war with an overwhelming attack on FS271 off Yarmouth. In one devastating rush Birnbacher's boats sank four coasters and damaged another. Most of the victims had no time to react and sank in just a few minutes. One of the first was the 1,571-ton collier *Joseph Swan*. Of eighteen men on board, there was just one survivor, named Beattie, who had just come off watch when *Leutnant-zur-See* Christiansen's *S18* struck: 'The Chief Officer called down the companion way "What does six short blasts mean?" I answered submarine or track of torpedo on starboard side.'[15] As Beattie turned to the code books to check, a violent explosion rocked the ship. It took only seconds to rush up on deck but by the time he got there the entire after part was under water:

> All those who were aft at the time had no chance whatsoever . . . I saw the master step off the bridge . . . and that was the last I saw of him. Then I felt the water round my ankles and the next thing I knew I was in the water. When I came to the surface the ship had completely disappeared.[16]

Beattie was alone in the water, surrounded by the terrifying sounds of roaring E-boat engines and machine-gun fire 'spattering in the water all around me'. The 'flat-iron' collier *Fulham V* passed within feet of him as he desperately waved a flare and shouted, but her Captain obeyed his orders and passed on by. Eventually Beattie found a raft. He was rescued at 2330.

As it happens, rescue by the *Fulham V* would have been no kind of rescue at all, although her Captain was haunted by the lonely figure in the water:

> The second ship ahead of me in the starboard column was blown to pieces. There was a terrific flash amidships, a column of smoke and she must have sunk in about one minute. Soon after that I heard a voice from the water shout . . . I didn't stop but put my engines at full speed and eventually came across the *Joseph Swan* with about nine feet of her bow sticking out of the water.'[17]

Minutes later the little flat-iron was torpedoed amidships on the port side, by *Leutnant-zur-See* Grund's *S2*. Captain Ramshaw was blown high into the air above his own bridge, while the *Fulham V* sank beneath him.

Captain Gibbens of the *New Lambton* actually saw the E-boats which sank his ship, one of which was *Leutnant-zur-See* Bernd Klug's *S21*. They were hard to miss given the circumstances:

> Two E-boats came along our port side about 200 feet off and started to machine gun us and they continued to do this while we launched the boat and for twenty minutes in the boat. We all lay flat in the boat and no-one was injured . . . the E-boats were about fifty to sixty feet long and had a certain amount of superstructure with a machine gun mounted forward.[18]

Eventually Klug delivered the *coup de grâce* with a torpedo and the *New Lambton* slipped beneath the waves. In the same bloody few minutes Birnbacher's flotilla also sent to the bottom the twenty-year-old Dutch collier *Nieuwland* and the British *Corbrook*, as well as damaging the *Ewell*, before vanishing into the night without loss.

E-boat attacks continued throughout the month. Leslie Sullivan was treated to one on his first trip out as a wireless operator in the V&W HMS *Vivien:*

> As a wireless operator . . . it's something like being in a big tin can and someone keeps banging the outside, if anything drops near then the vibration comes right through the ship, everything jumps, everything moves, you've got a pair of phones on your head, you're trying to listen to a signal and there's all this banging and crashing going on and it makes life very difficult.[19]

E-boat attacks in September culminated on 23 September with a raid on the trawlers of the Ipswich Auxiliary Patrol Group, in which the *Loch Inver* was sunk. In response more Hunt-class destroyers were introduced as quickly as they became available and the elderly V&Ws were modified for anti-E-boat work by replacing the forward armament with quick-firing twin 6-pounders.[20]

Between September and the end of the year the German offensive against coastal shipping began to rely almost entirely on the twin pillars of E-boats and mines, broken up with periodic 'tip-and-run' attacks. On a bad night as many as eighty aircraft could be found engaged on minelaying operations over the coast. Life in coastal waters was full of danger and uncertainty.

The experience of the collier *Jersey Queen* in the Channel was fairly typical. Making her way from Blyth to Plymouth on 4 October she was first strafed by a raider at 0750, described by Captain Colverson as 'black in colour' with 'twin engines'. Colverson was on the bridge as the aircraft demonstrated a new tactic, which was to become common in coastal waters – a silent gliding approach giving no warning to the target:

> I was on the bridge at the time and the first thing I knew he was machine-gunning us. The plane flew over us, banked and came back again, and by this time we had manned our guns. We got one shot away with the 12-pounder but I think we fired too early. One of this gun's crew was injured in the back by a bullet. Our machine gun was also firing but one of the bullets from the aeroplane pierced the machine gun shield and injured No 3 of the crew in the shoulder. The Gunner said he hit the aeroplane but I am not at all sure about this.[21]

The aircraft dropped six incendiary bombs, fortunately scoring no hits, before making off. Colverson took his ship into Milford Haven and landed his wounded before proceeding around the coast. At 1000 on 5 October he was putting into Falmouth when the hapless *Jersey Queen* triggered a mine, sinking in five minutes:

> I was knocked unconscious as the wheel house collapsed and all the concrete slabs on the bridge fell on me and I was trapped. When I came to I managed to struggle free . . . I found that the rest of the crew had lowered the boat and were just casting off. They had not bothered about me and when I asked about the Mate they told me he was missing.[22]

The Falmouth examination vessel picked up Colverson and his perhaps understandably self-centred shipmates.

As October began the government had serious concerns about the reliability of coal supply, in the face of constant attrition of the colliers by E-boats, aircraft and mines. An undated Mines Department memorandum spelled out the dangers as winter approached: London and the south required more than twenty million tons of coal to build up reserves and get through until March. Shipments in September had fallen to 60 per cent of the average monthly intake as a result of enemy action and the restrictions on shipping brought in to try to protect the colliers. To make matters worse the London Blitz had caused a similar drastic collapse in rail deliveries, down to 52 per cent of the average monthly intake. The report went on:

> It is clear that a very serious situation will arise if similar conditions persist . . . during the month there were numerous areas in London in which it was impracticable to deliver any supplies at all . . . the continuance of such conditions would mean a shortage of 350,000 tons a month.[23]

The government set up a committee of senior political and military figures under the Lord President of the Council, Sir John Anderson, to find a solution to the problem. In theory it was simple: more ships must be found, convoys must run more frequently and be turned around faster. In practice this would be rather harder to achieve. At the first meeting on 14 October, the Royal Navy representative, Rear Admiral Moore, bluntly spelt out the problems facing coastal shipping: 'Owing to enemy action in the Thames Estuary interruptions to arrivals were likely to take place from time to time and that in any circumstances the Admiralty could not provide for more than one convoy a day down the east coast.'[24]

Coal supply was in crisis and winter was coming. While the politicians held anxious meetings, the drama on the coast continued. German destroyers based at Cherbourg joined in the assault, sweeping through the Channel on several occasions. Mercifully they never reached a convoy but engaged British warships on several occasions, sinking the armed trawlers *Warwick Deeping* and the ex-French *L'Istrac* on 11 October.

On the east coast Lieutenant Commander Phipps was still in command of the V&W *Woolston* during this difficult time, and his diary again provides a grim testimony to the sheer grind of coastal escort work. On 16 October he reported that the northbound convoy was attacked by E-boats off Smith's Knoll buoy. After hearing heavy gunfire Phipps closed up *Woolston* at action stations for an hour 'but nothing came our way'.[25]

One of the ships in the northbound convoy, FN311, was the collier *Brian*. Captain Wilkinson watched in horror as the *Hauxley*, *Gasfire* and *PLM14* exploded around him. Almost immediately afterwards Wilkinson spotted what he thought was an E-boat on his starboard beam:

> She was about 1000 feet away when I first saw her . . . the E-boat was greyish white in colour and looked like a large motor launch. I could not see her armament but the craft seemed to have a ribbon bend below her gunwale. I swung the helm to starboard and gave the order to fire. We circled around the E-boat and fired 300 rounds of ammunition from our Lewis guns. After this the E-boat just disappeared and we heard cries from the water.[26]

Tragically, the reason why the 'E-boat' was vulnerable to the feeble Lewis guns and resembled a launch was because it seems to have been one, despatched by one of the escorting destroyers to look for survivors. Certainly this was the opinion of at least one other witness, Captain F.H. Cook of the torpedoed *Hauxley*. [27]

On 20 October, *Woolston* was attacked from the air, and on 27 October Phipps phlegmatically described the end of the Everards coaster *Suavity*, which had 'blown up an acoustic mine with her pop-pop engines'.[28] *Suavity* was part of FS321. Her Captain remembered little except 'a loud but sharp explosion' with 'no column of water, flame or smoke'. His ship sank rapidly without loss of life.[29]

Mines sank the V&W destroyer *Venetia* and damaged the new Hunt *Hambledon* during October, as well as sinking several minesweeping trawlers. As the mining offensive gathered pace again, life for the hard-pressed men on the sweepers grew correspondingly more dangerous. Their precarious existences were made yet harder with the introduction by the Germans of anti-minesweeping floats fitted with explosive charges designed to cut the wires used by oropesa sweepers when sweeping tethered mines. These floats were lethal even when washed ashore – one killed four soldiers on the beach at Yarmouth on 17 October.[30]

John Neale, Navigating Officer of the fleet minesweeper *Speedwell*, spent two years sweeping the east coast as part of the 4th Minesweeping Flotilla at Harwich. On 17 October he witnessed the dreadful end of the 1914–1918 vintage coal-burning minesweeper *Dundalk*, which triggered an acoustic mine near Bawdsey:

> *Speedwell* stopped immediately and lowered both whalers and the motorboat to start the rescue. We pulled over to *Dundalk* to pick up any we could and all the time there was a terrible roar as her high pressure steam escaped from her fractured steam pipe . . . some watch keepers had just come off watch and were washing half naked when the mine exploded and they were drenched with steam from a fractured pipe. I forget how many times we rowed across for survivors but all who were not killed were rescued including some terribly scalded men.[31]

Commander Grenville Temple of HMS *Sutton* was in command of the 4th Flotilla on that day. His report throws some light on the loss of the *Dundalk*. The flotilla had been sweeping northbound ahead of an FN convoy when a sweep wire parted. When the ships turned southbound to start their second run there was a fatal gap in the line, in which not one but two mines lurked, as Temple discovered when he took the *Sutton* alongside the *Dundalk* to take off survivors: 'When alongside her, the two ships being about seventy-five yards apart, a mine was observed between the two ships, amidships from *Sutton*, three feet from my port side. I immediately went full speed ahead and the wash of the propeller threw the mine clear.'[32]

Temple's assessment was that the mines had been laid by E-boats, as they were small and even the ancient *Dundalk* took a long time to sink after hitting one. This was in fact the case, as the E-boat flotillas had laid their second major east coast minefield on the night of the 11th.

In a subsequent report, written as he freely confessed after he had 'sat down with a bottle of whiskey', Temple summed up the multiple dangers present in coastal waters at the end of 1940: air attack, surface attack by E-boats and destroyers, submarine attack, 'the ordinary hazards of the mariner', long-range shelling, fog and of course mines – contact, magnetic and acoustic. With regard to the latter he grimly concluded that 'no antidote has yet been found for the acoustic mine, it is assumed that this will be found shortly.'[33] Fortunately, his optimism was well founded.

Towards the end of September, despite the careful regulations, a *Luftwaffe* aircrew had finally repeated the cardinal sin that had ended the malign reign of the magnetic mine; they dropped an acoustic mine on land, where it was dissected and the frequency of the sound waves to which it responded were discovered.[34] During October, with minings taking place at a rate of roughly one a day, the Admiralty began to get to grips with the problem, and by early November the solution had been found. What Roskill's Official History majestically calls 'the necessary counter-measures' turned out to be the humble kango demolition hammer, which generated sound waves capable of triggering the mines.

Brookes Richards had one fitted to his trawler, but it failed to work properly and was removed, much to his amusement. His laughter was short-lived, however; soon after the removal of the kango his drifter *Sevra* triggered an acoustic mine off Falmouth and was effectively vapourized: 'the ship went up about thirty feet in the air with an enormous column of water just clear of its stern on one side.' Richards broke his leg and, whilst recuperating, was recruited into the Naval Section of the Special Operations Executive. The remainder of his war was spent in very lively activities entirely unconnected to minesweeping.[35]

Sweeping on the coast was now a complex business, with every convoy preceded by combinations of acoustic, magnetic and conventional oropesa sweepers. The battle was being won, but it was a slow and difficult process, and as the new equipment was developed and installed, losses on the coast continued to mount. William Donald's sloop *Black Swan* triggered an acoustic mine on 31 October, and was towed into Rosyth, where he was able to reflect on the experience: 'Being mined is not particularly amusing. The unexpectedness of the thing leaves a permanent psychological effect, however slight . . . there is the added annoyance of having had a kick in the pants from the enemy without being able to hit him back: a distinct loss of dignity about it.'[36]

Many others were to experience such a 'kick in the pants' as the war's second long, deadly winter wore on. The Battle of Britain was to all intents and purposes over, but in an unexpected development Stukas returned to the Thames Estuary on 1 November, in one of the last mass daylight raids. They caught FS322, which had just arrived at Sheerness from Methil, and sank the coaster *Letchworth*, commanded by Captain Doughty: 'They dived at an angle of about 85 [degrees] coming down to a height of 400 feet over the ship, crossing us athwart ships. The machines followed one another in single line, each plane dropping two bombs, which I could see leave the machine.'[37]

As many as thirty bombs were dropped altogether, eight of them very close to the *Letchworth*, and as each aircraft passed over the rear gunner strafed the ship. To the crew it seemed inevitable that their ship would be hit, and when the blow came it was no surprise: 'The vessel was enveloped in steam and spray and it was difficult to see . . . the ship was lifted out of the water about six feet by the force of the explosions.'[38]

Their work done, the German dive-bombers made for home, leaving the *Letchworth* to roll over and sink. The whole attack lasted just one minute from start to finish, though it must have seemed a lifetime to men like Robert Stoves, who ended up in the water:

> We had a forty-five gallon drum of fuel oil on the boat deck and I went down with sea boots on and lifejacket and everything else, I shot up amongst all this fuel oil. This happened to about four of us, we were all covered in fuel oil. The tide was running fairly strong then, two or three were shouting, 'help help I can't swim'. Anyway a lifeboat eventually came off from Southend and picked us up and took us ashore, by which time it was dark and the railway line on the pier at Southend was electrified and all the chaps ahead of us were saying

> 'mind your feet . . . don't touch that rail it's electrified', in the middle of the night with no lights at all.[39]

Robert and the other survivors were taken to a hut at the end of the pier, where they gratefully warmed themselves, one at a time, in front of a gas cooker. They were then taken to a department store in Southend and given replacement clothes by the manager who opened up in the middle of the night to help them:

> I was standing in my underpants, [my] boots had come off with the suction of the water and so on, we were frozen stiff. We'd had a double brandy from the coxswain of the lifeboat, that was the only thing that had kept us warm, and this gas cooker, and we had to get dressed in this shop, although we were still covered in fuel oil . . . I couldn't ever wash that fuel oil off the shirt collar![40]

The following week, Stukas returned again to attack FN329, damaging three ships including the SS *Catford*, whose Captain remembered 'a mass of aeroplanes' diving 'almost vertically down on to us to a height of about 150 feet'. His ship was not hit but was left with twenty-nine holes in her side close to the waterline.[41]

Surgeon Lieutenant H.M. Balfour arrived on the east coast at this time, in the V&W HMS *Windsor*, and was caught up in one of these last massed Stuka attacks:

> I was appalled by the noise they made as they hurtled down out of the sky. 'Christ what a hideous din' I said to Johnny as we both crouched on the bridge and one of the planes deposited its bomb to our port side and flipped up again into the sky with tracers from our machine guns trailing after it. 'Yes they have special devices fitted to their wings' said Johnny 'supposed to spread alarm and despondency among those being attacked.' 'It works' I said 'a hundred per cent!'[42]

A surgeon in civilian life as well, Balfour was amusingly determined to make no concessions to the new world he had entered 'for the duration':

> As a matter of principle I insisted on maintaining my civilian language and referring to such completely un-nautical things as floors, walls and ceilings. [His Commanding Officer, Lieutenant Commander George Pepys Huddart RN] entered into this with relish and was able with great ease to tie me in knots with naval terms and naval traditions that were . . . completely unknown to me.'[43]

Balfour's description of his new comrades in arms paints a vivid picture of the crew of a typical coastal escort. Huddart, the Commanding Officer, 'a lean, fair man', was a regular Royal Navy officer who seems to have liked his amateur medical officer. The Sub Lieutenant was 'a solemn young man who had risen from the lower deck'. In keeping with the conventions of maritime fiction the Chief Engineer was 'a solemn grey haired Scot' and the First Lieutenant 'a harsh unsympathetic disciplinarian'.[44] And then, of course, there were the men: 'The ship's company were a mixed bunch of regulars and "Hostilities Only". The latter, like me, were bemused by the Navy and its traditions but were learning their lessons in a rather harder school than I was.'[45]

Balfour found himself taking on a variety of extra duties, from ordering the Wardroom drink, to running the cipher office (a never ending job given the volume of signals which plagued any Royal Navy warship at this time) and censoring the men's mail. The latter was a thankless task: 'Armed with a pair of scissors we had to read all the sailors' letters and snip out any statement which could possibly disclose where the ship was or what duties we were performing. It was a task that I found embarrassing and boring . . . what seemed most striking was their total inability to communicate.'[46] He goes on to illustrate some of the popular expressions he had to deal with, from the sentimental 'SWALK' ('sealed with a loving kiss') to the rather more lurid 'NORWICH' – 'knickers off ready when I come home'!

November was a busy month for the hard-pressed escorts and for the RAF. The south coast was far quieter than the east, at least for the convoys, but the *Luftwaffe* visited Dover twice and German destroyers continued to be a problem, badly damaging the destroyer *Javelin* on 28 November.

The east coast was livelier. On 9 November, Phipps' *Woolston* was bombed, and on the same day he lost one of the ships in his charge, the SS *Baltrader*, to a magnetic mine in the Thames Estuary. His journal records tersely that 'chaps got away and only two missing'.[47]

One of the 'chaps' who got away was twenty-year-old Wireless Operator Alec Clark. The 1,699-ton *Baltrader,* whose keel first touched salt water in 1919, was a typical older coaster:

> The wireless room must have been added some time after it was built . . . the only place they could put [it] was opposite the galley at the after end of the midships accommodation. So I was on from midnight to six in the morning . . . and of course I used to watch the cockroaches come in from the galley . . . with the heat . . . they thrived quite well there.'[48]

It was 1400 on a Saturday when the *Baltrader* found the mine with her name on it. She was the last ship in her column and several other ships had passed in safety, when there was 'one big bang'. Alec and the *Baltrader*'s Third Mate grabbed their lifejackets and ran for the upper deck, where they abandoned ship in the only undamaged lifeboat.

The two missing men noted by Phipps were at the stern of the ship, right on top of the mine when it detonated:

> The stern of the ship was blown off and . . . we never saw them again. One was an ordinary seaman and one was a carpenter, we called him Chippy. Two Londoners . . . the rest of us got off on the lifeboat and then we were picked up by a drifter patrolling nearby, taken into Southend pier about 5 or 6 o'clock that evening.[49]

As a wireless operator employed by the Marconi Company, Alec was given two weeks' survivor's leave, and £40 with which to buy new clothes. When he returned home to Buckie, in north-east Scotland, his father met him at the station: 'He says, "where's your luggage?" I said, "It's at the bottom of the sea." "Oh man!" he says.'[50]

By the autumn of 1940, nowhere in coastal waters could be described as 'safe'. Back in August, a new convoy series running northabout between the west and east coasts of Scotland had been introduced, prefixed EN (eastbound) or WN (westbound). This reflected the growing reach of the *Luftwaffe*'s Norway-based aircraft.

On 11 November, German torpedo aircraft attacked EN23, sinking the SS *Creemuir*, a 4,000-ton freighter bound for Oban in ballast. One of her few survivors was a seaman named Luckham, who described how one German aircraft carefully staged a half-hearted attack to draw off the convoy's air escort before a second struck at 1645, flashing random morse code signals to hide his identity for as long as possible while he closed the ship at 200 feet. The true identity of the intruder does not seem to have become apparent until he dropped his torpedo, which impacted the side of the *Creemuir* with 'a colossal explosion'. One minute later the ship's decks were awash and the crew were heading for the boats: 'The port boat had twelve men in it, and I was just trying to pull myself over the side when the *Creemuir* went down, pulling the boat with it. This was about three minutes after the explosion.'[51]

Luckham frantically tried to grab hold of floating wreckage as his ship went almost vertical in the water and sank. Afterwards he scrambled onto the upturned starboard lifeboat, which had floated clear. There followed a desperate struggle to save the life of the ship's cook, 'who was completely numb with the cold [and] said he couldn't manage it and we were to look after ourselves'. A deckhand called Smith managed to pull him in and tried to hold on to him but he too was exhausted and could not support the cook's weight indefinitely. Luckham tried to help as the tragedy reached its inevitable conclusion: 'The Rating shouted to me that the Cook was going. I grabbed hold of the rating's hand and with the other held on to the Cook but unfortunately the Cook slipped off despite our efforts and we didn't see him again.'[52]

As the *Creemuir* survivors struggled in the water, they witnessed the German aircraft turn on the 4,597-ton freighter *Trebartha*. 'In very little time it became a raging inferno. The men took to the boats and the enemy came back and machine-gunned them, being guided by the light of the burning ship which lit the whole scene quite plainly.'[53]

The *Trebartha* was hit on the bridge by a bomb, which blew the ship's gunners to pieces before penetrating into the Wireless Operators' cabin, killing both junior operators. There followed a scene of absolute horror:

> The Chief Wireless Operator was on watch in the wireless cabin which caught fire almost immediately, trapping him. We tried to get the hoses to bear, but the water supply failed. We could hear him shouting, his cries gradually growing fainter. He was under the table and the bulkheads had collapsed on top of him, we tried to get him out another way but it was impossible.[54]

The heat was so intense that the glass in the portholes melted. *Trebartha* burned for two and a half hours before finally drifting ashore and turning over on rocks south of Aberdeen. Of her crew, four were killed. The remainder, after surviving the ordeal of being strafed in their lifeboats, were eventually picked up, as were the men from the *Creemuir*.

The following day Trinity House lost their second tender. Ironically, THV *Argus* was on her way north to recover equipment from the first to be sunk, THV *Reculver*, mined off the Humber on 29 September. *Argus* was Trinity House's oldest tender, launched in 1909, and sank rapidly when she was mined in the Thames Estuary at 1600. All but one of her crew of thirty-four died, 'immobilised by broken legs and pelvises and finally drowned as the ship foundered'.[55]

Meanwhile the war of the *Woolston* went on. Phipps was attacked by torpedo aircraft on 17 November, and in early December whilst escorting FS353 he received a brutal reminder that the east coast in winter did not need the enemy to make life hard: 'an awful mix up with the northbound convoy' followed by a gale; 'very uncomfortable and blowing harder than I have ever seen it I think . . . bloody awful night.' The entire convoy was eventually forced to anchor and ride it out.[56]

On 15 December, while escorting FS360, *Woolston* was attacked by Birnbacher's *1. Schnellbootflottille*: 'The weather conditions were ideal for E-boat operations – sea slight, sky completely covered by light cloud which diffused the light of the full moon.'[57] Generally, the E-boats were less active in winter. Although more seaworthy than the British MLs and MASBs, they still could not stand up to a North Sea gale. And on 19 November the destroyer HMS *Campbell* had scored the first recorded success against them when she rammed and sank *S23* off Southwold. But they came out when they could, and when they did, it could be deadly. Phipps's after-action report gives a vivid impression of the breathless speed of these encounters:

> Detected fast HE [hydrophone effect – the sound of high-speed engines] bearing 110 [degrees]. It was not immediately recognised as the sound was somewhat

> quenched by the noises of the convoy . . . a minute later there was no doubt what it was – engines were put to full speed and wheel hard a port to close position as rapidly as possible. Before the ship had turned at all two torpedo tracks were observed on the port side. The first track appeared to pass underneath the bridge and the second under the bow . . . [It was] too late to do anything except wonder whether they were going to hit us.[58]

Phipps was luckier than many escort officers; he actually saw the E-boat and his gunners opened fire with *Woolston*'s forward 4-inch gun. After firing five salvoes they lost contact as the frantically jinking E-boat maneuvred behind a smoke screen of its own manufacture and headed for home at high speed.

Unfortunately the torpedo which passed under the shallow-draught destroyer found a mark, ripping open the hull of the Danish coaster *N C Monberg* and sending her to the bottom. Hugh Irwin of the sloop *Lowestoft* witnessed her end, a personal tragedy for him, as he was an acquaintance of the Captain:

> The worst experience I had, which I think was really terrible, was [when] . . . we came into the Tyne because of bad weather . . . and I found the Captain of a ship called the *Monberg*. This Captain recognised me, I had come back from France in 1937 to Newcastle in her . . . I said to the Captain 'any news of your family?' He said 'no' and I felt very sorry for him. Anyway we proceeded south. Now . . . close to the Thames estuary . . . we passed this buoy, it was very dark and we suddenly heard a revving up and it was an E-boat . . . then there was a big explosion astern of us, it was the *Monberg*, it had blown up, there were no survivors . . . it was terrible, it affected me.[59]

One of the few survivors of the *Monberg* was her English First Mate, Arthur Ryder, who recalled how the ship sank so fast that the boats were submerged before they could be launched. The ten survivors (out of twenty-two on board) were rescued by the trawler *Le Tigre*, but the unfortunate Captain died an hour later despite desperate attempts to give him artificial respiration.[60]

Luftwaffe minelayers also came out in force in mid-December, with no less than ninety-three aircraft out on the night of 12/13.[61] Two days after the loss of the *Monberg*, they claimed the Everards coaster *Aquiety*, as she left Southend with two sisters, *Angularity* and *Acclivity*. The entire bridge crew, including the Captain, were swept away and the ship sank in two minutes.[62] Christmas in coastal waters was going to be grim once more.

On Boxing Day the *Lady Connaught* ran over a mine in the Mersey, heralding a new campaign around the west coast ports. Coupled with the Liverpool Blitz, it wreaked havoc as the year drew to a close. Fifteen ships were sunk in harbour between 20 and 21 December, and mines claimed many more, including the *Elax* on 22 December, the *Victoria* on the 27th, the *Lochee* on the 28th, the *Catrine* on the 29th and the *Dorcasia* on the 30th.

The New Year brought some respite – records indicate that it was quieter, although doubtless to those involved it did not feel like it at the time. Mines still took down ships with depressing regularity, among them the brand-new Trinity House tender *Strathearn* and fifteen of her crew on 8 January, whilst engaged in the hazardous work of maintaining the 'war channel'.[63] Both H.M. Balfour's *Windsor* and Hugh Irwin's *Lowestoft* also ran over mines in January. Balfour returned to the coast almost immediately in the new Hunt *Holderness*, but for Irwin it was what he termed a 'comfortable' mining:

> By that I mean that I had had Christmas leave and I had by then got fed up with this ship and I wanted to move . . . we'd had a year of pretty hard going. We had one or two badly injured but nobody killed . . . I was up in the Director, I lost some teeth and had a gash in my leg.[64]

He got his wish, being transferred out of the ship to the Bristol Channel Balloon Barrage.

Phipps's *Woolston* survived another E-boat attack on 16 January while escorting FN385. Once again the attack began with the ominous high-speed hydrophone signals at 2038, and once again the men of the *Woolston* caught sight of their assailants: 'Got all ready to fire when Gunner . . . saw them. Looked at first like one long dark shape but soon split up and two then three appeared. About a thousand [feet] or less off.'[65]

The skilled and experienced E-boat commander turned into the *Woolston*, and her gunners were unable to depress their weapons far enough to hit him as he sped off into the night. 'I thought I was bound to ram, he was right under my bow but he just saw me in time and was away in a flurry of foam just as I was on him. Pity we did not hit one . . . but we put the fear of God into them and they ran like hell.'[66]

The following week the anti-submarine trawler *Tourmaline* scored a rare success, apparently sinking an E-boat during an attack on FN385.[67] This, then, was the pattern in coastal waters during the winter of 1940/41: long periods of enemy inactivity followed by sudden bursts of action. However, to describe this as 'quiet' would be doing the men of the convoys a grave injustice; it should never be forgotten that even without the enemy, the weather conditions and navigational challenges made coastal waters a dangerous place. Peter Wyatt was a junior officer aboard the Rosyth-based sloop *Grimsby*:

> The main action came from heaven. It was an extraordinarily cold and bloody awful winter, the Norfolk coast was the coldest place I've ever been, in spite of Arctic convoys and all the rest of it, that winter going from Hull down to the Thames and back again was absolutely appalling. We had a cycle of three

> trips back and forth, which took twenty-one days, then we had three days off in Rosyth and then another cycle of three trips. And we went through the whole winter doing that . . . It was very difficult to keep a convoy of fifty ships in two columns [but] they had to be narrow to get through the minefields, so the convoys were several miles long and in anything like a cross tide . . . the tail of the convoy was apt to be swept to one side and probably on to a shoal or sometimes into a minefield. Navigation was a very big problem . . . it's a bad coast, a difficult coast and particularly when there are minefields around . . . There were no lighthouses, all the lighthouses were put out. One had nothing except a finger up . . . to hear where the wind is.[68]

The men on the older destroyers, like Surgeon Lieutenant H.M. Balfour, suffered particularly badly:

> Although *Windsor*'s slim tough lines were built to cope with any sea she certainly did move a great deal. To get from the stern of the ship, where the Wardroom was, to the Bridge or Sick Bay was a hazardous procedure. She lay low in the water and the deck was not far above the sea so it was quite easy for waves to come swirling down adding to the difficulty of keeping one's balance. Overhead wires were fitted permanently and from these hung ropes attached by metal eyes so that they would slide along and provide a hand grip.[69]

Along with the weather, the escort commanders still had to deal with the coaster men. More than a year of war had increased mutual patience, understanding and respect, but at times there was still something of an empathy gap. In early 1941 William Donald was promoted to command of the sloop *Guillemot*:

> One day off Yarmouth we drew alongside an elderly coaster miles astern of the convoy, making about three knots with propeller high out of the water, thrashing away in the most inefficient manner. 'Can you go any faster?' I shouted through the megaphone. No reply. 'Can you increase speed a bit please?' There did not seem to be anyone on the bridge. Eventually . . . the wing window of the collier's bridge appeared and an angry red face appeared. 'What do you think I am?' it roared 'a **** Spitfire?'[70]

Luftwaffe tip-and-run raids continued through the winter, although with decreasing frequency. On 26 January, whilst northbound with FN392, the coaster *Cormarsh* was attacked by a low-flying Messerschmitt 110 – flying far too low, as it turned out, when operating in the vicinity of barrage balloons:

> He appeared to attempt to dive but straightened out and flew right into our kite which he carried away with him. He began to lose height very quickly but

> the visibility was so poor at that time that, unfortunately, we were unable to see him come down. However we saw smoke streaming from the plane and learned later that the plane had come down and that one airman was alive and the other dead.[71]

Such good fortune was rare, but fortunately so was the quite extraordinary inattention displayed by the men of the SS *Baron Renfrew,* who managed to be bombed at 1000 on 28 January, apparently without anyone noticing. The Chief Engineer, J. Kendrick, felt a shock and rushed on deck. Seeing sparks at the rail he assumed there was a fault in the ship's degaussing cable and ran down to the engine room to check the indicators. On arrival, he discovered a hole in the ship's side and an unexploded bomb nestling in the starboard coal bunker. His report does not include his feelings when he realized that the 'sparks' at the rail had been ricocheting machine-gun bullets fired by the raider which had swooped overhead unobserved.

The crew immediately and probably forgivably abandoned ship, but Kendrick returned later with a Lieutenant from a naval escort to find the engine room under twelve feet of water and the bomb rolling around in the coal. Kendrick and the Lieutenant hurriedly departed, only to return on 30 January to arrange a tow. The tug *Tenacity* did not arrive until 1 February, and did not fix a tow until the following day. On 4 February the line parted and the *Baron Renfrew* disappeared, probably to the relief of all concerned.[72]

At 1630 on 4 February, the SS *Gwynwood*, while anchored at Hawke Road anchorage in the Humber, encountered another aerial raider which passed overhead at 1745. The only surviving witness to what followed was a crew member named Collier: 'When I reached my station I saw a parachute at a height of 150 feet, of a lightish colour, coming down at a speed which I judged to be three or four times as fast as a man would fall.'[73] Collier opened fire with a Lewis gun but failed to hit the parachute. He heard the object hit the *Gwynwood*'s after deck, and then his ship quite literally vanished: 'Within one second there was a colossal explosion, a terrific flash and great volumes of smoke and I found myself being blown through the air.' He subsequently estimated that he had travelled 40 feet downward and around 50 feet horizontally. Although he felt no pain, Collier later discovered he had two broken ribs; he was also deaf, and lucky – every other man on the *Gwynwood* was killed. This was what happened when a ship received a direct hit from a parachute mine.[74] *Gwynwood* was unlucky enough to be on the receiving end of a huge operation. Hull was closed for a fortnight, while no less than ninety-four magnetic and acoustic mines were swept.[75]

New measures were already being taken to make Britain's river estuaries safer. In February 1941, a 43-year-old Liverpudlian First World War veteran named Cyril Punt was recalled to the colours as a Sub Lieutenant RNR and got on a train to Portsmouth. After three weeks training at HMS *Vernon*, he was sent to Newcastle:

> We started building little brick buildings, just big enough to hold a man and put a compass card in and an azimuth on top of it . . . You'd build these at vantageous [sic] points, we had forty-two on the Tyne, twenty-six on the Wear, five on Sale Harbour . . . when the men came along that were to do it, they were dressed in matelots' uniforms but they were all sorts of people, cab drivers, clerks, mostly people of higher ages . . . We had to . . . teach them to march [and] find digs for them somewhere near where we were going to post them, and their job as soon as the air raid [warning] went [was to] jump out and go down to their post, take the shutters down, and just watch out, if they saw anything coming out of the sky, take a bearing of it as it hit the water.[76]

The vigilance of the 'mine watchers' greatly speeded up the process of minesweeping in estuarial waters after early 1941.

The day after *Gwynwood* was vapourized, E-boats struck again. This time they chose as their victim the 500-ton Everard's coaster *Angularity*, straggling from a northbound convoy, probably FN401, on 6 February. William Lind was one of her crew:

> Shortly after leaving Harwich we could see in the distance ahead of us the northbound convoy; it was too far ahead for us to catch up with it . . . unfortunately the ship was in bad trim. Our cargo of phosphate . . . in Number 1 hold, that is in the fore part of the ship, had more in it than was required, thus putting the ship down by the head . . . It was a bitterly cold night and a snowstorm was raging with a heavy sea on.[77]

Angularity was thus alone and vulnerable when *Oberleutnant* Klaus Feldt in *S30* found and despatched her at 2030, condemning William Lind to a terrifying brush with death:

> There was a muffled explosion. I was in my cabin, having just come off watch. I opened my door to see what had happened but . . . a solid wall of water drove me back . . . The next thing I knew I was trapped in my cabin under water. Fortunately my cabin got airlocked through the vessel going down bow first. I reckon the whole thing happened within ten seconds. Strangely enough I did not panic. I was swimming in circles in my waterlogged cabin with just enough air space to keep the water below my nose. My head was bumping the bulkhead. I took one deep breath and dived through the open doorway. It seemed ages before I broke surface. The seas were high and the water was bitterly cold.[78]

Angularity struck bottom in shallow water, and William surfaced to see her stern rising above him, but before he could climb to safety he was swept away by the current. He was left clinging to a hatch, alone in the dark with no life-jacket, and feeling his body beginning to numb. Death seemed certain until salvation arrived from an unlikely quarter – Feldt's E-boat maneuvred alongside and William was hauled on board. Rudimentary first aid coupled with genuine kindness almost certainly saved his life:

> With some difficulty they hauled me on board. I could not help myself owing to my numbed legs. They bundled me in blankets when I got below. I was laid in one of the crew's bunks then three sailors sat on top of me to impart the warmth of their legs. They offered me a bowl of hot soup and a glass of schnapps. After that I fell into a deep sleep and did not wake till the E-boat arrived at her base.[79]

When he recovered he was interviewed by Feldt, who spoke perfect English, and was told that *S30* had also picked up 'Jimmy', the Second Engineer. He and William were the only survivors of *Angularity*'s crew of thirteen. Their treatment by the *Kriegsmarine* continued to be good, but after a few days of fresh clothes, food, coffee and sleep, they were transferred to the Gestapo, who interrogated them for six hours. They were then passed to the Vichy French police:

> For five days and nights we slept on damp palliasses, we were never even allowed to go to the lavatory, everything had to be done on the floor of our cells . . . to me the French were worse than the Germans. On the fifth day I was seized with violent shivering and a high temperature [and] I collapsed.[80]

Once again William's unlikely saviour was a German, this time a guard at the prison who arranged his transfer to first hospital and then Milag (*Marine Internierten Lager*) Nord, the Merchant Navy prisoner-of-war camp at Westertimke, in Lower Saxony, where he remained until May 1945. His remarkable experience seems to have been unique amongst coaster men. Two years after his release, his sleep was still being broken by 'terrifying dreams'.

Three days after the loss of *Angularity*, Lieutenant Commander Phipps of the *Woolston* recorded in his journal in celebratory capitals that FS408, between 9 and 12 February, was his 'ONE HUNDREDTH EAST COAST CONVOY'.

Just over a week later, celebrating was probably the last thing on his mind, when FN417 was attacked by E-boats off Harwich.

> At 2110 we were investigating a possible E-boat picked up on HE when suddenly astern there was the most terrific blaze up . . . two great balls of fire went up and the whole sea for about half a mile looked to be a roaring inferno . . . it was not until 2323 that I got a report from [HMS] *Shearwater* that she was picking up survivors from [the destroyer HMS] *Exmoor* who had been

> torpedoed by an E-boat, her magazine had gone up and all her oil fuel caught fire on the water.[81]

Exmoor, a brand new Hunt only commissioned in October, sank quickly, taking over a hundred officers and men down with her.[82] Her assailant was once again Feldt's *S30*. Phipps's terse comment on the affair was accurate enough: 'It was a bad night for us.' Soon afterwards he was transferred to Atlantic convoys, just before what passed for a lull in coastal waters came to a dramatic and bloody end.

Notes

1. NA ADM 199/2133 Survivors' Reports: Merchant Vessels 1 June 1940 to 31 August 1940, p. 190.
2. Foynes, *Battle of the East Coast*, p. 91.
3. NA ADM 199/2133 Survivors' Reports: Merchant Vessels 1 June 1940 to 31 August 1940, p. 218.
4. Roskill, *War at Sea*, vol. II, p. 326. Identities of lost ships from www.convoyweb.org. Roskill interestingly assigns the torpedo aircraft to 'The German Navy's Air Arm', which did not in fact exist – Hermann Göring never released them to the Navy.
5. NA ADM 199/2133 Survivors' Reports: Merchant Vessels 1 June 1940 to 31 August 1940, p. 246a.
6. Ibid.
7. Although it falls outside the scope of this book, the bombing of the London Docks was of course of great significance to the coaster men: according to J.P. Foynes's *Battle of the East Coast*, p. 147, thirteen ships were sunk or disabled on the first day of the London 'Blitz' alone.
8. Roskill, *War at Sea*, vol. I, p. 326.
9. IWM Sound 17394 Gueritz, Edward.
10. Ibid.
11. Ibid.
12. Lieutenant Derric A. Breen RNVR, Second World War Experience Centre.
13. IWM Docs 01/39/1 Syms, Commander James.
14. Captain Sam Kent Williams, Second World War Experience Centre.
15. NA ADM 199/2134 Survivors' Reports: Merchant Vessels 1 September 1940 to 30 November, p. 12.
16. Ibid.
17. Ibid., p. 9.
18. Ibid., p. 11.
19. IWM Sound 12549 Sullivan, Leslie.
20. Foynes, *Battle of the East Coast*, p. 93.
21. NA ADM 199/2134 Survivors' Reports: Merchant Vessels 1 September 1940 to 30 November, p. 67.
22. Ibid.

23. TNA Power 26/407 Minutes of Lord President's Coal Committee 10 October 1940 to 14 May 1941: Memorandum on Coal Supply Position in London and South, pp. 1–2.
24. Ibid.
25. IWM Docs 75/105/1 Phipps, W.J., p. 69.
26. ADM 199/2134 Survivors' Reports: Merchant Vessels 1 September 1940 to 30 November, p. 95.
27. Ibid., p. 102.
28. IWM Docs 75/105/1 Phipps, W.J., p. 70.
29. ADM 199/2134 Survivors' Reports: Merchant Vessels 1 September 1940 to 30 November, p. 133.
30. Foynes, *Battle of the East Coast*, p. 97.
31. IWM Docs 92/50/1 Neale, J., pp. 23–4.
32. IWM Docs 76/28/1 Cronyn, Captain St J.
33. Ibid.
34. Roskill, *War at Sea*, vol. I, p. 326.
35. IWM Sound 9970 Richards, Sir Brookes. Richards ended the war as SOE Head of Section in Corsica and southern France.
36. Donald, *Stand by for Action*, pp. 39–40.
37. TNA ADM 199/2134 Survivors' Reports: Merchant Vessels 1 September 1940 to 30 November, p. 141.
38. Ibid.
39. IWM Sound 11758 Stoves, Robert.
40. Ibid.
41. ADM 199/2134 Survivors' Reports: Merchant Vessels 1 September 1940 to 30 November, 178.
42. IWM Docs 95/23/1 Balfour, Surgeon Lieutenant H.M., p. 49.
43. Ibid., p. 32.
44. Ibid., pp. 31–5.
45. Ibid., p. 36.
46. Ibid., pp. 47–8.
47. IWM Docs 75/105/1 Phipps, W.J., p. 71.
48. IWM Sound 20939 Clark, Alec.
49. Ibid.
50. Ibid.
51. ADM 199/2134 Survivors' Reports: Merchant Vessels 1 September 1940 to 30 November, 181.
52. Ibid.
53. Ibid.
54. Ibid., 179.
55. Woodman, *Keepers of the Sea*, pp. 142–5.
56. IWM Docs 75/105/1 Phipps, W.J., p. 73.
57. Ibid., p. 77.
58. Ibid., p. 77.

59. IWM Sound 9956, Irwin, Hugh.
60. ADM 199/2135 Survivors' Reports: Merchant Vessels 1 December 1940 to 28 February 1941, p. 51.
61. Foynes, *Battle of the East Coast*, p. 100.
62. ADM 199/2135 Survivors' Reports: Merchant Vessels 1 December 1940 to 28 February 1941, p. 62.
63. Woodman, *Keepers of the Sea*, pp. 146–7.
64. IWM Sound 9956 Irwin, Hugh.
65. IWM Docs 75/105/1 Phipps, W.J., p. 80.
66. Ibid.
67. Foynes, *Battle of the East Coast*, p. 110. According to Foynes the bodies of four crewmen were washed ashore at Aldeburgh four days later. *Tourmaline* was herself sunk in an air attack the following month.
68. IWM Sound 12818 Wyatt, Peter.
69. IWM Docs 95/23/1 Balfour, Surgeon Lieutenant H.M., p. 53.
70. Donald, *Stand by for Action*, pp. 50–1.
71. ADM 199/2135 Survivors' Reports: Merchant Vessels 1 December 1940 to 28 February 1941, p. 169.
72. Ibid, p. 177.
73. Ibid, p. 203.
74. Ibid.
75. Foynes, *Battle of the East Coast*, p. 107.
76. IWM Sound 12245 Punt, Cyril.
77. IWM Docs 99/43/1 Lind, William. Page referenced elements of this account are taken from a typed account, whereas unnumbered references are from the accompanying handwritten notes.
78. Ibid., p. 7.
79. Ibid., p. 8.
80. Ibid., p. 9.
81. IWM Docs 75/105/1 Phipps, W.J.
82. For a detailed account of *Exmoor*'s loss see Foynes, *Battle of the East Coast*, pp. 110–12.

Chapter 7
Backyard Battle

1 March 1941 to 31 December 1941

March 1941 saw eighty-nine day and nineteen night-bombing attacks, and a third mine offensive in the Thames Estuary. Worse still, two new E-boat flotillas had arrived, but it was the well-established veterans which made their presence felt on 7 March, the night which one author has labelled 'the E-boats' greatest victory'.[1]

Two convoys were passing in the 'Alley' on the night of 7/8 March 1941 – southbound FS429 and northbound FN426 – a regular occurrence but one which meant that more than seventy ships would be passing through the narrow war channel off the East Anglian coast. Both convoys had already been heavily attacked by tip-and run raiders during the day and one ship, the 934-ton collier *Flashlight* in FS429, had been sunk by a Dornier 215 at 1115.

The repeated bombing and the highly visible loss of *Flashlight* meant that by the time night fell, many of the men in the two convoys were already on edge. Just after 2000, twelve E-boats of Birnbacher's *1* and *Kapitänleutnant* Friedrich Kemnade's *3 Flottillen* swept in at high speed, fanning out across more than 20 miles of sea as they powered towards the coast. Shortly before 2035 Chief Engineer T.G. Molyneux of the British and Continental Steamship Company's 1,385-ton coaster *Dotterel* spied *Leutnant-zur-See* Götz Freiherr von Mirbach's *S29* approaching at high speed, 'like a big ship's lifeboat with a fo'c'sle head and a runway and stern like a destroyer'.[2]

There was no time for evasive action before the torpedo slammed into the starboard side: 'The sound from the torpedo was like a sharp crack and the explosion broke all the electric lamps in the engine room. [It] released all our anchors and the steam pipes were carried away . . . After this the ship went down about eight feet by the bow.'[3]

What happened next is confusing. The corvette *Sheldrake* came alongside and picked up *Dotterel*'s survivors, before assembling a boarding party to try to salvage the ship, while the developing battle raged around them. The boarding party was led by the Chief Officer of the *Dotterel,* apparently acting against the orders of his Captain, William Nash. Nine volunteers returned, including the First Lieutenant of *Sheldrake*, 32-year-old Lieutenant Commander Cecil Checcucci, and two ratings:

> Shortly after the volunteers had got aboard, another torpedo was fired, time about 2045. This struck the small boat and Number 2 Hold on the port side of the *Dotterel*, killing all those who had gone back to her, with the exception of the Engineer Lieutenant and the Wireless Operator. I was on the bridge of the destroyer at the time and saw a huge column of water was thrown forty to fifty feet into the air and a great sheet of blue flame.[4]

Witnesses on land some 10 miles away apparently saw *Dotterel*'s funeral pyre. Nineteen survivors were rescued by *Sheldrake*.[5]

Oberleutnant Büchting's S27 sank the next victim, the 1,048-ton coaster *Rye*, which was lost with all hands off Cromer. Then *S28* found Captain Rees' coaster *Corduff*: 'A terrific bow wave swept between the two columns and the E-boat sped on a parallel course with the convoy at a speed of forty to fifty knots.'[6]

There followed perhaps an hour of nerve-jangling cat-and-mouse, as the men of the *Corduff* heard high-speed engines pass close by before vanishing into the night. Periodically her DEMS gun crews would respond with a wild burst of machine-gun fire into the night, or frantically train her 12-pounder in what they hoped was the right direction. Finally, at 2137, a torpedo impacted her starboard side, blowing the *Corduff*'s gun and most of its crew into the sea. As the coaster stood on her stern and slipped beneath the waves, the survivors were spotted by *Leutnant-zur-See* Bernd Klug's *S28*, which motored quietly towards their lifeboat, her powerful engines just about turning over:

> [The E-boat] was a dirty white. On the hull about two thirds of the way along the bow there was painted a horse with the front legs rearing up . . . the man who spoke to us was certainly someone in authority and we took him to be the Commander. It is difficult to describe him because he just appeared as a dark form looming over us. His English was excellent.[7]

Klug hailed the boat, asking for the Captain, but Rees was understandably concerned that he would be taken prisoner if his identity were revealed. He had instructed his crew to deny his presence, and made efforts to conceal his uniform with his lifebelt. The tension can only be imagined as the German officer continued to question the survivors, asking the name of their ship and her tonnage. Finally, the worst was over. Informing Rees that he had two injured survivors on board, and giving him directions to the coast, Klug moved away with a jovial 'Well I am now off to Germany – cheerio and good luck!' The following morning the survivors were picked up by the Cromer lifeboat.[8]

Elsewhere the slaughter continued. *S31* took down the coaster *Kenton* at 2210, which sank within a minute and a half, and at 2225 *S61* found and sank the big freighter *Boulderpool*. Captain J.N. Govan had already had a terrifying night. At the beginning of the attack a torpedo had missed his ship by about 3 feet, and two more passed directly underneath him at 2200, before *Oberleutnant-zur-See* von Gernet scored a direct hit forward of the bridge on the port side. *Boulderpool* took half an hour to sink. Like many east coast wrecks, she sank in water so shallow that part of her hull projected above the surface, another macabre grave marker amongst the many around the coast by that spring of 1941.

Later in the night E-boats sank the *Norman Queen* and Captain L. Lawrenson's fully laden collier *Togston* which sank in just two minutes taking nine of her crew down with her: 'There was no time to do anything . . . there was a bright flash, a rush of steam and a strong smell of cordite.'[9] Lawrenson was himself sucked down but managed to reach the surface despite an apparent inability to swim.

The night of 7/8 March, a 'Black Friday' for the east coast, heralded a truly awful month, during which E-boats sank nine ships, including Manny Raud's *Daphné II* on 18 March. Despite the provision of extra destroyer escorts the Royal Navy still found it all but impossible to find and strike the elusive enemy. William Donald summed up the problem in a sentence: 'A target presented itself for a few seconds only, and if you were not absolutely on the alert you lost [it].'[10] Midshipman A.G.F. Ditcham joined the Hunt-class destroyer HMS *Holderness* the day after the March disaster, and was unceremoniously dumped into the thick of the March action, where he got an object lesson in 'Donald's Law':

> Five days after my joining we were at sea patrolling with *Vanessa*. We were at action stations and I was down at the after guns with Petty Officer Flint and the crews. It was a perfectly calm night, ideal for E-boats. We were steaming about fifteen knots, operating the Asdic, and listening for the hydrophone noise of the E-boats' fast-revving propellers or – more importantly – those ever faster revving of torpedoes . . . down after, we were over the screws and I remember the thrill when suddenly the rumbling of the propeller shafts became thunderous as we increased speed drastically. Something was up!
>
> Suddenly I saw *Vanessa* turning to starboard and firing rapid broadsides. What a splendid, dashing sight! But at once our own gun got the order 'enemy in sight' and we began firing as rapidly as we could shove them up the spout. The Captain was maneuvring to keep the E-boats in the moon path. We chased them for twenty-three minutes before they escaped over the mine barrier but over which we were of too deep draught to follow.[11]

According to Ditcham *Holderness* engaged three separate E-boats during this action, and fired off every star shell in the ship along with 160 rounds of high explosive, all without scoring a hit: 'This was our life – excitement and routine, patrol and convoy escort, fair and foul weather.'[12]

Nor did the start of offensive sweeps by the fledgling motor gunboat flotillas of Coastal Forces in March prove particularly successful. Indeed, elsewhere in the service the gunboats were derisively christened 'costly farces', and in these first encounters with E-boats they generally came off worse. Jack Seal was serving in the destroyer HMS *Ambuscade*, and came across the aftermath of some of the early skirmishes:

> Invariably when we went out we would find the MTBs with two dead men in the gun . . . we'd go out and pick them up and escort them back with a couple of dead men on the deck and two dead men in the gun positions which couldn't be replaced once they'd been shot up.[13]

Nowhere on the coast was safe. In the Channel, night-time tip-and-run raiders hit CW28 the day after the East Anglian catastrophe. One of the victims was the collier *Sylvia Beale*, on her way to Poole under the command of Captain G.L. Alexander, strafed and bombed by 'a twin engined aircraft with all his lights on flying towards us straight out of the moon at a height of about 150 feet'.[14] *Sylvia Beale* suffered only superficial damage, but another collier, *Waterland*, was less fortunate when a torpedo bomber attacked her later in the night. A.N. McRea was her Chief Officer and was off watch when the torpedo struck at 0150:

> I was awakened [to find] myself on the floor with debris falling around me . . . the door to my cabin was jammed; I put my shoulder to it and with great difficulty forced it open and I was no sooner outside than the remainder of the roof came down. I dashed up [to] the boat deck where I discovered only half of the after port boat swinging in the davit and on the starboard side there was no boat at all. As I was making my way to the raft on No 2 Hold I noticed that the after end of the deck was buckled. There was one fireman sitting on the raft when I reached it and he asked me what we should do. I just told him to sit tight and we should float off eventually. In the meantime the men were coming from the forecastle; I gathered them all on the raft and we numbered seven altogether. Everyone was cool and level headed and carried out my instructions without question. It was not long before we began to float off; the port bulwarks were under water and just as we were crossing them a shower of debris began to fall . . . at that moment the ship rose stern first until she was absolutely perpendicular and then went straight down. I looked at my watch and it showed the time as being 0155 BST.[15]

Six men were killed. The remainder were rescued by an escorting motor launch and transferred to the balloon ship *Mammouth*. In the same attack the collier *Sparta* was also sunk, with the loss of nine men, and further to the west the big ocean-going freighter *Port Townsville* was sunk in the Bristol Channel.

April brought more of the same, with 124 day and seventy-two night air attacks by tip-and-run raiders, and another E-boat attack on FS464 resulting in the loss of two ships. May was even worse, with a staggering ninety-nine ships lost to enemy action in coastal waters. To try to limit the effects of sinkings, delays and diversions on the coal supply, the faster northbound coastwise traffic was grouped into a new series of convoys, coded EC, to try and return empty hulls to the coalfields as quickly as possible.

Defensive fighter sorties were also increased, but the enemy held the initiative and it was impossible to cover every ship at every time. Many ships found themselves unprotected at the critical moment. Henry Fellingham joined the tanker *Chesapeake* at the beginning of April 1941. When he arrived he was dismayed to see the consequences of his new ship's encounter with a raider off Fishguard a few days before: '[she was] peppered by machine gun bullets, there were machine-gun bullets everywhere you looked, pipelines, decks, lifeboats'. *Chesapeake* was also trailing oil in her wake and carrying an unexploded bomb as a souvenir.[16]

Shortly after he joined the ship in Avonmouth the port was raided and Henry found himself 'dashing round putting out incendiaries'. When she finally set sail for New York, on 13 June, she still had a wooden patch over the hole in her side, and was attacked yet again by Heinkels off Fishguard. This time she was lucky, unlike the 1,922-ton Irish packet ship *St Patrick*, which took a direct hit and sank with heavy loss of life.

In the desperate fighting between March and May 1941, 212 ships were lost in UK home waters, most on the east coast.[17] Losses exceeded those sustained in the North Atlantic during the same period. More than any other time, this terrible spring illustrates the awesome potential of the German war machine to interdict coastal trade, and there is little doubt that continued pressure at this level would have come dangerously close to stopping it altogether. However the end was in sight, even though it may not have felt like it at the time. On 22 June 1941, Germany invaded the Soviet Union. For the historian of high strategy, of course, this meant that Great Britain now had a powerful new ally, albeit one who was morally questionable and desperately unprepared.

For the coaster men and their escorts, the invasion of Russia was no magic wand and the German forces ranged against them did not suddenly vanish. The *Luftwaffe* strike aircraft and E-boats were only gradually transferred to the east, and it was some time before any significant change become apparent. Hindsight and statistics, however, show that sinkings from all causes noticeably decline from this point: in particular, just three E-boat sinkings were recorded between June and November 1941.[18] By August there was only one flotilla left in the west, and the long summer days did not make it easy for them. Early forays by Coastal Forces and RAF aircraft into German waters were beginning to play their part as well. Sinkings by air attack declined just as noticeably; between August and December 1941 there were just twenty-one losses to air attack, all but one at night.[19]

Minelaying was still widespread but decreasing in effectiveness. A new combined magnetic/acoustic mine was introduced in July, but British countermining specialists had correctly predicted this development and its effects were negligible. Shortly afterwards moored influence mines started to appear, with equally limited impact.[20] Of course, phrases like 'limited impact' and 'negligible' would be small comfort to those who had to endure such attacks, particularly when travelling on something as small and vulnerable as the 82-ton barge *Rosme*.

Rosme was making her way under sail from Gravesend to Ipswich on 3 July, with a cargo of wheat and a crew of two. The Master, F.W. Smy, was on watch at 1330:

> I was thrown into the air and struck my head on the roof of the wheelhouse. The mate was below having his dinner in the cabin and I at once called out to him; receiving no reply I went down the companion ladder and found him unconscious in the cabin. I got him up the ladder somehow and onto the raft, which had fallen down from above the wheelhouse, and as I scrambled on myself the stern sank beneath us. Almost immediately the bows went under also, the vessel disappearing within two minutes of being mined.[21]

Smy's modesty is touching but his eighteen-year-old Mate, G.E. Bruce, was in no doubt that he owed his life to his 'skipper':

> Almost immediately the water was up to my armpits and rising rapidly. I do not remember very clearly what happened, but the skipper leaned down through the hatch and somehow pulled me up; I should never have been able to get out by myself . . . if it had not been for him pulling me out and getting me on the raft I should not be here this morning. [22]

The following day, a mine vapourized the 363-ton collier *Lulan* 40 yards from the pier at Penarth. The only survivor was her badly scalded Chief Engineer who was blown out through the engine-room skylight and found clinging to a boat davit.[23]

Tip-and-run attacks continued to be a nuisance, with victims at the end of July including *Umvuma*, in the Humber on the 20th, *San Roberto* on the same day, and *Adam's Beck*, which was sunk in the Tyne on the 29th. *San Roberto* was something of an institution on the coast. A tanker operated by the Eagle Oil Company, she was too old and slow for transatlantic duty and so appeared on the coastal routes at the beginning of 1941. Patrick Mummery served on her for most of the war:

> No history would be complete without mention of the *San Roberto*, Captain Cyril Allison. While on the coast she sailed regularly between London and Grangemouth, frequently as Commodore ship . . . due to having 'deep sea' accommodation for the Commodore and staff. She carried a million tons of cargo on her coastal voyages for which Allison was awarded a richly deserved OBE.[24]

Naval signalman J.W. Booth remembered the *San Roberto* as well, albeit with rather mixed feelings: 'She was frequently used, and bitterly disliked by the signalmen because she . . . had the largest and bleakest bridge on the coast.[25] As far as can be established *San Roberto* took part in at least 111 FN and 116 FS convoys, and we shall certainly hear from her again.[26]

Life on the coast was still full of unexpected dangers, not all of them caused by the enemy or even the weather. The coasters shared the congested waters of the war channel with a variety of other users, including submarines. These were sometimes attached to convoys, a bizarre practice which caused regular complaints by escort commanders. One perhaps preventable accident had already occurred in April 1940 when HMS *Unity* was run down and sunk by the Norwegian coaster *Atle Jarl* with the loss of four men, but on 20 July 1941 a far greater tragedy befell one of her sisters, the brand-new boat HMS *Umpire*. She was following a northbound convoy when she was rammed and sunk by the trawler *Peter Hendricks*, an escort from a southbound convoy which had apparently drifted into the wrong lane in the dark. Just nine of the thirty-two men on board survived, most of whom had to make a nightmare ascent from the sunken hulk after it had settled on the sea bed.[27]

Another tragic accident at this time vividly illustrates the appalling navigational hazards on the coast, which did not require the enemy to make it dangerous at any time of year. FS559 was just another southbound coal convoy, albeit a very large one of forty-seven ships, which left Methil for Southend on 4 August 1941. Two days later, early in the morning of the 6th, the convoy was stretched over several miles of sea, labouring in a gale and poor visibility, when a vital course change was ordered. Midshipman A.G.F. Ditcham's *Holderness* was one of the escorts, and he takes over the story at 0400:

> Suddenly we saw a buoy about two miles on our starboard beam. I could not identify its flashes but the Captain could. We were not only two miles from the Channel but it was the corner buoy at which we should have altered course. The whole convoy was steering for the Haisborough Sands in a gale. At this dramatic moment, the Senior Officer of the escort appeared in his sloop, labouring and crashing about in the seas and flashing a signal asking if we had seen the buoy. We had. He ploughed away to warn the leading ships of the convoy and we all altered course drastically to regain the channel . . . the

> convoy, however, was about six miles long and – inevitably in such bad visibility – the 'corner' at which we altered course was prolonged, like a snaking rope. The last six [actually seven] of the deep laden ships steamed straight on to the Haisborough Sands and became a total loss . . . the trawler which was stern escort was never seen again. She must have struck and been rolled over and broken up. Many years afterwards, the east coast charts still showed six wrecks in line ahead.[28]

The lost ships were the British coasters *Oxshott, Aberhill*, *Afon Towy, Betty Hindley* and *Deerwood,* along with the French *Gallois* and Estonian *Taara*. The official enquiry into the disaster records that thirty-seven men died.[29] Remarkably, despite the conditions 134 men were saved, thanks to the extraordinary efforts made by local lifeboatmen, among them the legendary and much-decorated Coxswain Henry G. Blogg of the Cromer lifeboat, who was decorated with the British Empire Medal for his courage that day. The Commanding Officer and most of the crew of the escort trawler *Agate* were amongst the dead.

The coast may have been an unforgiving environment, but the enemy was nowhere near as active by August. It is perhaps an indication of the changed conditions that in mid-August a contemporary 'celebrity' was sent to travel with the convoys. Major Owen Rutter was a well-known travel writer and journalist who had been attached to the Admiralty Press Office for the duration and had already written several propaganda booklets on their behalf.[30] On 14 August 1941, he received an Admiralty pass allowing him to accompany a northbound east coast convoy, FN505. He kept a detailed diary of the entire process from start to finish, which gives the reader a fascinating insight into 'normal' life on the coast in the late summer of 1941.

Rutter was instructed to report to Naval Control at the rather unwarlike address of 7 Royal Terrace, Southend, from where he was escorted to the convoy conference, which was held in an even less likely location:

> The Conference was in the Solarium where in peacetime the holidaymakers of Southend drank their morning coffee. A number of masters, all in plain clothes, were already present . . . also six signallers (RN ratings) who were to accompany the Commodore [Commodore Mills, RNR]. Facing the audience was a blackboard with a list of the ships so far known to be joining the convoy, with their allotted pennant numbers, destinations, tonnage, speed and cargo.[31]

Blackboards bearing drawings and warning posters were scattered around the room. Mills addressed the assembled coaster men informally, 'a merchant seaman talking to merchant seamen'. He described the intricate system of pendant numbers, organized to allow ships to join and leave at particular ports without disruption. He showed drawings of E-boats and various types of German aircraft, and warned them of the difficulties of aircraft recognition. The briefing concluded with a dire warning of the importance of keeping station following the recent FS559 tragedy on the Haisborough Sands: '"Do keep closed up," he appealed to the masters . . . "repeat all signals and obey immediately you see."'[32]

At the end of the briefing Rutter was introduced to the Master of the Commodore ship, in which he was to travel:

> Before we left the Pier-Head, Kendal [the Naval Control Officer] introduced me to the Master of the *Bury*, with whom we were to sail. He [the Master of the *Bury*] seemed rather appalled at having to take both the Commodore and me. 'Where will I put them to sleep?' he asked . . . The *Bury* was a weekly ship, which meant that officers and crew provide their own food, so when I got back to town I went foraging. Having no ration book it was impossible to buy meat, bacon, tea or butter, but at the local Liptons I got some tins – soup, sardines, chicken and ham roll, cocoa and a Swiss Roll.[33]

Rutter's attempt to win friends and influence people was clearly unsuccessful, as both he and the Commodore were transferred to the venerable Polish collier *Kronan*, built in 1912, which was going all the way up to the Firth of Forth. The accommodation for visiting journalists was rough and ready, to say the least:

> A very hard settee with a very dirty blanket . . . A bare table, a great deal of cigarette ash on the floor, a plate of butter and an enormous quantity of flies. Glad of a slab of the chocolate I had brought with me and a few biscuits. Gave a slab to Mills and to each of his four signallers, who had spent a wretched night sitting up on deck. One . . . told me the quarters they had been offered in the fo'c'sle were verminous, Mills appeared unconcerned. The officer who had detailed them to him at Sheerness asked him to see that 'the matelots got treated rough' – apparently shore life was a bit soft for them.[34]

In command of the *Kronan* was the redoubtable Captain Drydeck, who at the outbreak of war had taken his ship out of Poland one step ahead of the Germans, first to Bergen in Norway, and then to Britain. When France fell he had almost been trapped in Dakar, in French Senegal, but he had charged the boom and broken out. His equally determined wife, trapped back in Poland, had fled overland to Slovakia, then to Budapest and Paris before joining her husband's ship in England. '[Mrs Drydeck] was on the ship's books as the Purser, kept the accounts and supervised the stores, cooking and stewards . . . she seemed completely happy and at home in the ship.'[35]

Wartime conditions and Drydeck's uncompromising nature – he had already removed his Chief Engineer for supposed Nazi sympathies and was deeply suspicious of his German-born steward – made the *Kronan*'s crew a bewildering mixture of nationalities. As well as Poles, there were British, Swedish and Norwegian sailors amongst the crew, as well as a complement of British DEMS gunners. *Kronan* was armed with seven machine gunners and the usual antique 6-pounder: 'In an attack she was known to throw everything into the air except the galley stove.'[36]

At first light the convoy set off down the Thames Estuary and out to the convoy lanes in a slow procession, ships with odd pendant numbers forming station to starboard and those with even numbers to port to form two columns. Rutter's diary provides a vivid impression of the war channel after nearly two years of fighting:

> As it grew lighter I could see on either side of the channel wreck after wreck of ships that had been sunk by mines, some with their topmasts protruding above the water, the latest marked with green flags . . . The course for east coast convoys is a narrow channel about three miles from the coast, buoyed every half mile or so, inside the minefields which extend far out into the North Sea. Each buoy is numbered and has a light at night so that constant vigilance is required day and night to check the position of the ship.[37]

As the convoy made its way around the coast towards the East Anglian bulge and 'E-boat Alley' Rutter fell into conversation with Commodore Mills, a career Merchant Navy officer with an RNR commission. Like most commodores, Mills was concerned about the perennial problem of straggling, which he attributed to a variety of causes: habitually cautious coaster engineers conserving coal, masters exaggerating their ship's speed to join faster convoys, and Naval Control Officers trying to get rid of ships as quickly as possible regardless of their suitability. Rutter amusingly described him as 'a maritime Little Bo Peep, who can't afford to lose his ships, for if he leaves them alone, it is highly unlikely that they'll come home, tugging balloons behind them'.[38]

Mills also waxed lyrical about the tensions between the Commodore, responsible for navigation, and the Senior Officer Escort, responsible for the protection of the convoy. For him at least, it seemed that little had changed since 1939, despite the shared hardships of the last two years:

> I had several talks with Mills about this divided control. It was a matter on which he felt keenly, as a merchant officer. His point was that the RN escort had no experience of commercial waters and could not realise that a Commodore, by getting a convoy into port earlier than the ETA (estimated time of arrival) might save 20 ships a tide, expedite their loading, and so enable 60,000 tons of coal to reach London a day earlier than schedule. Therefore the Commodore's idea is to push on all he can, while the E.0's [Escort Officer's] only idea is to keep to schedule and avoid trouble.

Mills, a veteran of the First World War when he had found this tension far less pronounced, put it down to 'professional snobbishness' between the RNR commodores and RN escort commanders. Privately Rutter reflected that 'he admits the same feeling does not exist against the [less working class] RNVR . . . therefore it must, apparently, be due to social snobbishness.'[39]

Joined by an air escort of Spitfires at dusk, FN505's night-time passage of 'E-boat Alley' was uneventful, and on the morning of 16 August Commodore Mills ordered an increase of speed, the flag signal apparently taking an hour to pass down the columns. Between Scarborough and Whitby they met the southbound convoy, prompting Rutter to muse eloquently about the largely unsung yet vital contribution made by the 'dirty little coasters':

> There is something tremendously impressive about these concentrations of little ships, most of them coasters . . . Off the East Coast there are always eight of these convoys at sea – something like 300 ships . . . northbound and southbound, dirty, ugly, but each doing her job, the northbound ships light as empty boxes, pitching and rolling, the southbound wallowing along with a couple of thousand tons of eagerly awaited coal. Does the British householder in the south realise that his coal comes to him by sea, brought by these little ships and their crews at the peril of their loss? I didn't, and in future I shall feel more grateful for every lump I burn.[40]

After Whitby the usual round of departures and arrivals began, with fifteen ships leaving for Blyth on the Tyne: 'they just pushed off without even a goodbye signal or a dip of the ensign.' Two little colliers bound for Aberdeen came out to replace them. Shortly afterwards Rutter had his only scare of the trip, an evening air-raid warning as they neared Methil:

> The Commodore shot through the saloon bar – I have never seen anyone move so quickly: one moment he was sitting in his blue overalls at the table and the next he had vanished, the Captain followed him, more leisurely. I grabbed my tin hat and struggled into my Vita-buoy [life jacket] and dashed up to the bridge. The bell rang through the ship, every gun and post was manned.[41]

No attack developed and by the morning of 17 August FN505 was picking up its pilot to enter Methil Roads. While Commodore Mills went ashore for two days rest before picking up his next southbound convoy, Owen Rutter returned to the south. Less than two weeks later he began the second of his two coastal journeys, this time with channel convoy CW48, travelling with the SOE, Lieutenant Commander Allan Noble RN, in the Hunt-class destroyer HMS *Fernie*.[42] The Commodore was the legendary 'Non-Stop' Newman:

He had a red pointed beard and a jocular manner which seemed to go down well with the masters. He begged them to report if they were due for dry-docking or any structural repairs, otherwise they would be unable to make the grade through the shelling area. They must make sure they got good bunkers [coal], not poor steaming coal: too much smoke might give away the whole convoy, especially in the moonlight or starlight when they stood out like a lot of black matchsticks against the shimmer of the sea.[43]

As CW48 set out Rutter recorded the very different rituals of the Channel:

The ship got under weigh and began to steam past the convoy which was getting into position – the ships for Southampton and Cowes coming first, then those for Shoreham and Newhaven, and last two for Dover, which would be the first to leave . . . By the time we were finished the convoy was under way, the Commodore leading in the balloon ship *Haslemere*, we steaming some distance astern on the port side and the convoy strung out behind us. Travelling in line ahead from the Commodore to the last balloon ship we are thirty-five vessels, two hundred yards apart, which makes the length of the convoy five miles . . . I noticed that the convoy password was bacon – this would enable the ship to signal Bomber Command ie 'I am being attacked by aircraft – Bacon.' Each naval ship had its own password, changed every voyage. Ours was 'peanut'.[44]

He found the young crew of the *Fernie* every bit as candid as those of the *Kronan*: 'There was nothing "cagey" or hush-hush about anyone. They spoke openly before me, answered all my questions frankly and made no difficulty about showing me anything I wanted to see.'[45]

One particular remark by the 33-year-old Noble is a telling indicator of the strain the men of the coastal escorts operated under, a constant corrosive pressure that they had no choice but to accept as their lot and cope with as best they could: 'Noble said that he had had to go to a specialist recently for an overhaul. The doctor had asked him "do you drink?" "Oh about the average [Noble had replied]." "The average for a civilian or for a naval officer?" asked the doctor.'[46]

It was doubtless particularly fascinating for the journalist Rutter to get the RN perspective on the tension between Commodore and SOE which he had discussed with Mills on the *Kronan*. Noble was certainly not a snob and had a great deal of respect for the merchant skippers with whose protection he was charged: 'Most of them don't look like seamen at all . . . but they're grand.'[47] However his experience of commodores was that sometimes the 'snobbery' could equally come from the opposite direction: 'His view was that the smart RNR officer was often inclined to look down on the RN professionally, and considered that they were better navigators – which as he candidly admitted they often were.'[48]

In line with accepted doctrine the convoy passed Dover in darkness, and at action stations:

> Unlike in the old *Kronan* everyone on board had his mae west blown up and had his steel helmet handy . . . The white cliffs . . . gleamed palely in the moonlight a mile away . . . the atmosphere on the bridge was tense. Everyone had binoculars to his eyes, watching for a flash from the German guns on the French coast. This was the most dangerous time.[49]

Rutter was lucky: an air raid on the Calais batteries was apparently underway. Sirens were heard wailing from the German-held coast and the flash of exploding bombs could be clearly seen as CW48 crept slowly through the Straits. No shells fell.

In fact like FN505, CW48 was a quiet convoy, although quiet should not be misinterpreted as entirely uneventful. One of the minesweepers reported mines being air-dropped in the path of the convoy, prompting a sudden course alteration, and later in the night there was an E-boat alert:

> At midnight a message was received that radio-location had detected a surface craft bearing 100 degrees from Dungeness, but no range was given. Vigilance was redoubled. Everybody [was] on his toes at the prospect of having a crack at an E-boat . . . Suddenly the destroyer, which had been jogging on quietly at seven knots, began to vibrate. Sparks came from the funnel, a white wake showed up in the moonlight, soon we were doing twenty-five knots, sweeping and turning . . . the chase went on for half an hour, scouring the sea – but without result.[50]

Owen Rutter's odyssey ended when the *Fernie* delivered her charges at St Helens Roads, Southampton, on 1 September, prompting a humorous signal from 'Non-Stop' Newman which typifies the spirit of the men who kept coastal trade flowing during the Second World War: 'Oh *Fernie*, my peanut, what have you done? You've scattered the E-boats and scared off the Hun! But what the heck matters, we've had a good run. Cheerio and goodbye.'[51]

Constant vigilance characterized life on the coast in the late summer and early autumn of 1941. The Germans may have been quieter but they were certainly not absent, and boredom or inattention could be punished in a heartbeat. Their longer-range aircraft were able to bypass the well-defended convoys of the east and south coasts, launching tip-and-run raids on defenceless independent shipping in the Irish Sea. Three days after Owen Rutter's uneventful passage of the Channel, the 489-ton coaster *Abbas Combe* was making her way from Liverpool to Watchet in Somerset when a Heinkel 115 seaplane dropped out of the night sky at 2315. Captain Carter:

> [The aircraft] flew over the ship at a height of about 250 feet and dropped a bomb which exploded in the stokehold or the engine room . . . the attack lasted less than one minute and we were all more or less dazed by the explosion . . . The wheelhouse collapsed and the concrete protection collapsed with it. The ship started to sink immediately, stern first. The starboard lifeboat was riddled with bullets and the davits of the port lifeboat caught and jammed the boat as it was being lowered and dragged it under with the ship.[52]

The aircraft made another pass, illuminating the rapidly sinking *Abbas Combe* with a searchlight and machine-gunning the wreck until it finally slipped beneath the waves. Four of the crew were killed. The seven survivors, one critically wounded, spent twenty-six hours on a life raft before being rescued.

As the nights drew in, the E-boats grew bolder. On the night of 7 September they struck at the fast northbound convoy EC70. *Oberleutnant-zur-See* Karl-Erhard Karcher's *S50* sank the 27-year-old collier *Duncarron*, which went down in seconds, her Master being washed out of the bridge door as she sank, before narrowly escaping being run down by the next ship in the column. Nine out of the thirteen crew were killed. The tiny 213-ton coaster *Ophir 2* and the superannuated Norwegian collier *Eikhaug*, launched in 1903, were also sunk, only four of *Eikhaug*'s crew of twenty-one surviving.[53]

E-boats were still almost invulnerable at this stage of the war, but the coasters and their escorts were more adept at fighting back against the *Luftwaffe*. Two nights after the attack on EC70, German aircraft hit the SS *Cormead*, northbound in EC72. Captain A.R. Emmott described how one *Luftwaffe* pilot misjudged his approach, flying straight over *Cormead*'s bridge and carrying away her balloon, then dropping two bombs that failed to explode. Three minutes later the aircraft returned and *Cormead*'s gunners blew its tail off: '[It] accelerated with a terrific roar, rose again, and finally plunged into the water about two miles away from the ship on the port beam.'[54]

It was not until the attack was over that the *Cormead*'s crew realized they had not escaped unscathed after all: 'We heard a most extraordinary noise going on each time the ship rolled so I sent the Mate to find out what it was. He came back and reported that the noise was due to a 500-pound bomb rolling about in Number 4 Hold.' There followed a nightmare journey into Yarmouth, the empty hold filling with water every time the ship rolled, and the unwanted cargo inside shifting from side to side.

Commander Frederick Halahan RN, Captain of HMS *Holderness*, found the nuisance raiders almost entertaining:

> It was especial fun for our fire-eating wildfowling Captain. He kept a 'stripped Lewis' on the bridge, loaded with 100 per cent tracer. He used this in night

actions to indicate a target, and as the permissive order to open fire. It saved valuable seconds if a ship or aircraft suddenly appeared at close range. But it also afforded him sport once action was joined with aircraft. As they passed overhead he would use it as a 12-bore, swinging on the target but hosepiping tracer at it.[55]

The EC convoys were fast becoming favoured targets for the Germans. E-boats returned on 17 September, sinking the SS *Teddington* in EC74. Captain Woodhouse of the *Tetela* heard the explosion and stepped out onto his bridge wings, only to see the bubbles of a torpedo track just 60 feet away from his ship. The assailant was Karcher again but this time he was out of luck – the torpedo blew a hole in *Tetela*'s side but failed to sink her.[56]

Mining also remained a threat, despite the precautions being taken. *Holderness* was rendered *hors de combat* for a few weeks on 16 September. Midshipman Ditcham recalled how the 'fire-eating' Commander Halahan incautiously carried out high-speed trials of a new main bearing in what was, unbeknown to him, a mined area:

'[We were] racing up and down to seaward of the convoy, who must have thought we had gone mad . . . it thus happened that all eyes were upon us when we went over a mine. These observers told us that the colossal explosion lifted the whole ship up two feet; when quite by chance the Captain and No. 1 were discussing mine danger . . . The Captain escaped decapitation by a whisker, as the gyro compass repeater in front of him (a solid brass device the size of a large pudding bowl) had sheered through the four metal plates holding it down and leapt into the air. Checked by the heavy flex which powered it, it had crashed down again, brushing the Captain's ear.[57]

Fortunately the mine was deep enough to avoid damaging the hull, but anything delicate or electrical was '*kaput*', and the ship was sent to London for repairs. Two days later the SS *Bradglen* was mined and sunk in the Thames with the loss of nine men, most of them in her engine room: 'Two firemen came out of the stokehold, one of whom, Hussein Awaleh, was badly scalded and one of his legs was injured . . . [he] was too badly hurt to swim, so the Chief Officer, H Fisher, and myself swam with him towards the destroyer [HMS *Vivian*].'[58] Hussein Awaleh, another sailor from the far reaches of the Empire caught up in a war which was not of his making, died later in hospital.

However dreadful such incidents, by late 1941 the British had the measure of the mines and the tip-and-run raiders. It was the E-boats that were still hunting the North Sea almost unopposed and in October the British started to put into place a new series of building blocks, which would ultimately lead to their defeat.

The answer lay with tried and tested methods: light coastal craft, destroyers and aircraft. The challenge lay in arming these forces with appropriate equipment and doctrine to find the E-boats, engage them and either sink them or drive them back into their own waters. Once they had been driven from the convoy routes, the Royal Navy could take the war over to the German side of the North Sea and the Channel, thus switching to the best defence of all: attack.

The gradual passing of the air threat with the invasion of Russia and the increased strength of the RAF meant that more resources were becoming available to deal with the E-boat menace. Wing Commander J. Constable-Roberts was on the staff of 16 (Reconnaissance) Group, attached to Admiral Ramsay's Dover Command. In October 1941 he initiated the first use of radar-controlled aircraft to defend the convoys. Six Bristol Beaufort torpedo bombers were directed by controllers at the Chain Home radar station at Swingate, adjacent to Ramsay's headquarters at Dover Castle. Their role was:

> (a) To intercept shipping in the Straits at night or in poor visibility by day.
> (b) In co-operation with Naval Forces under Vice-Admiral Dover, to silhouette by means of flares enemy forces attacking our convoys or approaching the coast.
> (c) To co-operate with surface craft in attacking enemy convoys at night.[59]

Constable-Roberts' plan was to first use this system to organize the defence of convoys, and then roll it out more aggressively into enemy waters through the winter.

At the same time steps were being taken to take advantage of one of the principle Achilles heels of the E-boats: the incessant short-range radio chatter of their commanding officers, which had been noted since the beginning of the year. Efforts were made in October to recruit German-speaking personnel to join the crews of coastal escorts, their role being to listen to and simultaneously translate German radio intercepts. Finding German speakers was by no means easy, but on 16 October a solution was proposed in a confidential report:

> It is proposed that endeavour should be made to transfer linguists from the Merchant Service . . . it is also proposed that German linguists should be sought in the Norwegian, Dutch, Polish or Belgian Navies now operating from this country . . . the future possibilities of the apparatus are considerable provided we can keep it a secret.[60]

Willing volunteers were found, mostly from the Dutch contingent. Others were recruited from the ranks of the Women's Royal Naval Service, and stationed in listening posts all around the coast. Hilda Hales, a nineteen year old who had lived in Germany before the war, was one of them:

> The places we did this were not famous places; we weren't famous people. It was done in very small stations all down the coast, mostly on the edges of cliffs. Places that you wouldn't suspect like Sheringham, Trimmingham, Hemsby, Southwold, Gorleston, Felixstowe, and then all round the South Coast as well . . . Those of us who were German speakers would listen in to their signals, hear what they were saying, and try to stop them doing whatever it was they had in mind. Some of the small stations we worked in were in houses. There were perhaps twelve to twenty girls in each of them, and we were doing shift work all through the day and night.[61]

The wireless intercept personnel were known informally as 'Headache' operators, for obvious reasons, and they soon made their presence felt on board the coastal escorts, including Midshipman Ditcham's *Holderness* when she returned from dry dock. *Holderness*'s Headache team was led by a Lieutenant Bacon:

> Sure enough, we soon picked up the 'carrier wave' of their R/T sets when they switched on as they left Ymuiden, and pointed at us with malice aforethought. They kept silence but the carrier wave betrayed them. Lieutenant Bacon . . . stood impassively at the back of the bridge. His job was to repeat in English what he heard in German. Suddenly he spoke. 'Hans this is Fritz. Are you receiving me?' 'Hans, Fritz, this is Hans. I hear you.' 'Hans this is Fritz report your position.' 'Fritz this is Hans – I am two miles on the starboard bow of the convoy.' 'Alarm' shouted the Captain. 'That's our position' . . . everyone saw it at once – the E-boat was right ahead and hardly more than fifty yards away, beam on and going slowly left. Their crew probably heard our Captain shout 'open fire! Full ahead together.' [62]

This particular E-boat 'got away with his instant 40 knots', but it was not long before Headache operators contributed to a much-needed success. By November two E-boat flotillas had returned to the west. One of them was 2. *Schnellbooteflottile*, under the command of the newly promoted *Kapitänleutnant* Klaus Feldt, rescuer of William Lind of the *Angularity*.

On the night of 19 November Feldt's flotilla launched a devastating attack on FS650 near Yarmouth. The first victim was the collier *Aruba*, torpedoed by *Leutnant-zur-See* Howaldt's *S105*, followed shortly afterwards by another collier, the *Waldinge*.

The crew of the *Waldinge* abandoned ship immediately but later reboarded, assisted by a naval motor launch and a party from the convoy's stern escort, the destroyer HMS *Verdun*, commanded by none other than William Donald. *Verdun* had been at action stations for hours, and had already seen the *Aruba* sink and the Sheerness destroyer *Campbell* accidentally fire on and damage her flotilla mate, HMS *Garth*. As usual the unexpected presence of a ML gave the edgy destroyer men a shock as they closed with the listing collier:

> 'Hello, here's another one,' said Toby, peering through his glasses. 'My God, there's an E-boat beside it,' he added excitedly. His remark galvanized everyone into action, but the E-boat turned out to be one of our MLs who called us up with a shaded blue light . . . we had an emergency party ready for such contingencies, and in a short space of time they leapt into the ML and disappeared over towards the dark form of the damaged collier.[63]

The boarding party soon discovered that *Waldinge* was in a bad way and flooding badly. They requested a tug and clambered back into the ML to await developments. When daylight came the collier had disappeared, the only visible reminder of her presence being the melancholy sight of her barrage balloon flying above her resting place on the seabed.

Verdun's boarding party were returned by the ML, which caused another panic for the destroyer's hard-pressed gunners as she came up from astern at high speed. The motorboat then went on to land the *Waldinge* survivors at Lowestoft.

In the meantime the E-boats had scored their greatest triumph of the night – in fact, one of the largest ships to fall victim to an E-boat, the 5,502-ton Royal Fleet Auxiliary tanker *War Mehtar*. She was full to the brim with Admiralty fuel oil for the Harwich destroyers when she wandered into the sights of *Oberleutnant-zur-See* Gerhard Rebensburg's *S104*. *War Mehtar*'s Captain was S.M. Woodward:

> As we turned to port I was on the bridge and heard the sound of engines approximately off our port beam. It was a high pitched humming sound, like the noise made by a circular saw, and lasted for about five or six seconds. The Chief Officer who was with me also heard the sound and remarked about it and I said I thought it was probably the turbines of some escorting ship overtaking us in the darkness. Then I saw the wakes of about eight torpedoes, approximately four on each side of the ship, travelling at about twenty-five knots. Only the wakes were visible.[64]

War Mehtar was hit astern, causing a terrible flash and a column of water as high as her mast. Her volatile cargo burst into flames, but fortunately the fire was contained within her hull, allowing the survivors to take to the boats. They were nearly run down by the SS *Greenwood*, which then redeemed herself by stopping to pick them up, while the tug *Superman* arrived to tow the blazing tanker. At daybreak her tortured hull finally gave up the fight, her back broke and she plunged to the seabed. William Donald, exhausted from a night of chasing shadows, witnessed her end:

> I clambered wearily onto the bridge. The ship was a casualty from the night before, and the tug was heading for Lowestoft. 'He'll never make it.' As I spoke the oiler took a heavy list to port. Men could be seen running along the upper deck, and a boat was turned out from its davits. At the same time a lamp flashed from the bridge – 'am abandoning . . .' But the signal was never finished, for the ship's lurch to port increased rapidly until she gave a lurch and disappeared; in the bubbling, muddy waters the ship's boat rocked and tossed about and men's heads popped up like currants in a bun.[65]

So far it had been a typical E-boat attack: a rush of powerful engines in the night, bubbling torpedo tracks, explosions and the enemy vanishing. This time, however, one of Coastal Forces' rising stars was there to intercept them as they sped home. Lieutenant Commander Robert 'Hitch' Hitchens had joined the 6th Motor Gun Boat Flotilla early in 1941, and since that time had pressed the Admiralty to upgrade the inadequate armament of the ex-MASBs. He had managed to obtain 20mm Oerlikons and 2-pounder Pom-Poms for his improvised E-boat killers, finally making them 'gunboats' worthy of the name. On the night of 19 November 'Hitch' was waiting at Felixstowe with three MGBs when one of the Wren-operated Headache shore stations sent out a warning.

As Hitch's force raced across the North Sea to await the returning German strike force, one of them broke down, leaving him outnumbered and outgunned. Despite this, he went ahead and laid his ambush, lying in the dark with engines cut, exactly as the E-boats waited for British convoys. At 0445 the MGB crews heard the sound of engines from the west. No less than five of Feldt's E-boats were approaching.

Despite the odds Hitch in *MGB 64* and his subordinate, Lieutenant L.G.R. 'Boffin' Campbell in *MGB 67*, raced into the attack. The E-boats, not expecting a fight so close to home, fled into the darkness at high speed. In the confusion, Block's *S41* was rammed by another E-boat and was abandoned in a sinking condition, to be found by Hitch's triumphant gunboats when dawn broke. Although an attempt to tow her home failed, the photographs and souvenirs obtained were more than enough to constitute a triumph. As a bonus, RAF Spitfires pounced on another of Feldt's boats later in the morning, badly damaging her. The days of unchallenged E-boat superiority in coastal waters were numbered.[66]

But to paraphrase Churchill, this was not the end, nor even the beginning of the end, of the E-boats' domination. It was merely a portent of the torrid time they were to have as the war went on. For the time being, such a bloody nose was a rarity, far outweighed by their successes during this new winter offensive. On 24 November, *4. Schnellbooteflottile* hit FS654, damaging the freighter *Blairnevis* and sinking the Dutch collier *Groenlo* and Captain N.R. Caird's 5,723-ton tanker *Virgilia*. Caird's crew were not as lucky as the men of the *War Mehtar*, whose flaming cargo had stayed inside the hull:

> When I came out on deck the fuel oil from the bunkers had caught alight and was spreading over the sea . . . the vessel at once started to go down by the stern, with the blazing kerosene and fuel oil mixing and quickly spreading out over the water to starboard . . . The flames were soon thirty feet high on the water and as the wind was blowing from starboard the fire was spreading to the port side.[67]

Understandably terrified by every tanker sailor's nightmare, there was a panicked rush to abandon ship. Captain Caird and four other men successfully got away in the starboard boat and began a nightmare circuit of the sinking *Virgilia* and her spreading pool of blazing kerosene and gasoline, trying to find other survivors. Their boat had only one oar, and was full of a greasy mix of oil and water, a result of being upended when it was launched. All around them the night continued to erupt with the sounds of the continuing battle:

> The flames were very close; however, the boat was a wooden one painted on the outside with asbestos paint, [otherwise] it would have been impossible to pass through the raging furnace of blazing oil . . . We were all covered with the greasy black fuel oil . . . and were half frozen and exhausted by the cold water.[68]

Eventually, and at great risk to themselves, the crew of a naval ML backed their flimsy craft to within 20 feet of the inferno, rescuing Caird and nine of his crew. But tragedy struck as the last of Caird's men tried to climb aboard:

> One of my crew who was swimming in the water managed to hang on to the net attached to a boom projecting from the ML. Unfortunately he was unable to pull himself up and I was paralysed from the waist downwards so could not assist him. The flames had almost reached us and the ML was forced to get away, leaving the man to his fate.[69]

Twenty-three of the *Virgilia*'s crew were burned to death or drowned. Five nights later, on the night of 29 November, the E-boats came back, striking at FN564 and sinking the colliers *Empire Newcomen*, *Asperity* and *Cormarsh*. It is always striking how completely incapable most of these small, often elderly, coasters were of standing up to a direct hit. Survival almost always seems to have been a matter of luck, a random outcome determined by where individual crew members were when the torpedo struck, and perhaps how well trained in 'abandon ship' routines they were. According to survivors *Asperity* took several minutes to sink, but took all but four of her crew of fourteen down with her; of the survivors, two were DEMS gunners who were washed off their gun platform, and one was a fireman who managed to climb out of the engine room skylight as the ship sank beneath him.[70] *Empire Newcomen*, on the other hand, sank in thirty seconds but twenty-two of her thirty-three crew survived.

December saw a new and intensive mining offensive, following a six-month hiatus. E-boats laid fields of the new magnetic/acoustic ground mines in the east coast war channel, which claimed twenty ships over the next two months – another grim Christmas for the coaster men. More mines were airdropped off the west coast ports, an unpleasant surprise resulting in the loss of five ships. There was also a spate of tip-and-run air attacks by the few aircraft remaining to the *Luftwaffe* in the west, which included the venerable He115 floatplanes. One victim was the 9,425-ton ocean-going tanker MV *Lucellum*, bombed on 19 December whilst crossing the Irish Sea in convoy BB13.[71] Her bridge collapsed and she caught fire immediately, with dreadful consequences for those on board: one ship's boy was so badly burned he later died, while thirteen crewmen were driven aft by the fire and eventually forced to make an appalling choice between the fire on board and the fire in the water. Most chose to jump, although ironically the ship was actually salvaged.

Of course, by December 1941 it was air strikes on the other side of the world which were grabbing the headlines, notably those which struck at the ships of the United States Pacific Fleet while they lay at anchor in Pearl Harbor, Hawaii, and those which sank HM ships *Repulse* and *Prince of Wales* off Malaya three days later. However grim the news, Britain now had a new ally, one whose industrial and military strength, once mobilized, was almost limitless.

Notes

1. Foynes, *Battle of the East Coast*, p. 112. I am grateful to the author for permission to use many details about the night of 7/8 March, taken from his very detailed account appearing between pp. 112 & 115.
2. ADM 199/2135 Survivors' Reports: Merchant Vessels 1 March 1941 to 30 April 1941, p. 6.
3. Ibid.
4. Ibid.
5. Foynes, *Battle of the East Coast*, p. 113.
6. ADM 199/2135 Survivors' Reports: Merchant Vessels 1 March 1941 to 30 April 1941, p. 27.
7. Ibid.
8. Ibid.
9. Ibid.
10. Donald, *Stand by for Action*, p. 57.
11. IWM Docs 96/456/1 Ditcham, Lieutenant A.G.F.
12. Ibid, pp. 34–6.
13. IWM Sound 12719 Seal, Jack.
14. ADM 199/2135 Survivors' Reports: Merchant Vessels 1 March 1941 to 30 April 1941.

15. Ibid.
16. IWM Sound 116509, Fellingham, Henry.
17. Roskill, *War at Sea*, vol. I, p. 618.
18. *British Merchant Vessels Lost or Damaged by Enemy Action During Second World War*, HMSO, London, 1947.
19. Grove, *The Defeat of the Enemy Attack on Shipping 1939–1945*, p. 159.
20. Ibid., p. 197.
21. ADM 199/2137 Merchant Navy Survivors' Reports 1 May 1941 to 31 July 1941, p. 281.
22. Ibid.
23. Ibid., p. 286.
24. Letter to the author, 20 August 2007.
25. IWM Docs 91/17/1 Booth, J.W.
26. www.convoyweb.org
27. For a first-hand account of the loss of *Unity* see IWM Sound 9578 McCurrach, Rob Roy. For *Umpire* see IWM Sound 13241 Band, Albert.
28. IWM Docs 96/456/1 Ditcham, Lieutenant A.G.F., p. 46.
29. NA ADM178/271 Board of Enquiry into Grounding and Loss of Convoy on Haisborough Sands.
30. Such as *His Majesty's Minesweepers*, HMSO, 1943.
31. IWM Docs 85/10/1 Rutter, Major O.
32. Ibid.
33. Ibid.
34. Ibid.
35. Ibid.
36. Ibid.
37. Ibid.
38. Ibid.
39. Ibid., p. 65.
40. Ibid., pp. 54–5.
41. Ibid., p. 69.
42. Noble was the son of the Commander-in-Chief, Western Approaches.
43. IWM Docs 85/10/1 Rutter, Major O.
44. Ibid., p. 96.
45. Ibid., p. 98.
46. Ibid.
47. Ibid., p. 89.
48. Ibid., p. 102.
49. Ibid., p. 112.
50. Ibid., pp. 115–16.
51. Ibid., p. 122.
52. ADM 199/2138 Merchant Navy Survivors' Reports 1 August to 31 October 1941, p. 99.
53. Ibid., p. 103.

54. Ibid., p. 141.
55. IWM Docs 96/456/1 Ditcham, Lieutenant A.G.F., pp. 47–8.
56. Ibid., 164.
57. IWM Docs 96/456/1 Ditcham, Lieutenant A.G.F., p. 40.
58. ADM 199/2138 Merchant Navy Survivors' Reports 1 August to 31 October 1941, p. 166.
59. IWM Docs 80/18/1 Constable Roberts, Air Commodore J.
60. NA ADM 199/670 Actions with E-boats 1941, 050028/41.
61. BBC PW A 3130183 Hales, Hilda.
62. IWM Docs 96/456/1 Ditcham, Lieutenant A.G.F., pp. 50–1.
63. Donald, *Stand by for Action*, p. 84.
64. NA ADM 199/2139 Merchant Navy Survivors' Reports 1 November 1941 to 31 January 1942, p. 49.
65. Donald, *Stand by for Action*, pp. 85–6.
66. See Cooper, *The E-boat Threat*, pp. 64–70, for a more detailed account of this action.
67. NA ADM 199/2139 Merchant Navy Survivors' Reports 1 November 1941 to 31 January 1942, p. 54.
68. Ibid.
69. Ibid.
70. Ibid, p. 57.
71. The BB series of convoys across the Irish Sea had begun in March 1941.

Chapter 8
Keeping the Home Fires Burning

1 January 1942 to 31 December 1942

New Year on the east coast was grim and subdued: 'The Third Mate rang in the New Year and rang out the old by striking sixteen bells at midnight . . . and took the risk of E-boats singling us out for their first attack of 1942.'[1]

In Dover, Admiral Ramsay was more upbeat: 'I feel justified now in stating that as a result of the implementation of . . . various proposals our grip on the Straits has in large measure been regained.'[2]

The entry of the United States into the Second World War spelled the end for the Axis, but like the entry of the Soviet Union, its effects were not immediately felt on the coast and the beginning of 1942 was very much business as usual. Hindsight is the privilege of the historian, and no one on the coast could know that the furious battering by the *Luftwaffe* which began in December 1941 and continued up to the end of January 1942 was to be the last serious air assault against coastal shipping. Such knowledge would probably not have made the attacks any easier to endure. On 12 January, the 7,025-ton freighter *Empire Masefield* was southbound off the Tees in FS698 when she was attacked by a Heinkel 111: '[The bomb] ploughed through Number 6 hold and into the Gunners' accommodation where it exploded and killed the three gunners . . . [who] were all badly burnt. We could not recover their bodies because of the debris.'[3]

Dreadful though such incidents were, the reality was that the *Luftwaffe* was all but spent as a strategic asset. From April much of its remaining strength in the West was diverted to retaliatory air raids, which became known as the 'Baedeker Blitz',[4] and just ten ships were sunk by air attack between January and June 1942. This was not just the result of German overstretch – the extraordinary efforts made by RAF Fighter Command to deny the daylight hours to the enemy also played their part in forcing this disengagement. At its peak in 1941 the RAF had flown as many as 8,000 fighter sorties a month.[5] Ramsay went on to acknowledge this in the positive report quoted above: 'The main factor in regaining that control has been the action of the RAF in establishing air superiority over the Straits and adjoining areas.'[6] Furthermore, the coasters were not the helpless targets they were in 1939. Many were well armed with close-range anti-aircraft guns, as were their escorts, and many reports from this period are characterized by raiders being driven off. In the Irish Sea the Dutch coaster *De Ruyter* lived up to her illustrious name, sending two Junkers 88s and a Heinkel 115 packing, and in the Channel on 31 January the SS *Cushenden*, on passage to Milford Haven with PW103, drove off another He115 using her PAC rockets, before apparently shooting down one of the deadliest raiders, a Focke-Wulf 200 *Kondor* long-range patrol aircraft: 'We saw our bullets entering the fuselage as the plane swerved sharply, making a perfect target as he swung across our bows. He was forced to turn almost at right angles and as he flew off towards the land . . . we all saw smoke pouring from him.'[7]

February saw the swansong of the *Luftwaffe* on the east coast: a series of fifty raids, many aimed at vulnerable minesweepers like the Yarmouth-based trawler *Cloughton Wyke*. A.H.Archer was a 21-year-old Hostilities Only rating, who had joined her the previous year:

> My visions of doing my service aboard one of the Naval vessels the like of which I had seen in Plymouth were shattered . . . I was deposited over the rails of a dirty and rusting trawler, with not a uniform in sight, all the crew, about a dozen of them, being in dirty overalls or 'civvies' . . . There was a sickly smell of oil, and there was coal dust everywhere . . . Everywhere was damp, our washing having to be dried either on lines in the messdeck, or over the burning engines, where they not only stank of oil, but were also covered with coal dust. Because of the dampness, we had to have frequent chest X-rays.[8]

Cloughton Wyke set out for her station on the morning of 2 February, a particularly filthy day even by the standards of the North Sea: 'The clouds were very low, the weather icy, there being snow in the rain, and the seas were very rough.'[9] What happened next typifies how suddenly death could come in coastal waters.

Cloughton Wyke developed a mechanical problem and was forced to break formation and heave to off Cromer. The dangerously isolated position of the little ship was not fully appreciated by her crew, most of whom were 'lounging about on deck, enjoying a brew up to keep warm' when another *Kondor* swooped down out of the lowering cloud cover:

> With a roar, we saw a four engined bomber bearing down on us, its machine-guns firing tracer bullets, and the noise was deafening . . . we saw four bombs leave the plane, and they straddled our ship, but with none hitting us . . . the plane disappeared, up into the clouds, and although it could still be heard, we gathered to discuss what had happened, and see if anyone had been injured.[10]

Before the men of the *Cloughton Wyke* could conduct their impromptu and rather ill-advised debrief, the aircraft returned:

> Again we scattered for shelter. Once again we saw the tracers, and four more bombs . . . one [exploded] beneath the ship, which promptly broke its back, the stern sinking like a stone. We were told to abandon ship [and] most of us rushed to our stations . . . mine being in the small boat, which we managed to lower into the rough sea. It took careful timing to jump into it, as once it was in the water, the heavy seas caused it to be one minute sucked away from the side, the next crashing into it.[11]

One young and inexperienced sailor, Eric, nicknamed 'Baby Blue Eyes' by the crew, mistimed his jump and was crushed against the ship's side before being dragged into the boat unconscious.

> Then we could see we were in great danger, as we were lashed to the fore part of the ship, which had by now also started to sink fast. Frantically we searched our pockets for a knife, but none of us had one on us. Our fate appeared to be either dragged down with the ship, or jump overboard into the icy water. Someone then thought to go through Eric's pockets, and there found [a] knife . . . and it went though the rope like butter.[12]

As the boat's crew pulled away Archer was horrified to see three members of the crew who had been left behind:

> As we pulled away, I saw what I have never been able to forget. In the water were three of my shipmates, struggling in the water trying to keep afloat, and being taken away on the tide. One was my friend the gunner, Arthur, wearing a heavy duffle coat. Another, by the name of Pellow, was wearing a heavy yellow oilskin fisherman's smock. His body was never recovered . . . On the way back to Yarmouth, radio messages between the two boats confirmed four were missing, and that five, including the skipper, had been injured . . . I often think back on to that day, especially at Armistice time.[13]

The beginning of 1942 also saw the last gasp of the German mining offensive. Although three ships were lost on the west coast in January, only one more ship was lost to a mine on the west coast during the war.[14] On the east coast, a new offensive was launched using both aircraft and E-boats to lay fields of magnetic/acoustic mines in the war channel. Although they claimed a number of ships, casualties have been accurately described by one author as 'considerable but entirely manageable'.[15]

The most serious loss of life was in the Rosyth-based destroyer HMS *Vimiera*, which was blown in half within sight of Sheerness on 9 January with the loss of ninety-two of her crew.[16] Her Captain, Lieutenant Commander Angus Mackenzie, was hauled onto a Carley float by his

RNVR Surgeon Lieutenant, who also saved four badly wounded ratings. Petty Officer Chapman was another *Vimiera* hero: 'caught below deck in a pitch-dark mess in the sinking wreck, he found an exit by striking matches and dragged two comrades to safety.'[17]

Notwithstanding these sporadic German successes, British defences by the beginning of 1942 had, according to Roskill, 'improved out of all knowledge since the tribulations of the early months of the war.'[18] Escorts were numerous and well armed, and radar and Headache intercepts allowed them to detect approaching E-boats well in advance of an attack developing. Aircraft patrolled constantly, protecting the convoys in daylight hours and making it harder for E-boats and enemy aircraft to operate. On 8 January 1942, Wing Commander Constable-Roberts reported from Dover that:

> The information of early approach of enemy light forces, obtained by Type 271 10cm R.D.F [radar] stations has enabled our own [air] forces to intercept before any damage could be done. This fortunate state of affairs has resulted in a complete cessation of enemy E-boat minelaying or torpedo attack along our convoy routes in this area.[19]

Constable-Roberts's strike force now consisted of radar-equipped Whitley bombers. By February he was arguing passionately that the new methods had been proven and should be rolled out around the east coast: 'We should now take the initiative and attack every available ship with the most advanced method whenever occasion to do so arises.'[20]

Anti-aircraft defences in the Thames estuary had also been dramatically strengthened. As well as extra batteries on shore, twelve radar-equipped anti-aircraft ships were introduced. They were mostly former Thames excursion boats, paddle steamers with names like *Royal Eagle* and *Crested Eagle*, and the class was unofficially christened the 'Eagle Ships': 'Their manoeuvrability [and] wide beam made them very suitable for this class of work.'[21]

Sub Lieutenant Michael Blois-Brooke was posted to one of these improvised ships. It was not exactly the ideal appointment for a destroyer officer who had survived the sinking of HMS *Imperial* in the Mediterranean:

> I was to report to HMS *Wildfire*, which I knew was the name of the base at Sheerness at the mouth of the Thames Estuary. To my horror I had been drafted to the anti-aircraft ship *Queen Eagle* whose duties were to go out into the swept channels of the Thames approach at night and there await the arrival of enemy minelaying aircraft.[22]

Even Blois-Brook was impressed by the firepower of his new ship:

> This new type of ship was simply bristling with anti-aircraft weapons of every type; .5 machine guns; quadruple Browning .303 machine guns; multiple 2-pounder pom-poms . . . anything would do; the ship was just a platform upon which were mounted as many guns as possible – and radar. But this was not destroyer work. And I longed to get back to the 'boats' again![23]

Work had also begun on a series of forts in the approaches to the Thames, to defend the estuary against E-boats and aircraft. Designed by and named after the architect Guy Maunsell, the 'Maunsell Forts' were monstrous 4,500-ton triumphs of engineering. Built at Gravesend and fitted out at Tilbury, they consisted of an 817-ton pontoon base resting on the seabed, from which two 60-foot-high hollow legs rose above the surface of the water, supporting a gun platform. The first four forts were to be manned by the Royal Navy and Royal Marines, and were armed with two 3.7-inch and two 40mm Bofors anti-aircraft guns. Stores and accommodation for the crew of 100 were inside the legs.[24]

The forts had to be towed out to sea and flooded, a hair-raising procedure the first time it took place, on 11 February, as no one really knew whether it would work:

> It was a case of suck it and see . . . after opening the flood gates, the fort took some fifteen minutes before sinking by the bow and hitting the bottom. It took a further one and a half minutes before the rest of the pontoon sank and the fort took an upright position. During this period there were many frightened crew and onlookers who thought the fort might tilt over sideways.[25]

The Naval forts were Tongue Sands Tower and Knock John Tower in the Thames approaches and Roughs Fort, the first to be deployed, and Sunk Head Fort, off Harwich. Later in the year three Army-manned forts were added, Great Nore Tower, Red Sands Tower and Shivering Sands Tower, which were even larger, consisting of seven towers linked by catwalks, and mounting four 3.7 inch guns, a 40mm Bofors and a searchlight. They were remarkably well appointed, with toilets, washroom, bathrooms and recreational areas available for the crew of 120.[26]

The day after the first fort was deployed, the wider war swept through coastal waters when the German battlecruisers *Scharnhorst* and *Gneisenau* and the heavy cruiser *Prinz Eugen* made their famous 'Channel Dash' home to Germany from Brest. Amongst the hopelessly inadequate forces which tried to stop them were six elderly coastal escort destroyers, one of which, HMS *Worcester*, was badly damaged.[27]

The following week, E-boats returned for the first time since Christmas, to find changed circumstances in their hunting grounds. On the night of 19/20 February a group of boats from Feldt's 2. *Schnellbootflottille* crossed the North Sea, heading for FS729. Warned by Headache intercepts, four destroyers from the 21st Destroyer Flotilla at Sheerness were waiting for them. The first Feldt knew of their presence was a shower of illumination rounds, swiftly followed by a concentrated barrage of shell-fire as the destroyers engaged them in a series of running battles well away from the convoy lanes. It was a typically confused night action, with the British optimistically (and inaccurately) claiming two E-boats sunk. What is certain is that one E-boat, *Oberleutnant-zur-See* Block's *S53*, was found wallowing in the swell, minus most of her bows, following a collision with *S39*. Midshipman Ditcham's destroyer *Holderness* edged close to her:

> As we approached it, I seized the Captain's stripped Lewis gun, cocked it and put the butt to my shoulder. The 10-inch signalling lamp was turned on them and as we swept past, 100 yards away, I called to the First Lieutenant 'open fire Sir?' 'Christ no!' he said, knocking the barrel up, 'they're hauling down their ensign.' I'd nearly become a war criminal.[28]

Holderness carried out a quick sweep of the area before returning to the stopped E-boat, her crew hopeful that they might be able to finally bring one back as a prize. Ditcham was already eagerly preparing: 'Before the order "Boarding party to stand by" was given, I had strapped on my .45 pistol and was down on the iron deck with the Gunner's Mate and my pirates. The ship came ghosting up to the E-boat to go alongside.'[29]

As Ditcham was about to step across, the stern of the E-boat swung away. Determined to make his capture he ran up to *Holderness*' fo'c'sle, and before he could stop to think he launched himself across the yawning 10-foot gap between his own ship and the E-boat: 'I reckoned I could just about clear the gap between us, and that if I landed with knees bent, I should not break my ankles. If I missed, wearing winter woollies, pistol and precious Gieves fleece-lined leather sea boots (not yet paid for) I should sink like a stone.'[30]

Clattering to the deck amongst the 'woebegone' German crew, Ditcham picked himself up and set off for the bridge. Before he reached it *Oberleutnant* Block blew the E-boat's demolition charges, killing himself and almost taking Ditcham with him: '[The Bridge] exploded upwards in a sheet of flame, blowing me back where I had just come from. Fortunately it did not blow me sideways and overboard, but along the fo'c'sle. The bridge was a raging fire.'[31]

There was little time to reflect on his good fortune. Ditcham and the Gunner's Mate passed their prisoners across to *Holderness* and made their way to safety. Ditcham was the last to leave:

> Looking around I found a rope; I coiled it up and threw it upwards and outwards to my shipmates, who caught it . . . I wrapped my feet around it in

> the approved fashion and shouted 'pull you so-and-sos!' and stepped off the E-boat's deck . . . I swung out like a pendulum, down and underneath the flare of *Holderness*' bow, striking the ship's side with a hollow bonk.[32]

With Ditcham safely on board, *Holderness*' crew tried to save their flaming prize, but it was too late. Within minutes *S53*'s ammunition began to 'cook off' and explode, and the fire started to creep dangerously close to her loaded torpedo tubes. As Leading Seaman W.R. Read turned a hose on the tubes, *Holderness* cast off and moved away.[33] Behind her the E-boat exploded and sank.

The journey home provided ample time for Ditcham to get an impression of his beaten enemies: 'We found that we had eighteen prisoners including one officer, Otto, who was very glum and would eat nothing. He had probably told his girlfriend that he would be back in the morning. Their uniforms were very inferior serge but they had good leather sea boots and soft leather wind-proof greatcoats.'[34]

Holderness having damaged her propeller, the entire crew was free to go ashore the following night, where they deservedly proceeded to 'stoke up a convincing Jolly of some magnitude'. Ditcham himself was smuggled back into the dockyard semi-conscious, supported by two ratings. For his actions on the night of 19 February he was later awarded the Distinguished Service Cross.

The following month the Germans avenged *S53* when *Oberleutnant-zur-See* Roeder's *S104* sank the Rosyth destroyer *Vortigern* while she was escorting FS749; 115 of *Vortigern*'s crew died. *The Cruel Sea* author Nicholas Monsarrat, serving in the corvette *Guillemot* which later reached the scene, described finding a solitary Carley float with 'a handful of black-faced, oil-soaked men, surrounded by prone figures sprawling in the lazy attitudes of death'.[35] There were just fourteen survivors. From a coldly tactical point of view the tragedy was offset when MGBs of the 7th Flotilla under the command of Lieutenant J.G.B. Horne RN intercepted the attacking E-boats on their way back to their base at Ijmuiden, disabling and capturing *S111* and nine of her crew.[36] At the same time RAF aircraft sent out to cover Horne's force caught another German group, sinking *S38*. The writing was on the wall for the E-boats, as the American journal *Time* reported exultantly the following week:

> Three British motor gunboats . . . caught an E-boat off the German base at Ijmuiden on the Dutch coast and left it sinking. In another engagement a British vessel fought off three E-boats until its ammunition was gone, damaged one, retired. A squadron of Spitfire fighters sighted four E-boats, one of them crippled from a previous clash. The Germans put up a screen of flak, but the British planes dived right through it, opening up with their 20-mm cannon. All four of the Germans were hit and one caught fire. The German fusillade punched 150 holes in one of the Spitfires and broke its

> elevator cable. But its pilot kept it in the air for a hundred homeward miles and landed safely. Reconnaissance planes found only a litter of wreckage mingled with Nazi corpses, bobbing up and down on the water.[37]

Tragic as losses like *Vortigern* and *Vimiera* were, they indicated that the E-boats no longer got a free shot at every convoy they went for. In 1942 the action was often far away from the convoys, which ploughed stoically up and down, sometimes unaware of the desperate game of cat and mouse taking place just over the horizon. It was not possible to guarantee them complete freedom from hazard, but the attrition rate was far lower than in previous years.

Life on the coast in winter was still exhausting, regardless of what the enemy did. Sub Lieutenant James Syms was the Navigating Officer on the Hunt-class destroyer HMS *Quorn*. Navigation was a peculiar activity on the coast, bearing little resemblance to the complex art he had learned in training:

> We were never, except in fog, out of sight of something, and tried not to be. But of course we did need to know where we were, all the time; there are tides and shoals along the east coast as well as mines and wrecks dangerous to navigation in those days. The swept channels, which the convoys followed meticulously, were marked every five miles by a centre line buoy. All the buoys were distinguished, in one form another, by name or number and by coded flashing lights . . . in addition to the swept channel buoys, there was a host of others, painted and flashing in green which marked the innumerable wrecks that had accumulated from enemy action along those frigid sea lanes. A lot of time on watch was spent peering for those bloody buoys.[38]

When not on the bridge peering into the gloom, James was huddled over a table updating charts, a tedious but vital activity in the ever-changing navigational environment of the coast. It is perfectly accurate to describe this work, easily dismissed as 'administration', as a genuine matter of life and death:

> All these floating aids to help keep us on the straight and narrow were liable to malfunction or change . . . so every day a stream of signals poured from the Admiralty to warn us . . . such signals were all identified by the letters QZ and became part of my life in the *Quorn* – QZS for swept channels, QZH for hydrographical matters like buoys . . . and so on . . . naturally the content of these signals had to be recorded, as they occurred, on the charts to which they referred . . . this meant a lot of charts and a lot of updating . . . the laborious work occupied most of my waking hours in harbour.[39]

This constant, monotonous, yet exhausting activity was only broken by the relatively rare but still adrenaline-charged and stressful intrusion of the Germans:

> When our wireless interpreter . . . announced up the voice pipe that he had E-boat 'carrier wave' we knew the E-boats were at sea and not far away. Binoculars swept the dark horizon, eyes strained, cocoa forgotten and the guns' crews bestirred themselves and manned their sights. E-boats, long, low, and fast, offered only fleeting targets and by night . . . they were extremely difficult to hit.[40]

In such conditions accidents were inevitable, the only surprise, perhaps, is that there were not more, with hundreds of ships crowded into such a small space and manned by dangerously tired crews:

> Trying to keep awake and alert on the bridge all night is not easily done, even with the sustaining cocoa and the occasional baked potato from the galley . . . I well remember one day when I had to remain as OOW [Officer of the Watch] . . . after an all night vigil. We were then zigzagging on the flank of the convoy as was the normal disposition of the Harwich reinforcement. 'Port Fifteen' said I to the wheelhouse in order to turn back towards the convoy. Fifteen degrees of port wheel was put on, the ship began to turn and I promptly fell asleep against the pelorus [compass]. Fortunately for me the Captain had remained on the bridge; I think we must have turned the best part of a circle before he quietly asked me if turning circles was what I intended to do.[41]

Such incidents were not confined to the men on the warships. The coasters were older ships, with few or no instruments, smaller crews and poorer training. These, combined with the weather and exhaustion, could be lethal. John Peters, a 21-year-old from Holyhead, was serving on the freighter SS *Llanover* in early 1942 when she was involved in a depressingly typical coastal accident:

> We were a very large ship there [4,959 tons] and of course you'd be mixed up with smaller fry around you . . . We were coming round . . . and it came on foggy – it's dreadful, fog in a convoy . . . They blew the whistle [to anchor] . . . from the wrong end of the convoy, they blew from the beginning, so ships at the head of the convoy were starting to drop their anchors while the rest behind were still lumbering up. I happened to be on the lookout and we saw this ship anchored in the gloom, just ahead of us, and of course put the engines full astern so we didn't hit it. The officer of the watch, I remember he ran up on the fo'c'sle and we dropped the anchor . . . next thing we knew, our stern has crashed into a coaster that had anchored right astern of us. Our rudder went in through the ship's side and she sank and we took their crew

on board.[42]

On the night of 12 April, *Kapitänleutnant* Niels Bätge's *4. Schnellbootflottille* carried out one of the last minelaying operations of the year, before the long summer days made trips across the North Sea impractical. The field was laid off Aldeburgh and immediately scored a success in the form of the Swedish coaster *Scotia*, ploughing north in FN680.

On the night of 20/21 April, Bätge's boats reinforced the field, just in time to catch the southbound convoy FS780, escorted by James Syms's *Quorn*. The new field snared the elderly Belgian coaster *Vae Victis* and the British *Plawsworth*, which both sank. *Quorn* was running late, having stopped to exercise her guns' crews, and was racing up to her station when the two freighters went up, followed almost immediately by the other escorting destroyer, HMS *Cotswold*:

> We [*Quorn*] accelerated a shade incautiously northwards outside the swept channel which was cluttered with the tail end of the convoy . . . As we moved up the line two explosions signified two more successes for the previous night's minelay, to be followed almost immediately by a third directly underneath us . . . the mine blew a large hole under our boiler room, we let out a piercing shriek of superheated steam and came to a stop with no power, steam or electric. We were to all intents and purposes dead in the water . . . a tug came out from Harwich, collected us some hours later and took us back to join the *Cotswold* in the invalid class.[43]

Aside from the occasional mining, spring and summer were quiet on the east coast. Both sides took the opportunity to reorganize. The British introduced a new patrol line, taking advantage of the hugely increased numbers of Coastal Forces craft now available – the base at Lowestoft, now grandly christened HMS *Mantis*, had thirty-seven, under another Coastal Forces legend, Peter Dickens, great-grandson of the novelist. The new line was known as the 'Z-Line' and ran hard up against the western edge of the east coast minefield for about 100 miles, from Cromer to Harwich – almost the length of 'E-boat Alley'.

Along this line, Coastal Forces provided an outer screen for the convoys, supported by destroyers and corvettes as 'goalkeepers'. Radar and Headache intelligence was passed to the Z-patrols, enabling the patrolling warships to respond to any emergency quickly. The Z-Patrols have been understatedly described as 'the less glamorous side of Coastal Forces': 'Once on station, the boats cut their engines and prepared for a night spent wallowing uncomfortably in the swell . . . [Z-patrols were] often operated in cold and wet conditions, in boats particularly prone to rolling, many of the crews would spend night after night, without ever seeing friend or foe.'[44]

One of the 'goalkeepers' was Michael Blois-Brooke, who after 'weeks of constant pressure' had finally arranged a transfer from *Queen Eagle* to the V&W HMS *Windsor* (Lieutenant Commander Derrick Hetherington), part of the 16th Destroyer Flotilla at Harwich. The work was not without excitement at times:

> One . . . calm still night with the sea like silk, we picked up an E-boat on radar only a few miles east of the convoy channel. A large convoy was due and he was obviously waiting for it to come within range. We sneaked up to him very carefully. Was he alone? . . . As a rule they worked in pairs. This one certainly seemed to be by himself; radar had picked up nothing else.[45]

Hetherington edged *Windsor* closer in the darkness until she was just a quarter of a mile away, then opened fire:

> Suddenly the sea was lit up by the starshell and there he was, lying stopped and waiting. The crew was not even at Action Stations! He was taken completely by surprise . . . we could see a German sailor scamper aft and turn on the smoke canister, putting his tin hat on at the same time. In seconds the enemy boat was under weigh and disappeared behind her smoke before we could get in more than a few rounds.[46]

Action was rare. Mostly it was just waiting in the dark empty waste of the North Sea, which could be an eerie place in the small hours of the morning. One night Michael heard a 'terrible moaning sound . . . what I can only describe as audible sadness'. On another occasion *Windsor* homed in on a small radar contact in the dead of night, only to find a grisly reminder of three years of war: 'An airman floating upright in his Mae West [life-jacket] but instead of a face all we could see beneath his flying helmet was a . . . yellow eyeless skull. It seemed to loll about in a grotesque way, mocking us.'[47]

The destroyers of the outer patrol line had little to do with the convoys but occasionally they would encounter the odd straggling coaster. The following incident is perhaps untypical, but does much to explain the gulf in empathy between the often elderly, veteran coaster men and the younger, impatient naval officers:

> One ship was always a straggler and returning from patrol we'd chase him up. This was a most extraordinary looking ship; it resembled a flat iron and rejoiced in the name of *Mister Therm*. She belonged, I think, to the Thames Coal and Coke Company and was commanded by an ancient mariner who always wore a trilby hat, smoked a clay pipe and hated the Navy! Just to annoy him we'd close him at high speed and tell him by loud hailer to put a jerk in it, get a wiggle on and in fact bloody well close up with the rest of the convoy. And then he would let fly! I cannot remember all that he called us . . .

> he always looked as if he was about to have an epileptic fit. The guns' crews loved it and word was soon passed below that the show was on and the sailors used to come up and enjoy it. When he got really furious, he would stuff his pipe into his mouth, bowl down, and stump into his wheelhouse for all the world like Popeye.[48]

No doubt this maritime bullying was a necessary pressure valve to release some of the tension of a night on the Z-Line, but it is hard not to sympathize with the master of *Mister Therm,* a veteran of coastal convoys since September 1939.

The new defences came a little too late to have a decisive effect in 1942, their introduction coinciding with a wholesale reorganization on the other side of the North Sea. The E-boats were reshuffled under a new *Führer der Schnellbooten*, *Kommodore* Rudolf Petersen, an experienced pre-war flotilla commander, and shortly afterwards he relocated them en masse to the Channel ports. Increasingly aware of their inferiority in numbers and the difficulty of finding replacement boats, E-boat commanders were also placed under restrictive orders compelling them to flee rather than fight when faced by British warships. The frustration of young officers like Lieutenant J.R. Gower, appointed to his first command at just thirty years old and itching for action, is palpable. He took over HMS *Winchester* on 31 May 1942, just in time for the lull:

> You can imagine my delight at having my command while still a Lieutenant: to be captain of a destroyer in war is to be among the gods. The East Coast was then rather quieter than the year before when E-boats had been such a trial but the convoys were getting bigger and bigger and sometimes it was left to just two destroyers, one ahead and one astern, to try and protect fifty ships. We were really mere shepherds.[49]

The action shifted back to the south coast, where three E-boat flotillas had assembled by July. As usual their operations were a mix of attritional minelaying, almost naval trench warfare, combined with the occasional high-speed torpedo attack.

On 9 July the Germans put together a devastating combined-arms attack on WP183, wending its way from Milford Haven to Portsmouth. Effective co-operation between the *Luftwaffe* and *Kriegsmarine* was rare at the best of times, and at this stage in the war almost unheard of, but this was doubtless no consolation for men like Captain P.P. Allen of the collier *Gripfast*, watching in horror as the battle unfolded around him; a shower of red flares, followed by the dull thump of the first torpedo, from *Kapitänleutnant* Felix Zymalkowski's *S6*, ripping into the hull of the tanker *Pomella* at 0125. This was followed by the sound of E-boat engines accelerating in the night as seven boats from Feldt's 2. *Schnellbootflottille* stalked the convoy.

With tanks full of crude oil it was fortunate that the *Pomella* merely lifted in the water and developed a list, before settling until her stern hit the bottom of Lyme Bay.[50] Captain Allen started to zigzag the unwieldy *Gripfast*, watching more flares slowly descend, punctuated by occasional gunfire and tracer rounds ripping across the night sky.

There was nothing to indicate from which direction the enemy was attacking except the sound of motor engines which changed bearings rapidly. I therefore gave the order for full speed and altered course to get away from the convoy. I saw the white wake and track of a torpedo pass across our stern.[51]

At 0230, Captain Allen witnessed the end of the SS *Konigshaug*, torpedoed by von Mirbach's *S48*, and shortly afterwards another track passed close by his ship: 'I did not know which way to turn for the best.' Overcoming his fears with the quiet stoicism that characterized many of the coaster men, Allen stopped his ship to rescue survivors from the SS *Rosten*, another torpedo skimming past his bows. Setting off on his own, towing a lifeboat from the *Rosten*, Captain Allen somehow survived the night. At dawn the *Gripfast* was alone but for two other merchant ships and one destroyer. WP183 was thoroughly scattered.

At 0545 Captain Allen heard the growl of aircraft engines, and two Messerschmitt 109 fighter-bombers powered over the horizon at wave-top height: 'There was a very loud explosion and I could see nothing but coal dust and steam . . . I jumped down on to Number 2 Hatch where the water was already up to my ankles.'[52]

Allen, a non-swimmer, was washed overboard but managed to find a floating ladder, to which he clung doggedly for forty minutes until rescue arrived. When it did, the selfless courage of one young crew member imprinted itself on his memory:

> The deck boy, aged sixteen, had managed to climb on to an upturned boat and was sitting astride the keel. He could see me in the water struggling with my ladder, which had several times turned over and ducked me. He also knew I could not swim. After about half an hour he saw the rescue boat coming towards him and I heard him shout 'go over there to the Captain, he is having a hell of a time with a ladder and can't swim, then come back here and rescue me because I haven't got any boots on.'[53]

Altogether, six ships were sunk in WP183. Fortunately this kind of catastrophe was now rare, and it is important to consider it in context. A total of 357 WP convoys passed through the Channel during 1942, and most went completely unscathed.[54] British offensive operations were more common during the summer of 1942. The ships of Coastal Forces were now numerous and deadly, equipped with heavier weapons and, crucially, radar.

They were supported by destroyers and aircraft, and they were confident and well trained.

This book is not a study of Coastal Forces, but it is important to remember that their activities on the German side of the Channel and the North Sea were an important reason why the E-boats were forced to stay away during the summer of 1942 – for much of the time they were too busy escorting their own convoys. Perhaps it is also worth remembering that German merchant sailors, and sometimes unwilling men from the occupied countries, fought their own bitter 'coastal convoy' battles during the Second World War. The following action should therefore be taken as representative of many.

Lionel Blaxell was a fairly typical Coastal Forces officer, a young RNVR Sub Lieutenant who had requested duty in small craft and had been appointed First Lieutenant of *MGB322*, based at Weymouth. On 19 July 1942, boats from his flotilla were sent to attack a German blockade runner, slipping up the Channel with a strong escort of E-boats and R-boats, the German equivalent to the Motor Launch.[55]

> [Lieutenant Henry] Cobb's boat [*MGB 328*] now began to close and opened fire, we followed in and [*MGB*] *601*. Cobb's boat appeared to be hitting the target continuously along the hull and below the bridge. We followed in doing the same thing and *601* joined in the fray. Hits could now be observed on the bridge. Suddenly all hell was let loose – on our way in we had in fact penetrated a very powerful escort and they all opened fire at us from what appeared every direction. The green tracer over our heads, the ricochets from the top of the sea and continual hits on our hull and upper deck made things very warm indeed.[56]

Suddenly Cobb's boat blew up in 'an enormous flash'. At the same time the forward pom-pom in Blaxell's *322* stopped firing, and while the hurtling MGB bucked and weaved underneath his feet he clambered forward to find out why.

> I left the relative security of the armour plated bridge and the security of the splinter mats and moved forward on the port side to the 2-pounder pom pom. The gunlayer was lying across the shield, apparently he had been trying to clear a jammed gun and had been killed by shrapnel, the trainer was at his side and beside himself with grief. We both tried to clear the gun but without avail – as it was such an exposed position and we were under heavy fire, I ordered him to go behind the bridge.[57]

The young Sub Lieutenant then had to struggle to the other end of the boat, where a similar problem had developed with the after 2-pounder:

> I found the gunner, a young Welshman, with a rope lanyard around the gun pedestal and the anti-flash muzzle against his chest, trying to recock the gun which had jammed with a shell 'up the spout'. He was weeping with frustration as an E-boat off our port quarter was pouring small calibre shells and bullets into our boat.[58]

MG322 was badly damaged. As well as losing her powerful 2-pounders, the hydraulic power lines had been severed, cutting power to the 0.5-inch machine-gun turrets, and leaving the little ship with no functioning weapons at all. Her Captain turned for home, but as he did so Lionel Blaxell's luck ran out:

> Just as I was about to move into the chart house I felt a hard punch on my left shoulder and I saw stars. When I recovered, seconds later, I was lying on the deck and found that my left arm was numb and that I was unable to move my head . . . my tin helmet had been knocked off my head and when I picked it up there was a slice of the metal flange hanging off the back.[59]

The boat's coxswain dressed Lionel Blaxell's wounds and when *322* returned to Dover he was taken to hospital. His wounds turned out to be serious: 'A piece of shrapnel had torn through the flange of my tin helmet and had deflected downwards taking a piece off the left clavicle and split open the left shoulder muscle bearing the left lung.'[60]

For his actions he was awarded the Distinguished Service Medal. He finished the war as Commanding Officer of his own MGB in the Mediterranean.

Such was life in Coastal Forces in 1942. On 2 August, MGBs of Robert Hitchen's 8th Flotilla, hurriedly transferred from Felixstowe after the WP183 disaster, intercepted a force of E-boats off Cherbourg, sinking two. At the end of August came the disastrous Dieppe Raid. George Barnes was passing through the Channel in the *City of Charleroi* at the time, and recalled how the coaster men were instructed: 'To keep a sharp lookout [and] fire at nothing that was coming from the French coast, like planes or any fast craft, they'd be our own . . . the last bell we got from a Convoy Commodore was "no lights, no bells, no sound".'[61] Passing by Dieppe George saw and heard gunfire. When he finally arrived at Newhaven the port was sealed off, while the sad evidence of catastrophe was discretely dispersed.

Luftwaffe raiders still made the occasional foray, with the Channel PW/WP convoys being a favoured target. The tanker *El Ciervo* was proceeding to Milford Haven in PW196 on 4 August when she was subjected to the unwelcome attention of a German torpedo bomber, at 2250 off Start Point. The torpedo ripped a hole 50 feet wide in the ship's hull, flooding her engine room, but she did not sink and a tug arrived to take her into Plymouth. Captain Davis reported what happened when they arrived: 'A diver went down to inspect the damage and found an unexploded torpedo in the stern of the ship. This torpedo had apparently entered the ship through the hole made by the first torpedo and remained there without exploding; it was found to be intact, the warhead being quite undamaged.'[62]

In September 1942, E-boat strength in coastal waters increased to four flotillas. In October they took advantage of the lengthening nights to return to their Dutch bases and once more threaten the east coast. From now on E-boat operations would be characterized by this switching of flotillas from one coast to another, like a versatile boxer changing effortlessly from his left hand to his right, although to continue the analogy he would get progressively more bruised as the years went by, and fewer of his blows would count. This, however, was small consolation to the men of FN832, which was attacked by a strong force from *4.* and *12. Schnellbootflottillen* on the night of 6/7 October.

The attack was the usual series of devastating blows, struck almost simultaneously. First to fall was the 2,730-ton collier *Sheafwater*, riding high in the water as she headed north in ballast. Torpedoes from *S117* opened her side in the small hours of the morning and the crew hurriedly abandoned ship, their Captain missing and the 2nd Officer badly wounded. The missing Captain eventually appeared on deck and the survivors were taken aboard a naval Motor Launch. When daylight finally came they reboarded their ship to try to salvage her, but the *Sheafwater* was beyond salvation.[63]

As the *Sheafwater* lurched to a halt, the cold waters of the North Sea filling her hull, more torpedoes tore into the 2,874-ton *Ilse*, as the usual running fight erupted around her: 'It was a violent explosion which threw the ship over to port . . . a tremendous amount of noise from gunfire was going on and in the general commotion it was not easy to tell whether all the noise was from our explosion or from other ships in the convoy which were being attacked.'[64]

There was little doubt in the minds of Captain H.E. Lawson and his men that their ship was mortally wounded. Her back was broken and down below 'the plates could be heard tearing and making a grinding noise.' Some of the crew began to panic:

> [They] rushed forward to the rafts but as there was still weigh on the ship I told them not to get on to the rafts. One of the port rafts was released and three men got on to it, but two of them climbed back, and the other tried to get back but slipped overboard and is missing.[65]

Lawson's Chief Engineer reported that the engines could not be stopped, so the dangerous evacuation whilst the *Ilse* was still in motion had to continue.

It seems remarkable that despite the chaos, when Lawson finally made a count of the survivors who had reached the boats, only two men were missing. The fate of one was clear to all: 'I made enquiries about the gun-layer Cumminger and a rating told me that he had seen him standing in the cabin where the explosion had occurred and that it was practically certain that he was killed.'[66]

The last coaster to fall to the E-boats that night was the elderly Danish collier *Jessie Maersk*, torpedoed by *S79* at 0330. As she slipped beneath the waves, taking with her twenty of her crew of thirty, the hopelessly outgunned Yarmouth-based Motor Launch *ML339* flew into the attack in the finest traditions of the Royal Navy. Captain H.H. Madsen of the *Jessie Maersk* witnessed her end:

> We did not see the E-boat but there was a British Motor Launch in the vicinity which gave chase and attacked one at a comparatively short distance from us. Later this motor boat passed us again but she was burning fiercely . . . I could see tracer bullets while she was fighting with the E-boat and gather she had been badly hit and caught fire.[67]

The E-boats also sank the rescue tug *Caroline Moller* before departing into the night unscathed. On board the other ships in the convoy, the crews desperately fought to stay out of harm's way as the battle raged around them. Captain Stevens of the SS *Ightham* was one such reluctant spectator; unfortunately, although his ship avoided destruction at the hands of the E-boats, she ran over a mine at 0850 the following morning. The first explosion 'was very violent and was followed by a terrific shattering noise which felt as though the whole ship was breaking up'.[68]

Shortly afterwards a second mine smashed the engine and flooded the engine room so that the *Ightham*'s pumps could not be started. With her steering gear wrecked and with no power, she had no direction to go but downwards, and Stevens ordered his men to abandon ship. To his disgust several of his men 'lost their heads', among them his own boat's crew which left without him. Fortunately his Chief Officer was made of sterner stuff: 'finding that I was not in my boat [he] promptly stripped and swam back to the ship.' The starboard boat was then 'persuaded' to come back and take them aboard.

Later in the morning Captain Stevens and a volunteer crew reboarded the ship to see if she could be saved. A salvage tug arrived at 1220 but by then it was too late. The *Ightham* sank, striking a third mine on her way down, and forcing the entire salvage crew to swim for their lives.

And so the convoys continued to run, as the nights grew longer and the E-boats bolder. A week later they attacked FN838, sinking the small and ancient (1907) Norwegian collier *Lysland* and blowing the SS *George Balfour* in half, despite her Master's frantic maneuvring. Her after end was eventually refloated and towed into Yarmouth. As if to emphasize the changing circumstances, the night before in the Channel, British destroyers and Motor Torpedo Boats had cornered and sunk the German raider *Komet.*

Despite growing Allied confidence, E-boats continued to bring the war into British waters whenever they could. On the night of 19/20 November they carried out a serious attack on PW250 off the Eddystone Lighthouse. According to eyewitnesses the boats, from *Kapitänleutnant* Bernd Klug's *5. Schnellbooteflottille* divided into two groups. The first swept in at high speed, drawing the escorting destroyer away into the night. In the meantime another six boats, which had been lying stopped, started an attack on the convoy from the opposite beam. The first torpedoes found their mark in the minesweeping trawler *Ullswater* (Lieutenant Cameron Ross RN), which blew up and sank at 0305. Within minutes, more torpedoes had found their mark in the coasters *Yewforest*, *Birgitte* and *Lab*, impacting almost simultaneously before their startled crews had even had time to process *Ulswater*'s destruction. Captain Terence Sheekey of the *Yewforest* was courageously ordering his engineers to slow the ship at the time, in the hope of finding survivors from the trawler:

> I saw a blinding flash astern and HMS *Ullswater* blew up. My ship was two cables astern and I decided that all I could do was to pick up survivors as we passed through them. I gave the men at the wheel instructions to steer so as to keep the men in the water on the starboard side, and reduced speed, and instructed the crew to get lines ready and to haul the men on board . . . [then, at 0310] . . . I assume that my ship was torpedoed, as the next thing I remember was taking my boots off in the sea . . . I must have lost consciousness immediately the torpedo hit the ship, as I remember nothing at all about it.[69]

Captain Sheekey was eventually rescued by the naval trawler *Notre Dame*, which picked up the only other survivors of the *Yewforest*:

> I did not know I had been picked up until I found myself being taken down to the forecastle or mess room, where I recognised my second engineer and one of my firemen, who had also been rescued. One gunner also survived. I could not speak to them, as my ribs were injured and my nose and face were badly smashed.[70]

When the *Birgitte* went down at 0321, most of the crew managed to board her lifeboats successfully, only to be caught up in an awful tragedy as the ship sank:

> The boat fouled the forward davit as the ship went down and was pulled under, it must have suddenly cleared itself for I saw the boat a few minutes

> later shoot up into the air and land on the water upside down, killing several members of the crew, including the Master, who were swimming in the water.[71]

The fourteen remaining survivors huddled together in one boat and a raft. Paddling away from the gunfire 'to improve the possibilities of a quick rescue and keep the survivors occupied and warm', they were eventually rescued by the trawler HMT *Cambridgeshire* and taken to Plymouth. On 3 December, Klug's flotilla returned to the Dorset coast, attacking PW257 and sinking the new Hunt-class destroyer HMS *Penylan* (Lieutenant Commander John Wallace, DSC, RN), as well as the coaster *Gatinais*. The latter ship had provided sterling service with the Channel Mobile Balloon Barrage before reverting to her original occupation.

Back on the east coast there was just time for one more strike before the year ended. On the night of 12 December, five coasters went down off Lowestoft in the space of a few minutes. It was a familiar story, easily told but far less easy to live through: SS *Lindisfarne* lurched to port, then rose vertically in the water and plunged to the bottom, whilst at the same time the *Avonwood* was blown in half. Tragically many of the survivors from the latter were run over by one of Fulham Borough Council's flat-iron colliers, doggedly obeying standing instructions and ploughing relentlessly through them as they struggled in the heavy seas:

> The SS *Fulham* which was astern steamed straight on through these survivors and they all perished . . . the Chief Officer has since reported that he saw our Steward W. Hutchinson supporting and swimming with the Mess Room Boy, whose leg had been broken by the explosion. This man was a very powerful swimmer and was supporting the Mess Boy when the SS *Fulham* steamed over them.[72]

The year ended dramatically, but once again, perspective is vital. For all the undeniable 'sound and fury' of the E-boat offensive at the end of 1942, by now they were operating unsupported by the *Luftwaffe* and their efforts were flea bites compared to the volume of shipping being passed along the coast. Losses in 1942 were by no means negligible but they were certainly manageable. Ninety-one ships were lost in coastal waters during the year, compared to 350 the year before and 650 in 1940.[73] Compare this to the total number of distinct passages made: 21,552 up and down the east coast in FN/FS convoys alone during 1942.[74] Most were exhausting, wet, cold and boring, but passed unthreatened by the enemy. Rather than ending 1942 with fire, then, let us leave the year with Patrick Mummery, in the veteran tanker *San Roberto*, trudging gamely up and down the east coast at the year's end:

> Astern, two shadowy grey lines of merchant ships, merging into the gloom. Ahead the faintly visible white wake of an escorting destroyer . . . night time in convoy. On the bridge, by the faint gleam of light from the compass, one can distinguish silhouettes. There is the officer on watch, propped up against the binnacle, a pair of binoculars glued to his eyes. The Old Man stumps up and down the bridge, breathing heavily, while a duffel-coated apprentice treads unobtrusively to and fro, steering a course that will take him well clear of the Captain. The gunners . . . are huddled in the lee of their charges, immobile but alert. There is a strong wind blowing – very nearly a gale. It crashes and thunders across the unprotected bridge, whilst chins are sunk into upturned collars, and hands thrust into pockets. Where it catches the rigging it literally shrieks. Suddenly there is a crack and a swish as a PAC rocket goes whirring up, fired by the tug of the wind. A blinding flash, followed by showers of golden sparks. Then silence and darkness again . . . now it begins to rain, gently at first, deteriorating into a heavy downpour. Rain drops land from cap-peaks, chins and noses, and tempers begin to fray . . . slowly the long hours of a routine night tick by.[75]

Winter on the coast was never easy. But the worst was finally over.

Notes

1. Batten, John, *Call the Watch*, Hutchinson, London, undated, p. 87.
2. Woodward, *Ramsay at War*, p. 80.
3. NA ADM 199/2139 Merchant Navy Survivors' Reports 1 November 1941 to 31 January 1942, p. 149.
4. So named because the target towns were supposedly selected using the famous travel guides.
5. Grove, *The Defeat of the Enemy Attack on Shipping*, pp. 159–60.
6. Woodward, *Ramsay at War*, p. 81.
7. ADM 199/2139 Survivors' Reports: Merchant Vessels 1 November 1941 to 28 February 1942, p. 213.
8. BBC PW A4183076, Archer, A.H.
9. Ibid.
10. Ibid.
11. Ibid.
12. Ibid.
13. Ibid.
14. Grove, *The Defeat of the Enemy Attack on Shipping 1939–1945*, p. 208.
15. Foynes, *Battle of the East Coast*, p. 219.
16. www.naval-history.net
17. Foynes, *Battle of the East Coast*, p. 219.
18. Roskill, *War at Sea*, vol. II, p. 147.
19. IWM Docs 80/18/1 Constable-Roberts, Air Commodore J.
20. Ibid.

21. Roskill, War at Sea, vol. II, p. 148.
22. IWM Docs 95/5/1 Blois-Brook, Lieutenant Commander M.S., p. 107.
23. Ibid.
24. Turner, Frank R, *The Maunsell Sea Forts*, published by the author, 1996, pp. 3–4.
25. Ibid, p. 5.
26. Ibid, p. 12. Several of the forts still stand at the time of writing and have been put to a variety of uses in the intervening years, including as pirate radio stations and a supposedly independent 'Republic' of questionable legal standing.
27. The Channel Dash has been extensively covered elsewhere: see, for example, Smith, *Hold the Narrow Sea*, pp. 145–54, and Potter, John Deane, *Fiasco*, William Heinemann, London, 1970.
28. IWM Docs 96/456/1 Ditcham, Lieutenant A.G.F., p. 57.
29. Ibid.
30. Ibid.
31. Ibid.
32. Ibid., p. 58.
33. Foynes, *Battle of the East Coast*, p. 222.
34. IWM Docs 96/456/1 Ditcham, Lieutenant A.G.F., p. 59.
35. Nicholas Monsarrat, *Three Corvettes*, quoted in Foynes, *Battle of the East Coast*, p. 223.
36. For a detailed account of this action see Cooper, *The E-boat Threat*, pp. 83–4.
37. *Time* Magazine, 30 March 1942.
38. IWM Docs 01/31/1/ Syms, Commander James Anthony, DSC, RN, p. 42.
39. Ibid, p. 42.
40. Ibid, p. 41.
41. Ibid, p. 41.
42. IWM Sound 12720 Peters, John.
43. IWM Docs 01/31/1/ Syms, Commander James Anthony, DSC, RN, pp. 43–4.
44. Jefferson, David, *Coastal Forces at War: Royal Navy 'Little Ships' in World War 2*, Patrick Stephens Ltd, Sparkford, Somerset, 1996, pp. 132-3.
45. IWM Docs 95/5/1 Blois-Brook, Lieutenant Commander M.S., p. 109.
46. Ibid.
47. Ibid.
48. Ibid., pp. 111–12.
49. IWM Docs 94/32/1 Gower, Captain J.R., DSC, RN, p. 40.
50. NA ADM 199/ 2141 Merchant Navy Survivors' Reports 1 June to 31 July 1942, p. 189.
51. Ibid., p. 184.
52. Ibid.

53. Ibid.
54. Hague, *Allied Convoy System*, pp. 120–2. The WP/PW Series convoys from Milford Haven to Portsmouth were introduced in July 1941 to bring shipping in the western Channel under the umbrella of convoy protection.
55. IWM Docs 91/7/1 Blaxell, Lionel H., OBE, DSC. Unpublished memoir *Through the Hawse Pipe 1939–1946.*
56. Ibid., p. 67.
57. Ibid., pp. 68–9.
58. Ibid., p. 69.
59. Ibid., p. 70.
60. Ibid., p. 71.
61. IWM Sound 11111 Barnes, George.
62. NA ADM 199/ 2142 Merchant Navy Survivors' Reports 1 August to 31 October 1942, p. 11.
63. Ibid., p. 274.
64. Ibid., p. 276.
65. Ibid.
66. Ibid. The lost gunner was Able Seaman Frank Cumminger, a 22 year old Londoner from Maida Vale.
67. Ibid., p. 294. Three men died when *ML339* went down.
68. Ibid.
69. ADM 199/2143 Merchant Navy Survivors' Reports 1 November 1942 to 31 December 1942, p. 152.
70. Ibid.
71. Ibid., p. 154.
72. Ibid.
73. Roskill, *War at Sea*, vol. III Part 2, p. 479.
74. Hague, *Allied Convoy System.*
75. Mummery, Patrick, letter to the author, 2007.

Chapter 9

Eye of the Storm

1 January 1943 to 5 June 1944

The year 1943 was a quiet one on the coast, even allowing for the 'wisdom of hindsight' which we have recognized before. Just twenty-five ships were lost, totalling a mere 52,484 tons – the equivalent of perhaps fifteen good-sized ocean-going freighters. It was also the year that John Batten, journalist, author and wireless operator 'for the duration' joined his American-built collier *Hamden Z Coney* (almost certainly a pen name). His book *Dirty Little Collier* is a remarkable snapshot of everyday life on the coastal convoys: hard work and the regular hazards of storms, drifting mines and fogbanks which lasted days, as well as the little things which made life bearable, like runs ashore, comforts from sympathetic civilians, Christmas dinner afloat, and the ship's 'adoption' by a girls' boarding school. But enemy action is rare. One or two E-boat alerts were all Batten experienced, although he recognized that things had been much harder: 'The worst of the enemy attack is over, and it's much more like peacetime, except for the convoy . . . [although] coasting seamen haven't lost the caution they learnt four or five years ago.'[1]

Batten visited a London power station while *Hamden Z Coney* was unloading, providing a vivid reminder of what the convoys were all about. The south's voracious appetite for fuel did not diminish just because the enemy were less active:

> We were a total of three days loading. It must have taken longer than that for the men in the pits to get the coal. We'd been three and a half days in convoy . . . and in spite of all this effort and work . . . we'd brought just enough coal to keep the power station generators going for forty-eight hours.[2]

The pressure on the coasters remained intense, and the convoys kept running. All around the coast hundreds of ships were in constant motion. By now the coastal convoys included increasing numbers of ocean-going ships as well as colliers. One such was the first casualty of the year, the 5,600-ton *Empire Panther*, mined on New Year's Day in the Irish Sea convoy BB50. A few days later, on 17 January, the Belgian ammunition ship *Ostende* also fell foul of mines, and was beached on the Isle of Mull. An attempt to salvage her cargo was brought to an abrupt halt when it started to explode, and crew and salvage party alike made for shore as fast as they could: 'When the boats were about fifty yards from the ship on their way to shore, another tremendous explosion occurred which blew away the fore part of the vessel and part of the midships accommodation.'[3]

The 'greater part' of the ship disintegrated, her after section remaining on the beach. Mines were still laid in relatively large numbers in 1943, but the unending vigil of the sweepers ensured that victims were few. During 1943, Nore Command alone swept 373 ground mines and eighty-six conventional tethered varieties. By now, the improvised trawlers and drifters had been largely replaced by modern, purpose-built naval minesweepers, making this dangerous work infinitely easier.[4]

Isolated losses like *Ostende* and *Empire Panther* should not obscure the wider picture of life on the coast in 1943, which was generally characterized by relentless grind rather than breathless action. The late John Terraine has summed up the dangers of giving a false impression of constant combat admirably, in his *Business in Great Waters*, actually a study of the Atlantic convoy battles but his words are just as applicable here:

> This is the sort of situation in which it is easy for history to project a false image of war. It is said that ninety per cent of war is boredom – but how does history convey that? . . . It is the day by day continuing experience, whose main feature is probably sheer fatigue, that presents the difficulty.[5]

Midshipman Derek Tolfree knew exactly what Terraine meant. He joined the east coast destroyer *Westminster* in December 1942, having transferred from the battleship *Nelson*. As a Midshipman part of his duties involved keeping a regular, assessed journal. The following extract is deliberately reproduced verbatim, and represents a fairly typical week in the 'day by day continuing experience' of a coastal escort:

> Friday Feb. 12th. We weighed at 1030 and mustered the convoy. This consisted of seven ships, the Commodore being the *Balmaha*. We were the only escort as from now on single escort convoys were to be in force. There was a very strong wind and heavy sea; several ships failing to sail.
>
> Saturday Feb. 13th. During the morning we met the Tyne contingent with *Sleipner*. This consisted of twenty-three ships. The wind and sea dropped slightly during the day but we remained in cruising watches throughout the night. Our additional escort [through E-boat alley] was the *Eglinton*.
>
> Sunday Feb. 14th. All was quiet throughout the night but we became a little behind of schedule time, shackling on to 5 Buoy at 1615. The Russians announced the capture of Rostov today.
>
> Monday Feb. 15th. We slipped at 0912 and proceeded at twelve knots through the gate and met our convoy. The Commodore was in the *Forth* and there were nineteen other ships in company. The weather was very fine but

there was a strong westerly wind blowing. There was a fairly strong sea running and owing to this fact we became far behind schedule, making an average speed of three knots. At dusk, we received warnings of enemy aircraft in the vicinity, and went to day defence stations until 2100, after which we reverted to cruising stations.

Tuesday Feb. 16th. Our additional escorts for the night were *Mallard*, *Greenfly*, *Quorn* and *Southerners*. [The latter were a group of minesweeping trawlers with names beginning Southern.] The Rescue Tug *Champion* was also with us. We became five hours behind our schedule at 4 Buoy.

Wednesday Feb. 17th. We estimated to lose time during the night but by midday the wind and sea had subsided and we made our ETA at May Island for 2130. During the afternoon we estimated eight knots with only two ships, all our ships except the Commodore's having left at Tyne. We received one Greek joiner from there. We took the convoy to Largo buoy and thence proceeded at twenty knots on our own.

Thursday Feb. 18th. We passed under the bridge during the early part of the Middle Watch and anchored at E2 berth. From there we proceeded to the oiler for fuel.

Friday Feb. 19th. We left Rosyth this morning at 0830 and proceeded to Methil for our convoy.[6]

Such actions as did occur often went against the enemy. As Derek Tolfree quietly entered the Forth on the night of 17/18 February, the southern North Sea destroyers of the 21st Flotilla intercepted a German minelaying operation, and HMS *Garth* sank *S71*in a lively action. The veteran east coast escort CO, Commander W.J. Phipps, now in command of another 21st Flotilla destroyer, the elderly HMS *Montrose*, was also present. His Headache operators gave him a blow-by-blow commentary: 'Two long sweeps out to the North-East to look for E-boats which were about, calling for Rödiger, who had reported his boat on fire and screaming for help. *Garth* in the meantime ran into him and captured seven prisoners from the boat and left it sinking.'[7] In addition to the prisoners the *Garth* also brought back *S71*'s canine mascot.

By now the Royal Navy was effectively in control of coastal waters; indeed, the presence of Coastal Forces craft in ever-increasing numbers caused Phipps and his fellow destroyer officers some confusion during night actions: 'One of the big snags of the night, the place was littered with our own light forces returning and going out to the battle.'[8] 'Friendly fire' incidents were common in 1943, and on 8 March, Phipps actually fought a full-blown engagement with Coastal Forces craft after the MGBs failed to fire the correct recognition flares.

The loss of *S71* was the start of a dismal year for the *Schnellboot* flotillas, in which fourteen of their number were sunk, but they remained deadly given the right opportunity. On 27 February, they hit WP300 in Lyme Bay, sinking two antisubmarine trawlers, the *Lord Hailsham* and the *Harstad*, as well as an unlucky tank landing craft on passage with the convoy, and the 4,858-ton ocean-going freighter *Moldavia* at 0120 in a joint attack by *S68* and *S81*. Her Captain blamed the company he had to keep for the loss of his ship: 'I consider that it is bad policy to put a large ship like mine in a convoy of small ships and it was perfectly obvious that my ship was picked out for the target.'[9]

Retaliation came the following month. On the night of 28/29 March an attack on FS1074 was driven off by the overwhelming firepower of the escorting destroyers. The fleeing enemy were intercepted by another of the 'aces' of Coastal Forces, the colourful and aggressive Lieutenant Donald Bradford.[10] Bradford, with just two MGBs under his command (*MGB 33* and *MGB 321*), engaged five of the returning E-boats, sinking two including *S29*, which he rammed, slicing off her stern.

Action may have been rare for the convoys in 1943, but life was still full of the normal hazards and discomforts. Lieutenant John Pelley joined the Harwich Hunt-class HMS *Eglinton* in February:

> It was hard, tiring and yet boring work . . . we had to be at action stations all night, every night, and when snatching an odd hour's sleep it was fully clothed and on the deck. Winter was very hard with long and bitterly cold nights, somehow no amount of clothing is sufficient in the North Sea. I've never been so cold even in the North Atlantic.[11]

Eglinton lost a man in exactly the sort of tragic, pointless circumstances which made service at sea so hard, wherever in the world you were. It was early in the morning, after an exhausting night rounding up a scattered convoy in a gale, when a dog-tired seaman was washed overboard:

> I immediately climbed the mast to try and spot him and it was a pretty nerve wracking experience with a howling gale, bitterly cold and the ship rolling all over the place. Luckily we saw him and closed him, but it was far too heavy weather to lower a boat. The man caught hold of a line thrown to him but he weakened and let go. Then John Mudford went over the side with a line round him and got him to the side of the ship but it was impossible to get him inboard and get a line round him owing to the heaving and violent rolling, and he was washed away again. But the Captain kept on trying and brought the ship round again and the man appeared near the port side so I, who was then on deck, put a line round me and jumped over the side. My God it was cold and the seas from that level appeared mountainous. Yet somehow I managed to close him and was just going to grab him when I was hauled back by orders from the Captain. Already I was three line lengths away and the Captain felt that it was far enough.[12]

Eventually, someone managed to snag the unfortunate man's clothes with a boat hook, and he was brought on board. By now he had been in the water for over an hour, and the destroyer had no doctor: 'Only once did they get a spark of life out of his body . . . on arrival in Harwich five hours later a doctor immediately gave injections to the heart etc but to no avail – he was dead.' Pelley and Mudford were commended for their actions.

Out on the Z-Patrol line, the Coastal Forces craft still waited patiently and uncomfortably. Graham Rouse was First Lieutenant of a Lowestoft-based ML in early 1943, and recalled how: 'We would stop engines and drift in the middle of the North Sea, listening with hydrophones for the propellers of E-boats.' During one cold, boring, vigil, his ML made fast to another, and three of the officers formed an impromptu jazz band: 'One played a sax, the other an accordion and I, using a biscuit tin and wire brushes, was the drummer.'[13]

Only the possibility of a run ashore relieved the monotony. The more adventurous, like Richard Bird of the destroyer HMS *Hambledon*, would do everything they could to make the most of it:

> We used to go one night up [the coast], one night back and into Harwich, and you were into Harwich for one night then you joined another [convoy]. That night we were in Harwich we had all night leave and I was courting my wife then and we weren't supposed to go up to London but we used to . . . All the ships, we used to get workmens' tickets from London back to Harwich . . . One and nine pence it was . . . I remember the booking clerk, this would be in the early hours of the morning, he'd have all these tickets ready and it'd be 'one and nine, one and nine' and he'd be passing your ticket . . . It was a hell of a fuss if somebody only had two shillings instead of one and nine because it was holding up the queue . . . We used to get back and of course we felt terrible, we had to go and do another two nights up on the convoys . . . the fellas used to be so tired.[14]

In the absence of action, frequent training kept the coastal escorts sharp. Commander Phipps found the exercises enjoyable, a welcome relief from boredom: 'Off again for one of these exercises with our coastal craft representing E-boats attacking convoy and minelaying . . . I had all the fun and hurtled around after two of them at twenty-nine knots for ten minutes and claimed to have sunk the lot.'[15]

And so 1943 went on, largely routine with odd bursts of adrenaline and moments of tragedy. On 12 April, the Coastal Forces 'ace' Robert 'Hitch' Hitchens finally ran out of luck and was killed instantly by a burst of cannon fire which swept the bridge of his MGB during an offensive operation off Scheveningen in Holland. In the Channel on the following night, E-boats from *Kapitänleutnant* Klug's *5. Schnellbooteflottille* successfully attacked convoy PW323 off Lizard Head, sinking the Norwegian-manned Hunt-class

HMS *Eskdale* and the elderly collier *Stanlake*. Once again, the presence of British light coastal craft among the escort caused confusion, as Captain H. Purvis of the *Stanlake* recalled:

> I observed an object on my port quarter and as I could not identify it I ordered the guns to be trained on it. This object had the appearance of an ML and was steering about a point inside our course, towards land, at approximately ten knots . . . if I had not had an ML on my port side, I would have immediately been able to recognise the E-boat.[16]

Stanlake was torpedoed, fortunately without loss of life, before anyone could identify the 'object', *Oberleutnant-zur-See* Klocke's *S121*, which 'immediately opened fire with her machine gun and then steamed off at full speed'.

Two days after the loss of the *Stanlake,* on 15 April, Midshipman Derek Tolfree met the enemy at last. Whilst on patrol just after midnight, *Westminster* received a signal reporting E-boats in the vicinity:

> Shortly after this high speed HE was heard, fine on the starboard bow. We then opened fire with starshell. [HMS] *Widgeon* was on the patrol to the south of us. Our starshell illuminated two E-boats and we increased to full speed engaging the enemy with the after mounting to starboard. We continued firing for about ten minutes during which time two E-boats were believed to have been destroyed and two damaged. We then had to break of the engagement as we were running into our Z-patrols.[17]

Having driven off this attack, the following night *Westminster* took a Channel Convoy through the Straits, Midshipman Tolfree recording 'no enemy activity'. The battle to secure coastal trade was almost won – *Moldavia* and *Stanlake* turned out to be the only mercantile losses to E-boats during the first half of 1943.

No ships at all were lost to air attack, although the *Luftwaffe* still sprung the occasional surprise, like the high-speed, low-level attacks by fighter-bombers which devastated Lowestoft on 8 May, killing thirty-nine people and wounding sixty-seven.[18] Patrick Mummery of the veteran tanker *San Roberto* experienced one such nuisance raid in the North Sea in July. His account is telling not only for its drama, but for what it reveals about the improved anti-aircraft capabilities of coastal convoys by the summer of 1943:

> Aircraft are swarming over the convoy, roaring in low from the east'ard. We can see some of them silhouetted against the glory of the young moon; and the ships begin to open fire . . . soon the thin red lines of tracer are stabbing upwards from every ship, and above the roar of engines rises the rat-tat-tat of machine-guns and the slower heavier rhythm of the barking Oerlikon cannons . . . a drone from ahead changes to a whine, to a diving howl; and above it a

> short shrill whistle. Everyone on the bridge ducks instinctively and three bombs burst close astern, sending columns of water high into the air. We gaze in silence at the falling masses of water . . . 'Bastards!' says the Old Man gruffly '**** off!' And obediently they do. Ten minutes later the raid is over.[19]

The anti-shipping aircraft of 16 Group RAF had now developed from the embryonic organization proposed by Wing Commander Constable-Roberts two years before into a lethal and highly trained Strike Wing. Their offensive operations, in conjunction with those of Royal Navy destroyers and Coastal Forces, were now greatly stepped up, paralyzing enemy coastal trade and keeping the E-boats penned in their own waters. They emerged only occasionally to carry out the minelaying sorties which characterized their offensive activity during the spring of 1943. Losses remained negligible, even after the E-boats were joined by the *Kriegsmarine*'s remaining destroyers in May and June: the small collier *Dynamo* on 17 April; the *Cormull* on 15 May; and the *Catford*, smashed to pieces on 31 May.[20]

One feature of 1943 was the increasing presence of ocean-going ships in coastal waters. Many were American and many carried military equipment, as the build-up to the Allied invasion of Europe reached a crescendo. On 26 July, Derek Tolfree recorded in his journal that: 'This convoy was quite the largest I have seen on the east coast. There were forty-seven ships, all except five being large ocean going vessels. There were three tankers and several large Liberty ships, both British and American. Many of these vessels had deck cargoes of tanks, armoured cars etc.'[21]

Commodore's Signaller J.W. Booth welcomed the Americans with open arms:

> The answer to every signalman's prayer was a 'Yank' . . . it was not only their open-handed generosity . . . but their great sense of hospitality. They treated us with a consideration rarely seen on British ships . . . Merchant ships generally serve meals earlier than places ashore and convoy conferences followed by embarkation usually meant that the signalmen were afloat too early for lunch ashore and arrived on the ship too late to get any there. This was no problem to the Americans who invariably enquired if you had 'et', and if you hadn't they made sure that you did. The food was unlimited and magnificent.[22]

Patrick Mummery remembered a small knot of Americans attending a convoy conference at Southend, 'listening intently, taking notes and occasionally raising a hand to ask a nasal question,' while around them veteran coaster skippers exhibited signs of profound indifference to what was for them a well-worn routine. Only a stern warning about firing on friendly aircraft aroused any interest, in the form of a 'flood of excited protest.'[23]

The increasing tempo of the Anglo-American bombing offensive against Germany in 1943 meant that most aircraft encountered over coastal waters were friendly. More and more airmen found themselves 'in the drink' after they were forced to give up the struggle to bring their battered aircraft home. Richard Bird saved the lives of one crew whilst escorting a convoy through the Channel with HMS *Hambledon*. He was on watch at the time, keeping a wary eye out for the flashes which heralded incoming shells from the German Channel guns:

> There were no flashes but by God I saw a dinghy! A yellow dinghy in the troughs of the waves . . . I reported this and nobody on board could see it . . . eventually the Captain said, 'Are you sure?' And I said 'I'm positive I can see it, I can't understand why you people can't see it!' And he said, 'Well I'm going to alter course . . . it's up to you. If I didn't think you were a good lookout, Bird, I wouldn't alter course!' And we picked up these airmen – the night before they'd come down on the way home.[24]

On 9 September 1943, after weeks of conspicuous preparations, the Allies mounted an elaborate mock-invasion of the port of Boulogne. Known as Operation 'Starkey', it was intended to test the German defences and, in particular, draw into action and destroy the *Luftwaffe*'s remaining fighter aircraft. No better reflection of the totality of Allied control of the Channel could be imagined than the presence of 255 naval and merchant ships, including ocean-going freighters, all loudly proclaiming their presence by radio. One of those taking part was William Hopper, on the 4,026-ton freighter *Empire Derwent*:

> We sailed out the Solent eastwards up the English Channel. We had MLs as escorts, we had French managed chasseurs . . . [and] a continuous escort of Mustangs and we were to identify these by black and white stripes [on] the underside of the wings . . . we went as far as Dungeness and then headed due south towards the French coast and then during the daylight . . . there appeared to be all sorts of planes going overhead bombing the French coast and we were told to put our balloons up. We headed south . . . well within range of the guns on the French coast and we were all alerted but no sign of the enemy whatsoever. And then, in the evening, at dusk, we were turned back . . . to the Solent where we were told the exercise had been highly successful, the idea had been to get the enemy's planes up in the air and see what his air defence was.[25]

Although perhaps a useful exercise, 'Starkey' failed in its principle objective: the armada was greeted with supreme indifference by the Germans.

By September, *Kommodore* Petersen's forces had been expanded to five E-boat flotillas, the strongest force in British coastal waters for some time, operating out of Ostend, Boulogne, Cherbourg and Ijmuiden, although they numbered in total just twenty-six boats. Against them Coastal Forces could deploy 324 MGBs, MTBs and MLs.[26] Like the British in 1940, the Germans were outnumbered and outgunned. It is therefore perhaps all the more remarkable that they were able to put together any offensive operations at all, let alone the most extensive on record in the North Sea. On the night of 24/25 September four flotillas probed to within a few miles of Harwich, laying mines and ambushing the local trawler patrols. *Oberleutnant-zur-See* Ritter von Georg in *S96* torpedoed and sank the *Franc Tireur,* and the *Donna Nook* collided with another trawler and sank while coming up to assist. Despite the entire action being tracked by coastal Headache stations, the British response was poorly organized, and only sheer luck prevented the Germans escaping unscathed: von Georg's *S96* stumbled into a Z-patrol on the way home, and was rammed and sunk by Lieutenant J.O. Thomas' *ML150*.[27] Commander Phipps of HMS *Montrose* recorded the melancholy tale in his journal:

> E-boats came to our doorstep as I knew they would. It was a perfect night for them and the area between 52 and 3 buoys only guarded by trawlers and [HMS] *Puffin*. In they came, torpedoed and sank two trawlers who happened to be in their way and were obviously fast asleep, and then laid their mines in the Channel.[28]

Phipps's own luck ran out the following month. On 20 October, he was given command of the brand-new Hunt-class *Limbourne*, and almost immediately afterwards he was ordered to take part in an offensive sweep in the Channel, Operation 'Tunnel', on the night of 22/23. The sweeps were regular operations, but this particular one went disastrously wrong. In a chaotic night action, *Limbourne* and the cruiser *Charybdis* were torpedoed and sunk by German destroyers with heavy loss of life. Phipps suffered a fractured skull and had to spend the next year ashore. His new command had lasted just three days.[29]

Operation 'Tunnel' shows how, whilst German naval forces in coastal waters may have been in decline by the end of 1943, they were not yet out. On the night of 24/25 October another strong force of E-boats under *Kapitänleutnant* Werner Lützow attempted to attack FN1160 and FS1264 off Cromer. In 1940 or 1941 it would probably have resulted in a massacre, but the east coast in 1943 was a very different place. Derek Tolfree of HMS *Westminster* recorded the action which followed in his journal:

> Just before midnight on the 24th, *Pytchley*, who was escorting the FN convoy, reported 'engaging E-boats.' We went to action stations at 0030 after receiving further enemy reports. Starshell was seen to seaward and *Worcester*, *Campbell* and *Mackay* reported being in contact with E-boats. Their signals continued for about two hours after which the E-boats were driven off. It appears that the E-boats attacked the FN in the outer channel sinking one trawler. *Worcester* reported sinking one.[30]

In fact, in a lively battle involving sixteen entirely separate actions, two E-boats had been sunk and a third damaged for the loss of just one patrol trawler, the *William Stephen*. One of the casualties was Lützow himself, whose *S88* was rammed by Lieutenant R.H. Marshall's *MGB607* at full speed. Both convoys passed by entirely unscathed.[31]

E-boats enjoyed greater success the following month, when nine boats of Klug's *5. Schnellbooteflottille* hit CW221. The eastern Channel Convoys had not been seriously attacked since 1941, German attention having been focused on the western PW/WP series, so the attack came as an unpleasant surprise. Twenty-two-year-old H.B. Knudsen was 3rd Officer of the Norwegian freighter *Storaa* bound for Cardiff with a cargo of tank parts. At 0010 the escorting warships started to fire 'snowflake' illumination rounds: 'Shortly afterwards I observed several E-boats, about half a mile away, approaching the convoy from the port quarter. "Action Stations" was sounded and we opened fire on the E-boats with the Oerlikon guns.'[32]

After ten minutes the attackers dispersed into the night, only to launch a second, more subtle attack. Approaching the convoy, quietly and unobserved, *S138* torpedoed the *Storaa* at 0035:

> I put on my lifebelt, and hastened forward to the boat deck, but owing to the debris blocking the door of the alleyway I was unable to get out. I then started to run aft and had just reached the door at the other end of the alley-way, when the vessel sank, bow first . . . It seemed as if I went right to the bottom with the ship before I managed to struggle out of the door and float to the surface.[33]

Storaa sank with heavy loss of life; Captain Jens Pedersen and twenty-four of his forty-three crew went down with her.[34] Ten minutes later torpedoes from *S100* found their mark in the collier *Foam Queen*. Built in 1922 and displacing just 811 tons, she stood little chance, as Captain R.E. Holt remembered:

> There was a terrific explosion, with a blue flash: a column of water and debris was thrown high into the air. The after magazine exploded immediately, and about fifty feet of the stern was completely blown off. Everything abaft the funnel completely disintegrated, the engines dropped out of the ship, the boiler being shifted twelve feet forward against the forward bulkhead of the stoke-hold. All the crew amidships were saved, but all those aft were lost.[35]

Captain Holt and his Second Mate carried out an inspection, but it was clear that the situation was hopeless, so the order was given to abandon ship. In the water they retrieved the only survivor from the obliterated after end of the ship, the DEMS gunlayer, who had been blown from the after gun position:

> We pulled him on the raft and found him to be in a very serious condition. Both legs were badly broken, he had lost an eye, and his face was covered with blood . . . We drifted on the raft for some time; it was very uncomfortable, as there was a rough sea, and the injured gunlayer was in great agony. The mate, although injured himself, and sea-sick, did his best to comfort [him], holding him in his arms throughout the whole time.[36]

From the raft the survivors watched the E-boats claim their last victim, the collier *Donna Isabel,* torpedoed by *S146*. The torpedo which hit her passed straight through the engine room without exploding; her Chief Engineer remembered 'a shudder and then something flashed in front of him, followed immediately by two arcs of water pouring into the engine room'.[37] *Donna Isabel* took an hour and twenty minutes to sink and her crew escaped into the boats without loss. Together with the *Foam Queen* survivors, they were rescued by a patrolling ML and landed at Newhaven. The battered remains of the *Foam Queen* were eventually salvaged and towed to Dover.

Back on the east coast, a similarly effective attack was made by 6. *Schnellbooteflottille* on FN1170 on the night of 4/5 November resulting in the damaging of the collier *Firelight* and the Commodore ship *British Progress*, although on their way back the German force was attacked by British aircraft, which sank *S74*.

Despite losing 30 feet of his bow Captain West of the *Firelight*, a veteran of nearly 200 convoys, managed to bring the remains of his ship to the safety of Yarmouth, stubbornly defying the orders of a naval Salvage Officer in the finest traditions of the coaster skippers:

> A Salvage Officer came alongside in a speed boat and told me to stop using the engines. On boarding the vessel he said that a tug was coming to my assistance, and that I was not to use the engines to steam ahead as he was of the opinion that something would carry away if I continued to do so. He said it would be all right to use the engines astern, but after several attempts I had to give it up as the vessel turned in a circle. The Salvage Officer then returned to his launch and while he remained in the vicinity I made a pretence at working my engines astern, but directly he was out of sight I put them ahead and managed to work the vessel clear of the [Haisbrough] Sands.[38]

A trickle of minings brought the year to a close, perhaps the worst among them being the collier *Morar* on 26 November in FN1188, which went down in seconds with the loss of all but four of her crew of twenty-three. One of the few survivors, Second Officer Macfadyen, went down with her and actually felt her hit the bottom before he was able to strike out for the surface. But despite this, as 1944 began it must have been hard not to believe that the war was coming to an end.

The New Year began much as 1943 ended, although by now it was perfectly clear to both sides that the long-awaited invasion of Europe was imminent. Many coastal convoys now contained vulnerable and unwieldy invasion traffic, tempting targets for the Germans if they could get near them. Jack Yeatman was serving on the RNPS trawler *Pearl* at the time, escorting PW and WP convoys from Milford Haven:

> The Coastal [convoys] contained the lot! Liners converted to troopships, 'Liberty Ships', tankers, 'flat-iron' colliers, small coasters, and tiny, usually Dutch, 'scoots' – all with different turning-circles and handling characteristics, especially in heavy weather. And, from 1943 on, 'flights' of basically unseaworthy Landing-Craft, and tugs towing the huge, unwieldy concrete caissons which would form the 'Mulberry Harbour'. Getting such a collection through the three turns necessary to round Land's End in an Atlantic gale, sorted out after having to anchor because of fog, or to reverse course when warned of E-boats off the Lizard or Start Point, could be quite a problem.[39]

But by this stage in the war it was almost impossible for the Germans to get near this great mass of shipping. Each convoy route interlocked seamlessly with the next, protected by strong escorts, total control of the air and excellent intelligence:

> [The coastal convoy network] operated rather like a bus service. A ship bound from Halifax, Nova Scotia, to Hull . . . would be brought into Liverpool by an Atlantic Convoy. Next day, the Irish Sea Coastal [convoy] would take her down to Milford Haven, we would take her on to Cowes Roads in the Wales-Portsmouth, the Channel East would deliver her to the Thames Estuary, and the East Coast take her up through 'E-boat Alley' to the Humber.[40]

Five E-boat flotillas were now operating in the West, mostly in the Channel. They were all led by experienced flotilla commanders and their armament had been strengthened during the winter, but they were outnumbered and without air support: 'The *Luftwaffe* had practically dropped out of the battle in the narrow seas.'[41] They were also under constant pressure in their own waters from Allied air and sea attack, and minelaying.

Nevertheless, with a little luck it was not impossible for them to score the occasional success with such an enormous volume of coastwise traffic in transit. On the night of 5/6 January 5. and 9. *Schnellbooteflottillen* took advantage of bad weather grounding air cover to penetrate the screen of WP457, sinking two freighters and the escorting trawler *Wallasey*. The victims were the tiny 403-ton *Polperro* and the 1,990-ton freighter *Underwood*, carrying a cargo of invasion craft.

The attack followed the familiar pattern: a shower of flares, panicky gunners loosing off rounds, a violent explosion in the night. Things were made worse by *Underwood*'s cargo; quite inexplicably, the invasion craft seem to have been fully fuelled, and immediately caught fire. The crew rushed for the boats and managed to cut one free, launching it as the *Underwood* quite literally sank beneath them. Fourteen of her crew of twenty-three were killed.[42]

On the last day of the month the Germans repeated their success with CW243, sinking the minesweeping trawler *Pine* and the coasters *Emerald* and *Caleb Sprague*, torpedoed at 0200. *Caleb Sprague* sank terrifyingly quickly, taking down all but seven of the thirty-one aboard. Chief Officer A.H. Mackie was one of the lucky ones: 'I was wakened by the explosion, which vibrated in my ears. I jumped off my settee, seized my lifejacket and rushed out on deck to find the ship already sinking beneath me. I was taken down as she sank, which could not have been more than fifteen seconds after the explosion.'[43] Swimming to the surface, he saw the ship broken in two and sinking: 'I swam desperately to clear the suction, which was so strong that I felt as if I was in the centre of a whirlpool.'[44] He survived by climbing on to a piece of timber from the *Caleb Sprague*'s deck cargo. In a touching testament to the changed perceptions of merchant seaman at the end of the war he makes a point of acknowledging the 'splendid treatment and kindness' shown to him and his fellow survivors at Haslar Royal Naval Hospital, an institution which had been known to reject Merchant Navy casualties in the early years.[45]

Perspective is again helpful. Tragic as the losses of *Polperro*, *Underwood, Caleb Sprague* and *Emerald* were, their combined tonnage was far outweighed by that of the German blockade runner *Munsterland* (6,408 tons), which was sunk by the British coastal batteries at Dover on 20 January. In one night the British batteries had done more damage than their German equivalents had in three years of pot-shots at Channel convoys, and proved beyond doubt that coastal waters were under Allied control.

On the east coast, E-boats sank the coaster *Phillip M,* Commodore ship of FS1371, just before midnight on 24 February, but the raiders were immediately driven off and subsequent attacks both here and in the Channel all failed. By the time E-boats managed another mercantile kill, Allied forces were ashore in Normandy. But between now and then a new and entirely unforeseen development would make the coast deadly once again. Battered and bloody, driven from the North Atlantic convoy lanes, but still full of fight, U-boats were back in coastal waters for the first time since 1939.

The first five U-boats which were ordered into coastal waters were sent out in February 1944, as part of an early effort to disrupt Allied invasion preparations. One was lost on the way, but the other four were able to reach their stations. One was *Kapitänleutnant* Gustav Poel's *U413*, stationed off The Lizard: 'I remember that day under the coast of Cornwall in the neighbourhood of Trevose Head. I had already been there with boat 413 for several days, but owing to the changing of convoy routes I had not had the opportunity of making an attack.'[46]

Gustav Poel was a tenacious and experienced commander, a pre-war submariner who had brought *U413* through five North Atlantic patrols. He took up position amongst a group of fishing trawlers, counting on them to conceal his presence, but was sighted and reported. A pair of destroyers arrived from Plymouth and began to hunt, but Poel was not one to back away from a fight, however dubious the circumstances.

One of his opponents, in command of HMS *Warwick*, was Commander Denys Rayner, DSC, RNVR, another experienced veteran of the North Atlantic, but his Asdic was not functioning correctly and he was finding the war on the coast to be very different:

> This was a new sort of war for us. Convoys in line of two columns were passing up and down the war channel, and the sea was littered with fishing vessels of all sizes. As our radar screen was confused with the echoes from the small craft a determined U-boat commander could have done what he liked.[47]

In short, Rayner was having a bad day. Poel carefully noted what happened next in *U413*'s War Diary:

> 1137 Fired spread salvo of two torpedoes from tubes 1 and 3 at the fast escort vessel. Enemy bow right, angle on bow 96.5 [degrees] right. Enemy speed twelve knots. Range 1200 metres. Torpedo depth setting four metres, magnetic pistol engaged. Hit after running time of four minutes fifty seconds, second explosion follows immediately. Destroyer has stopped and taken a list, column of smoke and vapour rising to about 300 metres. I assume a boiler or ammunition explosion. Loud sinking noises heard in boat, several fishing boats run out to the position of the torpedoing, within fifteen minutes there is nothing more to be seen of the destroyer. Five aircraft of various types . . . circle over the spot. Rafts are dropped. The destroyer has gone.[48]

Escorting a nearby convoy was the coastal Hunt-class HMS *Wensleydale*, of the 15th Destroyer Flotilla. Stores Petty Officer Henry Lehmann was standing by the ship's port 0.5-inch machine-gun mounting and watched in horror as a mushroom of smoke erupted alongside *Warwick*, accompanied by a shattering magazine explosion which blew off her stern.

At first *Warwick*'s after part remained afloat and under weigh, but the immense pressure of water forced in her bulkheads and she began to founder.[49] One of those fighting for his life was twenty-year-old Telegraphist K.G.Holmes:

> I was in my mess about 1154 when an explosion shook the ship violently and a cloud of dust fell from the overhead pipes that ran through the mess. My first thoughts were to get to my lifebelt and head for the upper deck . . . on looking up I could see some burning wreckage across the hatch top . . . I proceeded on

> to the upper deck to find oil, some of it burning, on the deck and seemingly spurting up somewhere near the funnel.[50]

Holmes's action station, in the High Frequency Direction Finding (HF/DF) office at the stern of the ship, had vanished, and in any case by now Commander Rayner had given the order to abandon ship. He was helping to try and lower the badly jammed motor boat when *Warwick*'s tortured remains finally gave up the struggle to remain afloat. As she heeled over, Holmes climbed over the rail and jumped into the water, where Radar Operator Jim Gold was also fighting for his life:

> As I landed in the sea by the mast I became entangled in a wire rope and at much the same time someone with no lifebelt grabbed onto me but as I was being pulled under with the ship I managed to push off my fellow traveller, hoping he would find a better insurance risk. I seemed to spend hours under water trying to free myself when suddenly I was aware of brilliant lights all around me and as my head broke the surface I realised it had been shafts of sunlight in the bubbles I was creating. When I looked around I was surrounded by debris, bodies, oil which was ablaze in places, and deciding this was no place for me started swimming my way through. The burning oil was the biggest hazard as when you swam into a clear lane you had no guarantee there was a way out but the bodies were the most upsetting and I remember one in particular which I automatically identified as the buffer [Chief Boatswain's Mate].[51]

The exhausted survivors, many half-blinded by oil, watched with relief as *Wensleydale* began to turn towards them, her crew deploying scrambling nets. But the Hunt could not stop with a U-boat in the area and increased speed to begin a depth-charge attack on *U413*: 'I can still see them in the sea as we steamed through them to make our attack.'[52] For K.G. Holmes it was a terrible blow: 'Just as I thought I was going to be saved, the destroyer sped away from me. To make matters worse, a few minutes later she started dropping depth charges and although I was a good distance away from her as each one exploded it was like being punched in the stomach.'[53]

Swimming away, he was seen by a nearby trawler, hauled unceremoniously on deck, stripped, washed and taken below. The survivors were eventually landed at Padstow and bussed to the Royal Naval Air Station at St Merryn, where 'we were greeted by a PO with a basin full of navy rum . . . It was only after that that I began to feel human again!'[54] Sixty-six men died in HMS *Warwick*. Gustav Poel, watching the hunt for his boat increase in intensity, finally decided discretion was now the better part of valour, retiring discretely at periscope depth. *U413* returned home safely.

The return of the U-boats was greeted with dismay by the Merchant Navy. Deep-water sailors thought they had seen the last of the underwater predators when they had been driven from the Atlantic the previous year, and the coaster men had started to think their war was coming to an end. P.K. Fyrth was serving on the SS *Kimble* at the time: 'It should have been a quiet way to end the war but . . . we were constantly on the alert for attack.'[55]

The U-boat offensive was given added impetus by the gradual introduction of schnorkel breathing apparatus. This gave the submarines greater underwater endurance as they could use their diesel engines whilst submerged, rather than having to rely on the short battery life of their electric motors.

Schnorkel was not a 'magic bullet'. Submerged boats using it had to proceed at a crawl, otherwise the mast would break, and it easily became blocked, causing great discomfort for the crews. Nevertheless it made it far harder to find U-boats, particularly for aircraft. Having fought so hard to provide appropriate levels of air cover for merchant shipping during the painful years of struggle in the Atlantic, Coastal Command found itself almost blind at the critical moment of the European war. The U-boat Command War Diary records how: 'Only a few months ago it seemed impossible that a boat could proceed submerged for forty-two days without once breaking surface. Only through schnorkel has it become possible to operate again close to the English coast, and to bridge the interval until the new type of boat becomes available.'[56]

The 'new types of boat', Type XXI and Type XXIII, were the so-called 'electro-boats', with three times the battery power of the older types. Capable of 17 knots submerged and able to operate underwater for up to three days before recharging, they would have been difficult to deal with, but few entered service before the end of the war. It was the old Type VIIs which bore the brunt of the new campaign.

Facing them were the veteran U-boat killers of the North Atlantic Support Groups, recalled into home waters as part of the invasion preparations. By 1944, their motivation, training and equipment were excellent, and their morale was high. They had defeated the U-boats once, and they could do it again. Reg Harris was an Engine Room Artificer on board the brand-new, American-built frigate HMS *Stayner*, commanded by the experienced and aggressive Lieutenant Commander Harry Hall, DSO, DSC, RNR: 'Every time we got the ping from a submarine, he'd take over from the ASDIC operator and listen himself and make the decision, "yes it's one", "no it's not" and so forth. It was always quite exciting with him because he'd have a go.'[57]

So both sides prepared for the inevitable, while the German light forces continued the war as best they could. Several of the *Kriegsmarine*'s remaining destroyers were destroyed or damaged in air attacks and a series of running battles in the Channel during April and May, and in March and April twelve separate E-boat incursions were beaten off without significant loss.[58] Three E-boats were sunk, all by the legendary Free French destroyer *La Combattante*, one of them, *S141*, carrying a naval doctor along for the ride: *Leutnant-zur-See* Klaus Dönitz, 24-year-old son of the *Großadmiral.*

The enthusiasm of *La Combattante*'s crew sometimes made them a danger to both sides. Twenty-year-old Dennis Watkins served alongside them in the sloop HMS *Retalick*, and described them as 'rogue elephants' who 'used to fire at anything they saw'.[59]

Retalick was a Coastal Forces 'Control Ship', commanded by Lieutenant Commander J.S. Brownrigg RN. By now Coastal Forces was a well-oiled machine, organized into killer groups which crossed the Channel into enemy waters looking for trouble. Frigates or sloops with better radar and communications equipment, like *Retalick*, guided the MTBs and MGBs to where they were needed and provided extra firepower: 'We had many a pitched battle with E-boats and sometimes German destroyers if they were guarding a convoy.'[60]

Often fought at night, between small high-speed craft, these actions resembled aerial dogfights more than naval battles. As a Gunnery Control Rating, Dennis was right in the thick of the action, which was fast and furious and almost impossible to interpret:

> I can remember the appalling choking cordite smoke that used to hang around the ship after you'd been bashing off a few rounds for ten minutes . . . it was pretty well turmoil. When you're in action it's very difficult to tell what's happening, in fact I used to have a great deal of admiration for the way the Captain kept his cool and conned the ship and got us in and out of these attacks we were in.[61]

Like most servicemen, Dennis was able to find humour in his dangerous existence. On his first patrol *Retalick* had a radar contact and set off to intercept, the men on board feeling the adrenaline surge of imminent action as their ship steamed at high speed through the darkness: 'We chased it for ten minutes and fired star shells and found it was a rogue barrage balloon . . . floating about ten feet above the water trailing rope . . . So we all got keyed up and found our target was a barrage balloon. We duly sunk it [and] had a laugh about it afterwards.'[62]

The only E-boat success during the spring of 1944 took place on the night of 27/28 April, when a strong force from 5. and 9. *Schnellbooteflottille* caught a convoy of American tank-landing ships on their way to carry out Exercise 'Tiger', a practice landing at Slapton Sands, in Devon. Two were sunk and another badly damaged, with enormous loss of life. Nineteen-year-old Geoffrey Cassidy of the frigate HMS *Curzon* was on a torpedo course at the time, and was sent to Weymouth to guard the dead as they were brought ashore:

> Ships of the US Navy, LCIs, started to unload dead US soldiers and sailors. They were laid side by side on Weymouth quay. I was told that there was a thousand dead from three LCIs . . . By 9pm that night the US ambulances were

> taking the dead away, six bodies to a van, by 4pm the following morning all had been taken away . . . the people at Weymouth did not know what had happened. It was endless to me . . . it took from 9 o'clock till four in the morning to put them in the vans and take them away.[63]

At the end of his macabre shift an officer came up to Cassidy and instructed him to 'forget what you've seen.' According to British and US official sources, 197 sailors and 441 soldiers had died, more than would be killed at Utah Beach on D-Day.

Notes

1. Batten, John, *Dirty Little Collier*, Hutchinson, London, undated, p. 31.
2. Ibid, p. 85.
3. ADM 199/2144 Survivors' Reports: Merchant Vessels 1 January 1943 to 31 March 1943, p. 52.
4. Foynes, *Battle of the East Coast*, pp. 231–2.
5. Terraine, *A Business in Great Waters*, p. 272.
6. Tolfree, Derek, Midshipman's Journal made available to the author, October 2007.
7. IWM Docs 75/105/1 Phipps, Commander W.J., p. 165.
8. Ibid.
9. ADM 199/2144 Survivors' Reports: Merchant Vessels 1 January 1943 to 31 March 1943, p. 124.
10. As well as being educated at the French Military Academy at St Cyr, and serving in the Merchant Navy, Bradford volunteered for the Bolivian Army during the Chaco War and the International Brigades during the Spanish Civil War. Bizarrely, after the war he became a branch manager for Marks and Spencer. Wilson, Alastair and Callo, Joseph F., *Who's Who in Naval History*, Routledge, London, 2004.
11. IWM Docs 91/51/1, Pelley, Lieutenant John G., RNVR.
12. Ibid.
13. BBC PW A3536462 Rouse, Graham.
14. IWM Sound 12424 Bird, Richard.
15. IWM Docs 75/105/1 Phipps, Commander W.J., p. 190.
16. ADM 199/2145 Survivors' Reports: Merchant Vessels 1 April 1943 to 30 September 1943, p. 35.
17. Tolfree, Derek, Midshipman's Journal made available to the author, October 2007.
18. Foynes, *Battle of the East Coast*, p. 261.
19. Mummery, Patrick. Letter to the author, 20 August 2007.
20. ADM 199/2145 Survivors' Reports: Merchant Vessels 1 April 1943 to 30 September 1943.
21. Tolfree, Derek, Midshipman's Journal made available to the author, October 2007.

22. IWM Docs 91/17/1 Booth, J.W., pp. 22-3.
23. Mummery, Patrick. Letter to the author, 20 August 2007.
24. IWM Sound 12424 Bird, Richard.
25. IWM Sound 10800 Hopper, William. This seems to have been the first time the famous 'D-Day stripes' were used in action.
26. Cooper, *The E-boat Threat*, p. 108.
27. Foynes, *Battle of the East Coast*, pp. 235–6.
28. IWM Docs 75/105/1 Phipps, Commander W.J., p. 192.
29. For a detailed account of the 'Tunnel' disaster see Smith, *Hold the Narrow Sea*, pp. 184–200.
30. Tolfree, Derek, Midshipman's Journal made available to the author, October 2007.
31. See Roskill, *War at Sea*: vol. III Part 1, p. 101, and Foynes, *Battle of the East Coast*, pp. 289–91.
32. ADM 199/2146 Survivors' Reports: Merchant Vessels 1 October to 31 December 1943, p. 27.
33. Ibid.
34. The *Storaa* became the subject of a High Court action in December 2005, when a test case was launched to establish whether the presence of DEMS Gunners and the nature of the cargo was sufficient for the ship to be considered to have been lost 'on military service' and therefore subject to the Protection of Military Remains Act, 1986; in other words, to be designated as a 'war grave'. The wreck had been purchased by a local salvage company and relatives of the deceased were anxious to prevent it being interfered with. Ultimately the Judge supported the wishes of the families.
35. ADM 199/2146 Survivors' Reports: Merchant Vessels 1 October to 31 December 1943, p. 29.
36. Ibid.
37. Ibid., p. 31.
38. Ibid., p. 33.
39. BBC PW A4189098 Yeatman, Jack. The two Mulberry Harbours were built in Britain as prefabricated sections, towed across the Channel and assembled off the invasion beaches of Normandy.
40. Ibid.
41. Roskill, *War at Sea*, vol. III Part 1, p. 283.
42. NA ADM 199/2147 Merchant Navy Survivors' Reports 1 January 1944 to 31 December 1944, p. 5.
43. NA ADM 199/2147 Merchant Navy Survivors' Reports 1 January 1944 to 31 December 1944, p. 30.
44. Ibid.
45. Ibid.
46. Letter from Poel in Docs Misc 182/2736 HMS *Wensleydale*.
47. Rayner, D.A, *Escort*, Futura, London, 1974, p. 171. Rayner went on to an illustrious post-war career as a novelist and boatbuilder. Amongst his work

was *The Enemy Below* (1956), which was later made into a film starring Robert Mitchum.

48. Extracts from War Diary of *U413*, in IWM Docs Misc 182/2736. HMS *Wensleydale*.
49. Letter from Lehmann in IWM Docs Misc 182/2736. HMS *Wensleydale*.
50. Letter from Holmes in IWM Docs Misc 182/2736. HMS *Wensleydale*.
51. BBC PW A8707296 Gold, Jim.
52. Letter from Lehmann in IWM Docs Misc 182/2736. HMS *Wensleydale*.
53. Letter from Holmes in IWM Docs Misc 182/2736. HMS *Wensleydale*.
54. Ibid.
55. IWM Docs 88/42/1 Firth, P.K.
56. Grove, *The Defeat of the Enemy Attack on Shipping*, p. 125.
57. IWM Sound 14875 Harris, Reginald.
58. Smith, *Hold the Narrow Sea*, p. 209.
59. IWM Sound 21575 Watkins, Dennis.
60. Ibid.
61. Ibid.
62. Ibid.
63. IWM Sound 17509 Cassidy, Geoffrey.

Chapter 10
Endgame

6 June 1944 to 8 May 1945

The long-awaited invasion finally came on 6 June 1944, when the Allied navies put ashore around 133,000 men along nearly 40 miles of defended Normandy coastline.[1] The story of Operation 'Overlord' is huge, there are many fine books on the subject and as before, this book will not try to go over such well-trodden ground, or explain the complex grand strategy of the most ambitious amphibious operation ever undertaken. But 'Overlord' changed the dynamic of the war on the coast for one last time, bringing about one final battle for many of the convoy veterans, and it is always their perspective which concerns us.

One of them was an old friend, George Barnes of the *City of Charleroi*. The invasion was in many ways one of the worst-kept secrets of the war, and for George the clues came when *City of Charleroi* went into dry dock:

> The ship was equipped and ballasted and derricks strengthened because we knew what we were going to do, and then when the hatches were battened down, tarpaulins [were] laid on, [and] there was what we call a ridge wire laid across to make a long tent. This was to carry troops, the idea being [that] these forty-eight ships . . . were to support our landing craft in that section. It turned out it was mostly ammunition we were carrying and stores, compo ration boxes for troops. So we were loaded up with that and then we laid in the Thames at Bowaters Paper Mill and we waited.[2]

The one secret which was kept was the most important, the location of the landings, despite the thousands of men and women who must have known it:

> We had charts on board to land in Norway, Spain, France, anywhere, so no-one on board knew anything about where you were going. Your bunkers were kept topped, you had a full head of steam, we laid like that for six days in the Thames awaiting instructions as the convoys went through.[3]

Against the thousands of Allied ships in the invasion fleet, the Germans had only a few destroyers, supported by E-boats. The four small destroyers of 5. *Torpedobootflottille* and twelve E-boats of 5. and 9. *Schnellbootflottillen* sortied on 6 June, but wisely fled after firing torpedoes at maximum range.[4] After years without success, the German batteries at Calais fared better, hitting the 7,219-ton troopship *Sambut*. Her Captain was Mark Willis:

> The first shell burst on striking the port side of the ship . . . it blew a hole in the ship's side . . . Approximately thirty seconds later, a second shell struck the port side a little forward of the bridge, making another large hole above the water line, and completely wrecking the two port lifeboats.[5]

The forward end of the ship was packed with inflammable stores, cases of petrol and diesel, and lorries with full fuel tanks, which caught fire in minutes.[6]

At 1215, 1,200 pounds of gelignite in a lorry exploded. The crew of the troopship realized they were fighting a losing battle to save her, and by 1230 she had been abandoned. Tragically 130 of the embarked soldiers were killed, some apparently due to an understandable reluctance to jump into the sea. The *Sambut* burned until 1900, when she finally sank.

City of Charleroi went across to Normandy soon after the assault waves. Like many of the coaster men, George Barnes was phlegmatic about the experience: 'Well, we were going over ground that we knew well, having been running over it for two or three years with these cargoes of coal.'[7] Arriving off Juno Beach, in the Canadian sector, the coaster's Captain was ordered to use the fastest method of unloading:

> The Beachmaster came up and said that you will run your engines full ahead and at that particular buoy . . . stop your engines and glide up the beach. When we did that we had a terrific bump, and what we'd done, we'd run over the top of a Sherman tank that had been knocked out on the landings and it just sliced the bottom of the ship. However we passed on, got out of the sand and stopped, then everything was opened up, and the 'ducks' [DUKW amphibious trucks] would come alongside.[8]

All along the beaches, in scenes eerily reminiscent of the Dunkirk evacuation four years earlier, the coasters were run up the beaches. Their crews discharged their cargoes, sometimes under shellfire, with the dogged courage which had got them through years of attritional warfare around the coast. Appropriately enough, one of them was the *Summity*, survivor of the CW8 disaster in July 1940.

George Clark went over soon after the invasion with another coaster, the 336-ton Everards collier *Aridity*. After discharging their cargo of petrol cans, George and two comrades persuaded their Captain to let them visit the battlefield, a sobering experience:

> We went into the German trenches. They had been abandoned and you could tell that they had left in a hurry . . . we saw a [dead] soldier who had been placed in a sitting position on the edge of a trench. We did not get too close in case he had been booby-trapped as we could see that he had been shot through the head . . . we decided that we had seen enough.'[9]

Marking the way for the coasters once more were the Trinity House tenders, six of which were tasked with buoying the swept channels across to the invasion beaches. On 15 June, THV *Alert* was mined and sunk carrying out this hazardous work. Mercifully the last Trinity House ship to be sunk during the war went down without loss.[10]

The invasion precipitated a wholesale restructuring of the coastal convoy network. The old Channel CW/CE and PW/WP series were replaced by new routes servicing the invasion area coded ETC/FTC, from Southend, and EBC, from Barry in South Wales. The coasters were joined by ocean-going ships and a bewildering variety of unwieldy invasion craft. For the long-suffering escort commanders, the latter meant yet more recalcitrant charges to whip into line. RNR Lieutenant P.F. Cole was commanding the veteran east coast destroyer *Holderness* at the time. 'I remember taking a large number of LSTs [Landing Ships, Tank] across and in the tide they trailed behind the leaders making a crab-like process across the Channel. In spite of signals the leading LST refused to do anything about their course.'[11]

A pre-war Merchant Navy cadet with Elder and Fyffes, Cole was an experienced veteran who had served in the Arctic and in the Mediterranean, where the destroyer HMS *Jaguar* had been sunk underneath him: 'To be in command at the age of 28 was really quite something.'

Those who manned the remaining *Kriegsmarine* and *Luftwaffe* assets in the West threw themselves at the invasion traffic with desperate courage in one last furious orgy of destruction – mostly their own. Before the invasion, ten schnorkel and seven non-schnorkel U-boats were en route from Norway, where a further twenty-two, known as *Gruppe Mitte*, were on standby. The thirty-seven mostly non-schnorkel boats of *Gruppe Landwirt* were stationed in various French ports: 'In this hour of crisis the role of the U-boats was to be decisive to the outcome of the war and every available boat had to be flung into the battle, regardless of cost.'[12]

This they duly did. Between May and July, Coastal Command aircraft sighted a staggering seventy-five U-boats in northern waters trying to make their way south. They attacked fifty-one and sank seventeen. A further eleven operating from French ports were sunk in the Channel and the Bay of Biscay during June alone. In exchange they claimed just five ships.[13]

John Pelley's HMS *Eglinton* was escorting one victim, the 2,386-ton troop transport *Maid of Orleans*, a former Southern Railways train ferry which was returning from the beaches in ballast when 25-year-old Erich Dobberstein's *U988* struck:

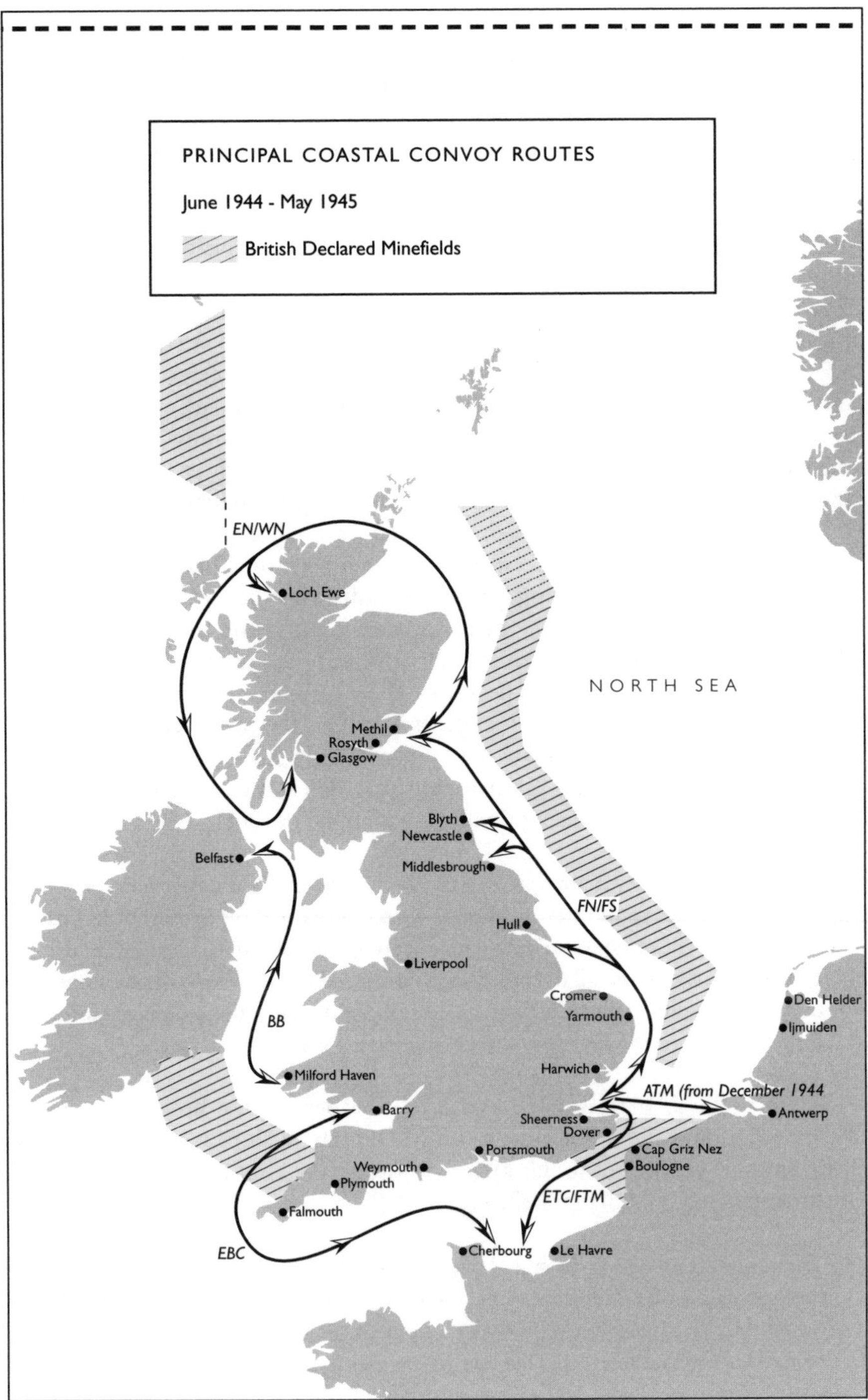
PRINCIPAL COASTAL CONVOY ROUTES
June 1944 - May 1945
British Declared Minefields
NORTH SEA
EN/WN
Loch Ewe
Methil
Rosyth
Glasgow
Blyth
Newcastle
Middlesbrough
Belfast
FN/FS
Hull
Liverpool
Cromer
Yarmouth
Den Helder
Ijmuiden
BB
Harwich
Milford Haven
ATM (from December 1944
Antwerp
Barry
Sheerness
Dover
Portsmouth
Cap Griz Nez
Boulogne
Weymouth
Plymouth
ETC/FTM
Falmouth
EBC
Cherbourg
Le Havre

> [*Maid of Orleans*] suddenly blew up and heeled over and sank. In a choppy sea and almost complete dark we took off ninety-three out of ninety-seven of the crew and clothed them, fed them and so on. What a night . . . her boat drill was magnificent and the conduct of her men very wonderful. Their boats picked up all the numerous seamen who were bobbing about each showing a red light and we never had to lower [our boats] at all.[14]

Dobberstein's experience is illustrative of the precarious operating conditions and desperate inexperience of the U-boat arm by 1944. *U988* was his first command, and this was his first patrol, other than a two-day run from Kiel to Norway. It had taken him more than a month to make his way slowly around the north of Scotland and south through the Western Approaches into the Channel. The previous day he had hit and critically damaged the veteran corvette HMS *Pink* with a 'Gnat' acoustic homing torpedo, and the day after sinking the *Maid of Orleans* he sank the freighter *Empire Portia*. Immediately afterwards *U988* was hunted to destruction by four frigates and a Liberator aircraft. All fifty men on board were killed.

Dobberstein was more succesful than the majority of U-boat commanders, most of whom perished having achieved no kills whatsoever. For the E-boats, it was a similar story. With their customary dash, the much-diminished flotillas continued to emerge from their concrete pens to attack the invasion fleet, but proved too weak to penetrate the overwhelmingly strong protective screen of warships. Both sides must have had the early years in mind as the formerly invincible E-boats made increasingly futile attempts to break through. Aboard an MTB control ship was Peter Wyatt, formerly of the Rosyth sloop *Grimsby* during the dark winter of 1940/41:

> We used to sail every night at 6 o'clock. We had about eight destroyers spread around in an arc round the anchorage, we had usually three groups of MTBs . . . and we went off in our frigate with a lot of beautiful radar . . . and watched Le Havre harbour and all the other harbours roundabout. When we saw something coming out, rather like fighter direction we'd send in the groups of motor torpedo boats or the destroyers to go and have a wag at these forces.[15]

Some of these battles were absolutely desperate, for both sides. John Pelley's *Eglinton* did some time as an MTB control ship, for coastal forces attacking Le Havre, although after witnessing the results of one action he rechristened her a 'mortuary ship':

> The gunboats used to go in and . . . fight some bitter, very close actions . . . On their return, if they did, they came alongside us in the early hours and transferred their dead and dying. How well I remember unstrapping dead gunners from their Oerlikon guns . . . the wardroom was a scene of blood, carnage and swaying plasma bottles and sailors sewing up bodies in hammocks; and then

as it grew light the dead were weighted and slipped over the side to a mournful pipe.[16]

In the end sheer weight of numbers coupled with courage and determination won the day for the Allies. Between 7 and 13 June E-boats sank three tank landing ships, two landing craft, three small coasters totalling just 1,812 tons, and three small warships. In exchange for what one author has called these 'pinpricks', four E-boats were sunk, and ten damaged.[17] Switching their efforts to more vulnerable shipping further out in the Channel, they enjoyed a dramatic success on the night of 10/11 June, sinking three ships in ETC4W off the Isle of Wight. They included the small tanker *Ashanti,* torpedoed at 0315 by *Oberleutnant-zur-See* Kurt Neugebauer's *S179* and vapourized in a dreadful holocaust of fire. Her wend was witnessed by a floating survivor of an earlier victim, Chief Officer Johansen of the coaster *Brackenfield*:

> As she drew abreast of me there was a terrific explosion from her port side, amidships, accompanied by a brilliant flash. The cargo of cased octane caught fire, which rapidly spread throughout the ship. The vessel completely disintegrated and sank immediately, leaving the surrounding water blazing for hours afterwards.[18]

Johansen was 50 yards from the flames and drifting inexorably closer when he was plucked to safety by a patrolling Motor Launch. There were no survivors from *Ashanti.*

The Allies were swift to exact revenge. On 14 June, fourteen E-boats were destroyed and more damaged in a devastating RAF saturation air raid on the pens at Le Havre, where most of the flotillas had concentrated. Three of the *Kriegsmarine*'s remaining small destroyers and thirty-nine other naval craft were also sunk. When the bombers left, only one operational E-boat remained in Le Havre. *Vizeadmiral* Theodore Krancke, the *Kriegsmarine* Commander-in-Chief in the West, rightly called it a catastrophe, and it drastically limited further surface naval operations against the invasion beaches.[19]

In a new twist, the first V1 flying bombs were launched against London on 13 June, and those that fell on the docks added to the risks faced by the shipping which serviced the beachhead. The novelist and playwright A.P. Herbert, now a 54-year-old RNVR Petty Officer in the Thames auxiliary patrol boat *Water Gypsy*, remembered 'the little lights [of V1 exhausts] appearing far off, like fireflies, over the Kentish Hills'.[20] One 'firefly' hit Captain John Edwards's 7,167-ton *Empire Tristram* in Surrey Commercial Docks on 23 June:

> I was in my bunk at the time, but not asleep, as several flying bombs had passed over during the night. I heard this one approaching for about two minutes,

> faintly at first, then gradually developing into a terrific roar. I believe it was flying very low; it exploded in less than ten seconds from the time when the engine cut out. It struck on the port side in the 2nd Engineer's cabin . . . the Chief and 3rd Engineers' cabins were on either side . . . All three Officers were blown to pieces.

Damage to the ship was light 'in comparison with the violence of the explosion' but, in perhaps the worst example of bad luck encountered during the research for this book, the *Empire Tristram* was hit by another V1 on 12 July, with the loss of another nineteen men, including many dockyard workers.[21] Another merchantman, *Fort McPherson*, was sunk by a V1 in Victoria Dock on the 4th, but not all the rockets were so successful, as Peter Wyatt recalled:

> One night while we were sitting out there looking at Havre a whole succession of flying bombs, V1, started to come out from somewhere behind the invasion line flying over us upon their way to Portsmouth . . . the extraordinary thing was that every single one, as soon as they'd passed us, turned 180 degrees and went straight back to where they'd come from. The sailors got intrigued by this, especially since they had families in Portsmouth, and as each of these things came trundling along and did a 180 degree turn and went straight back to the firing point the cheers from the sailors were terrific. All twenty turned, something wrong with their gyro.[22]

Other German attempts to hit back had an unmistakable air of desperation. In July the *Kriegsmarine* deployed its *kleinekampfverbände*, or 'small battle units' against the invasion beaches: human torpedoes, miniature submarines and explosive motor boats. Their successes were few and their casualties were immense. Peter Wyatt encountered *Linsen* explosive motor boats operating out of the little harbour of Honfleur:

> They were small, fast planing little motor boats with a driver who sat on the back end, the front end of the motor boat was all high explosive and they were sort of able to steer themselves. They came out of Honfleur going at high speed, straight to the anchorage, and the idea was the [pilot] . . . ran his ship into the anchorage till he was pointing at a nice big target . . . he'd then lock the steering on to that course and then he himself would fall over backwards into the water and the motor boat would go on and explode on the target. I think there was something like fifty of these things but they were directed up to the anchorage by some . . . controlling ship and in order to do that each of the motor boats had a little light on the back . . . so once they'd passed you they were pretty easy to see and we had some glorious shooting . . . I don't think one actually got through to a live target.[23]

After the *Linsen* came the *Neger* human torpedoes:

> [They] had a little cabin for one chap, with a little Perspex dome, they didn't go very fast, the whole thing went about five or six knots . . . They were soon spotted and our particular method of dealing with one . . . was to lower the motor boat with some sailors with axes and they'd roar off and catch these things and open the Perspex dome with the axe. What we wanted to do was catch one whole . . . We actually did manage to get one back to the ship and we actually got it on to the davit when the bloody little man inside went and let off some explosive charge which disengaged the torpedo from the rest and he was left dangling from the davit and his thing disappeared into the sea . . . They were nasty little men, they were all young eighteen [and] nineteen year old Nazis, spotty, cropped fair hair, thoroughly nasty little men. We didn't like them a bit.[24]

In command of these 'young eighteen and nineteen year old Nazis' was a veteran naval officer, *Kapitänleutnant* Friedrich Böhme, who has left an eloquent account of just how helpless his tiny craft were in the face of such overwhelming Allied superiority:

> Frequently day broke before my one-man submarines had returned and Allied fighters strafed them on the way back . . . of the submarines I sent out I recovered only ten or fifteen per cent. Approximately 200 submarines were lost through Allied strafing attacks. I have seen at one time as many as 50 to 100 fighters circling the bay like hawks.[25]

A more serious threat was posed by yet another new mine, code-named 'Oyster' by the Allies, which responded to changes in water pressure caused by a ship passing overhead at high speed. The Germans were careful to avoid using the new device until enough had been built to sustain an offensive, and more than 5,000 were laid off Normandy, mostly by air.[26] Some losses were inevitable, but an example was soon retrieved and dismantled. Although there was no effective sweep, a table of safe speeds was worked out for every type of vessel, which effectively defeated this new mining offensive.[27]

The 495-ton coaster *Oranmore*, built in 1895, triggered a pressure mine on 17 July while carrying petrol to Juno Beach in ETC39. The explosion threw the little ship sideways but her hull remained sound, her engines were still running and when asked if he required assistance the typically robust response from her Captain, H.H. Henson, was 'No, not yet.'

Oranmore put into Port en Bessin to discharge. After being tied up alongside for two days, Captain Henson was surprised in the middle of the night by his DEMS Corporal Gunner, who reported two stowaways on board: 'I investigated and discovered two men from the East Lancashire Regiment, who said they had boarded from the back of the pier. Apparently there had originally been five deserters but three of them decided to return to their Regiment.'[28] After surviving hard fighting around Tilly and Caen, the unfortunate soldiers had apparently 'decided they had had enough'. It is hard not to sympathize with them, but Captain Henson's duty was clear. The three deserters were taken back to Southampton and handed over to the authorities.[29]

The battle against the U-boats continued throughout July. In one of the most startling patrols of the war, *Kapitänleutnant* Ernst Cordes accidentally took *U763* into Spithead, perhaps the most heavily defended anchorage in the world at the time. Cordes had become understandably disorientated during a thirty-hour attack by escorts attached to convoy ETC26, during which no less than 550 depth charges were dropped around him, but remarkably, he and his crew survived the experience and returned home safely.

Most commanders were not as skillful, or as lucky, as Cordes, a veteran U-boat officer who had commanded his own boat since 1942. In July, three U-boats were sunk in the Channel, and a further six transiting from Norway or across the Bay of Biscay. Geoffrey Cassidy's *Curzon* caught *U212* on the 21st. His matter-of-fact style is typical of the Royal Navy's anti-submarine forces by 1944 – these were men who were used to success: 'It was a night action . . . we just dropped the depth charges and it was reported sunk, we saw the oil and that was it, it was classed as a kill.'[30]

In a rare success, the troopship *Prince Leopold* fell victim to *U621* (*Oberleutnant-zur-See* Hermann Stuckmann), one of the *Landwirt* boats, south-east of the Isle of Wight on 29 July. Twenty-seven-year-old Petty Officer Richard Hughes was the former Belgian ferry's senior gunnery rating:

> At about 7 o'clock in the morning there was an unholy thump, we'd caught a torpedo. It hit us astern . . . so we had to get the troops off so we put them aboard a destroyer and got them so they could go on their way. Fortunately there was only one or two that got a scratch, they weren't badly hurt . . . we were left to try and keep the old wagon afloat. I spent time down below with one of the young ERAs [Engine Room Artificers], he was trying to keep the pump going.[31]

A tug arrived and tried to tow the rapidly filling *Prince Leopold* but after a while it became clear that the pumps were losing their battle. Her commanding officer, Commander F. Bayles, gave the order to abandon ship, and Richard Hughes and his comrades took to the boats without further loss of life.

Two days later the surviving E-boats of *Korvettenkapitän* Felix Zymalkoski's *8.* and *Korvettenkapitän* Jens Matsen's *6. Schnellbootflotillen* attacked FTM53, which mostly consisted of ocean-going freighters. Only one ship was sunk, the 7,219-ton Liberty ship *Samwake*, after a four-hour battle to save her. Captain Owen John described her dignified end: 'At 0540

I saw my ship beginning to tip. She dipped by the head, the stern reared up vertically and held for a few minutes, then very slowly she rolled over to starboard and disappeared at 0545 in a small fountain of water.'[32]

The Liberty ships proved to be more challenging targets for the E-boats, however tempting they may have been. Four others were hit during the attack on FTM53, but none were lost and casualties were few.

At the beginning of August, Allied land forces broke out of the Normandy beachhead, threatening the U-boat bases in the ports along the Bay of Biscay, so the U-boats were ordered to abandon the Channel and make for Norway. This ended the first phase of the coastal U-boat campaign, which was directed against the invasion beaches, and led to what one account has called 'a rich harvest' for antisubmarine forces – fifteen were sunk in coastal waters, in exchange for just six merchant ships.[33]

Increased use of schnorkel meant that the responsibility fell mainly to the warships. On the night of 4/5 August, the destroyer HMS *Wensleydale* and the frigate HMS *Stayner* detected *U671* at 0112 during an asdic sweep south of Brighton. After a twenty-minute depth charge attack survivors and wreckage came to the surface, but years of grim experience had taught the British that this was insufficient evidence to guarantee a kill, and the two ships remained in the area until 0415 trying to 'crack' the U-boat's hull. The three survivors, *Oberleutnant-zur-See* Hans Schaefer, *Bootsmaat* [Petty Officer] Bruno Ehlers and *Maschinenmaat* [Stoker Petty Officer] Ernst Meyer, were lucky men indeed, as their interrogation report revealed:

> After the first of these attacks all lights were extinguished and water began to come into the boat. The second attack lifted the submarine and after it she remained heavy and on the bottom. The third attack apparently turned her on her side but neither of the ratings who were picked up by *Wensleydale* had a very clear recollection of anything except the water rushing into the boat.[34]

The morale of the three men was described as good, but 'neither rating had any enthusiasm for service in submarines and Schaefer, while having faith in the cause for which he was fighting, was pessimistic regarding the outcome of this war.'[35] At last, it seemed, the end was in sight.

For HMS *Wensleydale* the wheel turned full circle on 20 August, when, with the destroyers *Vidette* and *Forester*, she cornered and sank *U413*, the slayer of HMS *Warwick*. Karl Hutterer, the U-boat's Chief Engineer, was her only survivor. Inspecting damage at the forward end of the boat, he managed to get out through the escape hatch as depth charges from *Wensleydale* split her open near the wardroom. Hauled on board *Wensleydale* he was offered brandy and a cigarette, whereupon he was promptly sick over the destroyer's freshly polished quarterdeck.[36]

Pressure mines were still a problem. Another victim was the 5,205-ton freighter *Iddesleigh*, whose Captain, J.P. Herbert, preserved his cargo by beaching his ship on 10 August. Stranded, the *Iddesleigh* was vulnerable, and ultimately gave a *Marder* human torpedo one of the beleaguered *Kleinekampfverbände*'s few successes of the Normandy campaign, on 17 August: 'The torpedo struck with a terrific explosion in Number 2 Hold . . . and it is thought that it struck a rock before hitting the ship . . . many rivets were blown out . . . and many of the plates were corrugated.'[37]

The *Iddesleigh* was not holed but her starboard side was badly smashed. The human torpedoes returned for a second go two days later, this time with more typical consequences:

> At approximately 1900 on the 19th . . . the Chief Officer of the salvage vessel observed something moving in the water on his port quarter, and a moment later I saw a swirl in the water, as if a small underwater craft was passing round our stern . . . I gave orders for the Oerlikon to open fire, also several MLs searched the area and dropped numerous depth charges.[38]

A *Marder* also sank the balloon vessel *Fratton*, veteran of many Channel convoys, during the same attack. In exchange the *Kleinekampfverbände* lost twenty-six human torpedoes.[39]

As the Allied armies cleared or cut off German bases, life became noticeably easier in coastal waters. In August 1944, the *Luftwaffe* carried out its last recorded minelaying sortie into British waters, and in September the E-boats evacuated their French bases, slipping through the Straits of Dover and regrouping in Holland. Oceanic trade resumed through the Straits for the first time since 1940, and the last Coastal Forces action in the Channel was fought on the night of 1/2 October.

Towards the end of the month *Kommodore* Petersen, the *Führer der Schnellbooten*, reported that with total Allied control of the air 'the last possibility of E-boats advancing undetected into the operational area and affecting a surprise attack' was lost.[40] But despite the terrible odds, his men threw themselves back into the fray towards the end of the month, initially focusing on their old east coast hunting grounds. By October a force of twenty boats had been assembled, rising to as many as fifty by December, and as the last winter of the war approached a steady trickle of mostly ineffective operations were mounted. Only one ship was lost to E-boats between August and December 1944, the tanker *Rio Bravo*, in Ostend Roads on 2 November. Losses amongst the E-boats, on the other hand, were high. Geoffrey Cassidy's frigate *Curzon*, along with two other frigates and the veteran V&W *Walpole*, sank *S192* and *S185* in a night action two days before Christmas. Cassidy guarded the prisoners with a stripped Lewis gun as they were brought aboard. One of the first to arrive was the E-boat's Captain, with his ensign wrapped around his waist. Immediately *Curzon*'s officers began a rather unseemly squabble for this attractive souvenir, until 'the Captain saw it and shouted "it's mine" and the officer handed it over.'[41]

The plight of the German survivors touched Cassidy:

> One or two were crying, I think it was just the shock of being in the water. I treated them all right. I think someone asked me for a cigarette and I gave him one. I thought well it could be us couldn't it? We got them all down and we gave them something hot to drink . . . For all survivors we had a store of clothing . . . the size of a sandbag, and in there was a pair of grey flannels, socks and slippers, a jersey, underwear and toothpaste and toothbrush, so I gave each German one each.[42]

On 28 November, the great Belgian port of Antwerp had finally been cleared, and new convoys, coded ATM, began from the Thames Estuary in early December. Appropriately the approaches were pronounced clear by the sweepers of the Royal Naval Patrol Service, who according to Jack Yeatman 'came back down the river with the Commodore flying the signal "Channel now safe for straight-ringers" i.e. regular Navy Officers'.[43]

Antwerp was vital – on one typical day, 3 January 1945, more than half of all stores landed on the Continent passed through it.[44] It was the target for Adolf Hitler's grandiose Ardennes offensive and showers of V1s were fired at it. Even the *Luftwaffe* made efforts to interrupt trade. The tanker *San Roberto* carried aviation spirit on the Antwerp route and at 0930 in the morning on 1 January was anchored 25 miles downriver from the port. When Captain Allison heard gunfire, he assumed that the guns were engaging flying bombs, until he saw four Messerschmitt 109s and a Focke-Wulf 190 making straight for his ship. Despite his volatile cargo Allison showed no hesitation in taking on the enemy:

> The third plane came on, the starboard Oerlikons kept up their barrage and forced him to sheer away round the stern. He was flying at least 350 mph and was not an easy target, but the shooting of the gunners . . . was superb. Our 20mm shells were bursting all around him, as he passed about 1000 yards astern, and at least three shells scored direct hits in the way of his engine causing smoke to pour out of him. The pilot managed to get his aircraft into a steep climb before bailing out at the lowest possible height, about 500 feet. The pilot's parachute opened all right and I saw him land on the shore; the plane continued for about a mile then crashed on land and threw up a tremendous column of smoke.[45]

The new routes were a magnet for E-boats, still operating out of bases in occupied western Holland. They were supported by new and supposedly more effective miniature submarines, the larger *Biber* and *Seehund* varieties. Veteran convoy signaller J.W. Booth encountered one during a run back from Antwerp in early 1945. The first he knew of the presence of the enemy was an explosion which ripped apart a Liberty ship in the same convoy: 'by the time the column of water and debris had subsided she had broken in two at her after mast and the stern sank at once.'[46]

Every ship in the convoy started firing at a wreck, near which a periscope had been sighted, 'until the destroyer escort came pelting down the line flying the "Cease Fire" on one halliard and a black pennant [I am attacking an underwater object] on the other'.[47]

> The destroyer made a tight turn around the wreck and dropped a pattern of depth charges. Water, sand, and pieces of wreckage were hurled high in the air and it was incredible that anyone could have survived, but the midget was actually forced up and the intrepid one man crew picked up unhurt. We later saw him walking on the escort's deck apparently on the best of terms with her officers.[48]

Full-size U-boats also operated right to the bitter end, having reorganized themselves in Norway. This second phase of the campaign struck all around the coast, some submarines making the long, dangerous trip around the north of Scotland to attack targets in the Channel. On 18 December, the freighter *Silverlaurel* was torpedoed by *Oberleutnant-zur-See* Gerhard Meyer's *U486* not far from Falmouth. The damage was not serious and although Captain Duncan and his crew abandoned ship according to protocol, they were considering reboarding when a second torpedo ripped the *Silverlaurel*'s hull apart:

> There was a bright red flash, and a column of oil, debris and smoke was thrown up to about masthead height . . . flames and smoke shot up though the funnel, engine room skylights and ventilators . . . the ship heeled ten degrees to port, righted herself, then settled rapidly forward. As she sank by the bow she slowly turned over to port until the bottom was uppermost. The stern reared up, she hung upright for about ten minutes, then turned completely over and sank at 1745.[49]

Despite being repeatedly depth-charged the determined Meyer had kept his boat in the area to give the *coup de grace*. He went on to sink the packed US troop transport *Leopoldville* on Christmas Eve, with the loss of 763 US soldiers, and the Royal Navy frigates *Affleck* and *Capel* on 26 December, before escaping back to Norway. It was Meyer's first operational patrol. On his second, *U486* was sunk in the North Sea on 12 April 1945 by the British submarine HMS *Tapir*.

Success like Meyer's was unusual. A more typical experience was that of Hans Baum in *U1058*, in February 1945. *U1058* took a month to painstakingly circle around north of Scotland and west of Ireland, penetrating British defences north of Orkney and in the Bristol Channel, before operating in the Irish Sea for four weeks without success. The Irish Sea was used by the British as an antisubmarine warfare training area, and three boats had already been sunk there in January, in exchange for six merchant ships sunk. Baum's last two days 'were spent on the sea bed because three English destroyers found us and attacked us with depth charges for fifty hours'.[50]

> We had to lie horizontally in our bunks to conserve oxygen, food was brought to us . . . one depth-charge ripped the fastening mechanism of the big cannon and every time the current moved us from left to right the cannon went round and banged against the railing . . . It was a very frightening experience, our commander, his name was Bruder, he always came to us and said 'my name is Bruder and I am like your *bruder* [brother] . . . I'll get you home again.'[51]

The inspirational and confident *Oberleutnant-zur-See* Hermann Bruder was just twenty-three years old, and this was his first war patrol.[52] Eventually he was forced to admit defeat:

> After fifty hours we prepared for surfacing because we had reached the end of our oxygen supply . . . whilst we were doing the preparation the [hydrophone] operator who kept a constant watch on the British destroyers reported that the destroyers were departing. The captain listened to the noise of the destroyers, they were getting further away . . . and he realised that the destroyers were probably thinking that we couldn't possibly be alive after fifty hours.

In fact the naïve British destroyers had interpreted oil spilling from a ruptured diesel tank as a kill, and had left the area:

> Everything on deck was destroyed through the depth charging bombardment. Our diesel engine . . . had been rendered unserviceable, one electrical engine had burned out but we managed to make six knots and got out of the Irish Sea into the Atlantic . . . We crawled back to Norway at about six knots and we were reported missing already . . . we got home about four weeks late.[53]

In total nine merchant ships were sunk in home waters in February 1945, in exchange for five U-boats sunk. Three more were sunk off Shetland while making their way to their patrol areas, an exchange rate which the *Kriegsmarine* simply could not afford.

It is tempting for historians to ignore the operations of the last four months of the war, concentrating instead on bigger issues like the discovery of the concentration camps or great powers jockeying for post-war advantage. But for coastal shipping there was no anticlimax. The battle for coastal trade ended as it had begun: in fire and destruction.

The E-boats, in particular, came out more often and fought harder than they had at any other point in the war, hurling themselves at the east coast and

Antwerp convoys with magnificent, albeit misguided, skill and determination. Between 20 February and the end of the month operations were mounted every night, including a successful attack on FS1734 on the night of 21/22, in which two ships were sunk. Appropriately enough, one of the escorting destroyers, HMS *Valorous*, was commanded by J.A.J. Dennis, formerly First Lieutenant of the Harwich destroyer *Griffin* in the winter of 1939/40:

> We were between Immingham and Sheerness, going south. The Senior Officer, in *Verdun*, was ahead and I was bringing up the rear and trying to keep the stragglers in the swept channel. It was very dark and rather blowy and cold. A little after 0100 there were several heavy explosions somewhere up ahead in the convoy. After a while it became clear that at least two ships were sinking and it was important to know the cause – mine or torpedo. I closed one of the stricken ships and they reported that they had been hit by a torpedo from one of a number of E-boats which were still around.[54]

Approaching one of the sinking ships, the 2,780-ton coaster *Goodwood*, Dennis dropped rafts before increasing speed to catch up with the convoy:

> We arrived just in time. There were several E-boats milling around, ready to fire again . . . [There was] a lot of tracer fire from both sides and then quite a shattering explosion in our boiler room which at first I could only imagine was a torpedo; light guns couldn't have done it. On these occasions there nearly always seemed to be an ear-splitting escape of steam, which certainly happened now and didn't help one to think clearly. We were stopped in the water, a nice target for our own erstwhile targets. But after a few minutes of all kinds of gunnery, they shoved off and were no more seen . . . we suffered one man killed and two seriously wounded . . . On investigation we found that we had been struck by a 5-inch shell, which had come from one of the big merchant ships in the convoy, which must have mistaken us for the enemy in the melee.[55]

Other familiar faces returned to the coast for the endgame, including Commander W.J. Phipps, recovered from his injuries and now in command of the destroyer HMS *Mackay*. His journal for 1945 is just as busy as it had been in 1940. Already on 15 January he had been involved in a brush with E-boats off Dunkirk, which had torpedoed an LST, and on 22 February he had taken part in a fruitless seven-hour sweep for a U-boat which had torpedoed another one off the east coast. On the night of 28 February he fought a running battle with E-boats attacking an FS convoy. The battle began at 2351, and it is clear that Phipps had lost none of his combative spirit:

> Enemy were sighted in the moonlight at 2500 yards and I closed on them on a steady bearing until at 1700 yards they were two miles from the channel. I could not afford to wait any longer, I thought, and I opened fire. Shooting was

really very wild and the rate of fire of the 6-pounder was exploited to detriment of accurate shooting. It was Thompson's first experience in close action and I suppose excusable but very annoying as it was a perfect example of good positioning and handed to us on a soup plate. The result that though we hit them once or twice they were not hit vitally and they turned and ran for it under dense smoke as usual and the opportunity was lost.[56]

Mackay engaged a second group at 0015 and a third at 0200, all inconclusive and 'bloody maddening'.

March was no less busy, with as many as fifty U-boats operating in British coastal waters.[57] Nine were sunk. In exchange just nine merchant ships were lost – *worldwide* – in convoy. Perhaps the strangest fate to befall any coaster took place on the night of 7/8 March, when German soldiers from the isolated garrison in the Channel Islands raided the Allied supply depot at the French port of Granville, damaging several ships and abducting the veteran Channel collier *Eskwood*. The war did not in any sense 'wind down' on the coast, as Phipps's journal illustrates:

10 March . . . Got back to patrol at 0040 and almost at once got news from Ekins to the eastward of another group coming down from the north-eastward sliding around her patrol and then heading for the usual danger spot . . . I picked him up at five miles coming along the channel obviously minelaying. Cracked on to twenty-seven [knots] to engage as soon as possible and after being on the channel for three minutes at thirty knots he turned north again . . . with me in hot pursuit. The range was 3,100 yards and him in full cry as I opened fire blind and star shell hoped for some lucky hits again. By the time illumination had taken effect he had put up a dense smoke screen and I never saw him.[58]

The following night the *Kriegsmarine* threw all its remaining assets at shipping in the Scheldt. Not one ship was sunk, and in 'a lively night' the defences accounted for thirty-eight *Kleinekampfverbände* craft of various types.[59] The 'small battle units', however heroic, were a costly disaster. In 415 sorties of all types during 1945, they accounted for only fifteen ships totalling just 17,792 tons, in exchange for 159 craft lost.[60]

On the night of 18/19 March, E-boats attacked FS1759, and claimed their last victims, the coasters *Crichtoun* and *Rogate*. Three nights later Phipps was in action yet again:

I saw them streaking for the channel at 3,500 yards and taking not the least notice of me. Held on until 1,200 yards when I opened fire . . . on the leading ship with 6-pounder, Pom Pom and Oerlikon. To my astonishment the leading ship turned directly across my bow while the others streaked off for home to the northeastward . . . I thought 'here he is coming across my bow and will drop a [depth] charge under it.' Closing at about fifty-five knots I had less than

> half a minute to do anything. I put the wheel hard a port in the hopes that I might hit him instead and also made the speed across less for the guns. 6-pounder hit him six times they said, Oerlikon fired a belt into him, Pom Pom fired sixteen rounds before he ran out of their sight, the Gunner's Mate fired a magazine of Bren into him and I bloody nearly threw my cap at him. Although peppered to hell he got away with it though I saw his smoke toy on fire as he shot across my bow.[61]

Mines were laid by the Germans in large numbers right up to the end of the war, particularly in the approaches to Antwerp. Doubtless being mined was still an unpleasant experience for those who had to endure it, whether the war was won or not, but only eleven ships were sunk, out of the hundreds moving in and out of the port.

April saw six more U-boats sunk in coastal waters, as well as the first patrols of the new Type XXI and XXIII types, far too late to make any significant difference to the outcome of the war. Only thirteen merchant ships were lost worldwide, several in coastal waters, including the *Gasray*, which had her stern blown off by *U2321* on the 5th, and the French troopship *Cuba*, torpedoed by Ernst Cordes of Spithead fame the following night. Cordes was now in command of a new boat with an untried crew, *U1195*, which was sunk soon afterwards by the destroyer HMS *Watchman* with the loss of all on board.

Robert Atkinson, commander of the new corvette HMS *Tintagel Castle*, was typical of the opposition faced by these often young and inexperienced U-boat crews. A Royal Naval Reserve officer with six years of pre-war experience afloat, he had earned his command after years of hard fighting in the Atlantic. On 10 April, he cornered *U878* (*Kapitänleutnant* Johannes Rodig) and despatched her in a display of ruthless efficiency which could stand alone as a testimony to why the Allies, and the Royal Navy in particular, ultimately defeated the U-boats:

> A periscope and a schnorkel were sighted about twelve miles astern of the convoy . . . *Vanquisher* [the SOE] opened fire and put him down, and he ordered me to go and search and he returned to the convoy. Now luckily as it happens we soon obtained a contact, the equipment was very good and we had very experienced officers and crew. The submarine had made the mistake of going very deep and remaining almost stationary, about 500 feet deep, which was quite deep for a submarine, the pressures on his hull are simply enormous. We had this latest Squid [antisubmarine mortar] equipment and we obtained contact very quickly. Calm sea, stationary U-boat, the latest Squid, the latest echo-sounder and radar. I was almost sorry for the U-boat.[62]

Atkinson's pity was soon forgotten as Rodig skillfully manoeuvred his boat, turning away at the last moment and presenting his churned up propeller wash to confuse *Tintagel Castle*'s asdic:

> We hunted that boat all night from about half past five at night till five in the morning, seeking, waiting, being cruel. Once or twice I held back from an attack, that would unnerve him, he'd wonder what was happening. We would try to attack at what we thought would be the change of watch time, so we gave him no peace. I think we had had about six to ten attacks during the night with depth charges. Finally we got him, there was a huge underwater explosion which shook the *Tintagel Castle* and put all our lights out. HMS *Inman* heard the explosion and felt it five miles away. [63]

The following week *U1274* under *Oberleutnant-zur-See* Hans-Hermann Fitting scored one of the last U-boat successes of the war, when he torpedoed and sank the tanker *Athelduke*, bound for Hull in FS1784. The tanker caught fire and started to settle by the stern. Abandoned immediately, only the Chief Engineer, W. Mackenzie, lost his life out of her crew of forty-seven. Casualties would have been worse had it not been for the actions of 3rd Engineer Speed:

> [Thomas Wilson, the Mess Room Boy] had been trapped in his room below decks aft by the inrushing water and had attempted to escape via the porthole. Unfortunately he had become jammed in the porthole and Mr Speed . . . heard the boy's cries. He immediately leant over the side whilst sitting . . . on the poop deck and, getting his feet on the boy's chest, took hold of his arms and hauled him out of the porthole and back on deck, undoubtedly saving his life.[64]

Athelduke was immediately avenged by the V&W *Viceroy* (Lieutenant John Manners, RN), which ran over *U1274*'s presumed location and dropped a pattern of depth charges, before returning to Rosyth. However, without evidence, a 'kill' could not be presumed, and *Viceroy* was sent back to look again. Frederick White takes up the story:

> We went over the charted spot and we dropped more depth charges and the next thing, up came a sailor's hat, toilet paper, one or two oddments and a huge canister broke the surface . . . this was hoisted on board and we opened it up and it had four dozen bottles of German brandy inside, all intact. We sent two bottles to Winston Churchill and two bottles to the First Sea Lord.[65]

Churchill wrote back, thanking *Viceroy* for the brandy, and offering his congratulations to all concerned.[66]

Still the enemy kept coming. April saw engagements between E-boats and Coastal Forces in the North Sea reach 'a peak of intensity', with actions on the nights of 6/7, 7/8 and 12/13. [67] But by the end of the month only fifteen E-boats were fit for sea, and these were critically short of fuel. This most determined of enemies had finally been defeated.

On 3 May, Phipps recorded the collapse of the Nazi régime: 'Death of

Hitler and Goebbels and Dönitz taken in Führer and all kinds of signs of general crack-up and end of the war which really must come now any time. This was our last convoy and the end of the war came six days later.'[68]

Despite this the U-boats continued to set off on patrol, although by now their crews knew that the end was only days away. Hans Baum's Commanding Officer, *Oberleutnant* Bruder, later related Dönitz's words as he personally sent another group of his 'boys' out to fight a war which was all but over: '"I know the war is practically finished but I've got my duty to send you out again . . . I've still got my duty to the Führer" . . . but he said . . . "Bring your boys home again . . . never mind whether you sink shipping or not, bring your boys home."'[69]

U1058 sailed on 28 April. A week later instructions were sent to all U-boats to cease hostilities and prepare to surrender.

Not everyone received them. On 7 May, the Type XXIII 'electro-boat' *U2336,* under the command of *Kapitänleutnant* Emil Klusmeier, manoeuvred into position in the Firth of Forth. His target was EN591 and he sank two ships, the *Avondale Park* and the little Norwegian coaster *Sneland 1.* Thus the last merchant ships lost to enemy action during the Second World War were in coastal convoys.

The following day, Germany surrendered unconditionally, and the U-boats began to turn themselves in. Hans Baum's *U1058* was one of them:

> We celebrated the end of the war . . . we had a few bottles of spirits and eventually surfaced . . . and reported our position to the British Navy who sent a Catalina flying boat out which circled us . . . We destroyed all secret log books and decoding machines, destroyed the cannons, disarmed the torpedoes and four hours later a destroyer came and boarded our boat and escorted us into Loch Eribor.[70]

On 13 May, the last of the E-boats crossed the North Sea, under a white flag, to surrender at Felixstowe. Coastal shipping had survived its great trial.

Notes

1. Dear, I.C.B. and Foot, M.R.D., *The Oxford Companion to World War II*, pp. 666–7.
2. IWM Sound 11111 Barnes, George.
3. Ibid.
4. Tarrant, V.E, *The Last Year of the Kriegsmarine*, Arms and Armour Press, London, 1944, pp. 56–9.
5. ADM 199/2147 Survivors' Reports: Merchant Vessels 1 January 1944 to 31 December 1944, p. 126.
6. Ibid.
7. IWM Sound 11111 Barnes, George.
8. Ibid.

9. BBC PW A5675538 Clark, George.
10. Woodman, *Keepers of the Sea*, p. 151.
11. IWM Docs 98/1/1 Cole, Commander P.F., p. 21.
12. Hessler, *Fregattenkapitän* Günter, *The U-boat War in the Atlantic 1939–1945*, HMSO, London, 1989, p. 67. Hessler was a staff officer, former U-boat commander, and Dönitz' son-in-law. He was commissioned to write an official account of the U-boats from the German perspective after the war.
13. Grove, *The Defeat of the Enemy Attack on Shipping*, pp. 125–6.
14. IWM Docs 91/15/1 Pelley, Lieutenant John G., RNVR.
15. IWM Sound 12818 Wyatt, Peter.
16. IWM Docs 91/15/1 Pelley, Lieutenant John G., RNVR.
17. Tarrant, *The Last Year of the Kriegsmarine*, p. 67.
18. ADM 199/2147 Survivors' Reports: Merchant Vessels 1 January 1944 to 31 December 1944, p. 137.
19. Tarrant, *The Last Year of the Kriegsmarine*, pp. 69–70.
20. Foynes, *Battle of the East Coast*, p. 267.
21. ADM 199/2147 Survivors' Reports: Merchant Vessels 1 January 1944 to 31 December 1944, p. 156.
22. IWM Sound 12818 Wyatt, Peter.
23. Ibid.
24. Ibid.
25. Lucas, James, *Kommando: German Special Forces of World War Two*, Grafton, London, 1986, p. 218.
26. Grove, *The Defeat of the Enemy Attack on Shipping*, p. 201.
27. Ibid.
28. ADM 199/2147 Survivors' Reports: Merchant Vessels 1 January 1944 to 31 December 1944, p. 197.
29. Ibid.
30. IWM Sound 17509 Cassidy, Geoffrey.
31. IWM Sound 25525 Hughes, Richard.
32. ADM 199/2147 Survivors' Reports: Merchant Vessels 1 January 1944 to 31 December 1944, p. 219.
33. Grove, *The Defeat of the Enemy Attack on Shipping*, p. 126.
34. NA ADM 199/1462 Sinking of *U671*.
35. Ibid.
36. IWM Docs Misc 182/2736. HMS *Wensleydale*.
37. ADM 199/2147 Survivors' Reports: Merchant Vessels 1 January 1944 to 31 December 1944, p. 252.
38. Ibid.
39. Tarrant, *The Last Year of the Kriegsmarine*, p. 99.
40. Grove, *The Defeat of the Enemy Attack on Shipping*, p. 202.
41. IWM Sound 17509 Cassidy, Geoffrey.
42. Ibid.

43. BBC PW A4189098 Yeatman, Jack.
44. Roskill, *War at Sea*, vol. III Part 2, p. 265.
45. ADM 199/2148 Survivors' Reports: Merchant Vessels 1 January 1945 to 8 May 1945, p. 1.
46. IWM Docs 91/17/1 Booth, J.W., p. 27.
47. Ibid.
48. Ibid.
49. ADM 199/2147 Survivors' Reports: Merchant Vessels 1 January 1944 to 31 December 1944, p. 296.
50. IWM Sound 20364 Baum, Hans.
51. Ibid.
52. www.uboat.net
53. IWM Sound 20364 Baum, Hans.
54. IWM Docs 95/5/1 Dennis, Commander J.A.J., DSC, RN, p. 279.
55. Ibid.
56. IWM Docs 75/105/1, Phipps, Commander W.J., p. 223.
57. Grove, *The Defeat of the Enemy Attack on Shipping*, p. 130.
58. IWM Docs 75/105/1, Phipps, Commander W.J., p. 225.
59. Roskill, *War at Sea*, vol. III Part 2, p. 273.
60. Tarrant, *The Last Year of the Kriegsmarine*, p. 224.
61. IWM Docs 75/105/1, Phipps, Commander W.J., p. 236.
62. IWM Sound 25182 Atkinson, Robert.
63. Ibid.
64. ADM 199/2147 Survivors' Reports: Merchant Vessels 1 January 1944 to 31 December 1944, p. 38.
65. IWM Sound 13240 White, William.
66. Letter from Churchill reproduced at www.uboat.net
67. Cooper, *The E-boat Threat*, p. 124.
68. IWM Docs 75/105/1, Phipps, Commander W.J., p. 248.
69. IWM Sound 20364 Baum, Hans.
70. Ibid. Hans Baum was a prisoner of war until 1948. He remained in Britain, becoming a British citizen in 1953.

Conclusion

Life returned to normal on the coast fairly quickly and a grateful nation soon forgot. According to one coaster man, P.K. Fyrth, war bonuses were cut just a month after the cessation of hostilities, putting salaries back to 1939 levels.[1] Danger money ended, although the coast could still be a dangerous place, not least because of the thousands of mines which still littered it. Peter Charman was on board the coaster *Dorien Rose* when she set off an acoustic mine well after the end of the war: 'the sea on the starboard side simply erupted . . . there was no damage or problem, except the worry that there may have been more about.'[2]

Like the Battle of the Atlantic, albeit far less recognized, the battle to secure Britain's coasts began on 3 September 1939. Although it would be fair to say that, like the Atlantic, it had largely been won by 1943, it was by no means over, and ships continued to be attacked and sunk until the very last days of the European war.

Altogether, 1,431 merchant ships were lost in coastal waters during the Second World War, totalling 3,768,599 tons,[3] while 5,182 convoys had ploughed the principle FN/FS, CW/CE and PW/WP routes, a total of 130,435 individual voyages.[4] The contribution made by these ships, and the men who crewed them, to the war effort is hard to quantify but inarguably important.

At first it was all about coal, and this story still belongs to the scruffy little colliers first and foremost, ploughing their way down the coast bringing London its 40,000 tons a week. It is worth repeating one last time that the railways and roads simply could not have carried this volume of material without sacrificing other loads, to the detriment of the war effort.

But later the coast became a vital artery for other goods as well: military equipment, transferred into coasters in the secluded privacy of 'Emergency Ports' on the west coast of Scotland; ocean-going ships bound for the east coast ports, whose capacity was too important to be simply 'written off' for the duration. Later, the traffic which made the liberation of Europe possible passed along the coast: landing craft, troopships and sections of Mulberry Harbour. And finally, the experienced Merchant Navy and Royal Navy veterans of the coastal convoys helped sustain that great army once it had landed, first through the Normandy beaches and later through the continental ports.

If coastal shipping had not been maintained, the war would have been infinitely harder to win, and it could be argued that Britain might not have survived in the early years. The coasters were vital, and they had to get through.

And get through they did. Coastal shipping was a success story. Battered from the sea and air, the coaster men had their crisis convoys, just like other theatres: the *Luftwaffe* assaults on OA178 and CW8 in the Channel in July 1940, or the great battle for FS429 and FN426 in 'E-Boat Alley' on the night of 7/8 March 1941. The campaign was long and hard, and losses to enemy action and weather were at times severe, especially during the first three years. But none of this can overshadow the fact that millions of tons of shipping passed successfully around the British coast between 3 September 1939 and 8 May 1945, a fine memorial to the bravery of those who worked the coast and the skill and courage of those who defended them.

Let us, therefore, leave the last word to one of those men, Telegraphist Jack Yeatman of the Royal Naval Patrol Service trawler *Pearl*:

> These Coastal Convoys have 'slipped through the net' of History, . . . yet they were absolutely vital to the survival of the nation and, later, to the invasion of Europe. For just one thing, the London River Power-Stations . . . were all fuelled by Welsh coal, which had to be brought round daily, without interruption . . . and the Mulberry Harbour and the great flocks of Landing-Craft for D-Day didn't just spring up in the Solent – WE brought them there![5]

Notes

1. IWM Docs 88/42/1 Fyrth, P.K.
2. Charman, Peter, letter to the author 15 February 2008.
3. Roskill, *War at Sea*, vol. III Part 2, tables.
4. Hague, *The Allied Convoy System 1939–1945*, tables.
5. BBC PW A4189098 Yeatman, Jack.

Appendix I
Tables

British and Allied Merchant Ship Losses by Theatre
(after Roskill, *War at Sea*, 1954)

Month	United Kingdom Coastal Waters Tonnage (ships)	North Atlantic Tonnage (ships)
1939	455,953 (165)	249,195 (47)
1940	1,793,748 (650)	1,805,494 (349)
1941	740,293 (350)	2,421,700 (496)
1942	214,885 (91)	5,471,222 (1,006)
1943	52,484 (25)	1,654,379 (284)
1944	277,905 (77)	175,013 (31)
1945	233,331 (73)	122,729 (19)
Total	**3,768,599 (1,431)**	**11,899,732 (2,232)**

Principal Coastal Convoy Statistics
(after Hague, *Allied Convoy System*, 2003)

FN/FS Convoys

Year	Convoys	Total Ships	Losses in Convoy	Straggler Losses	Losses out of Convoy
1939	107	2,224	7		
1940	613	19,369	46	3	4
1941	505	18,333	72	6	10
1942	613	21,552	38	1	1
1943	636	19,502	7		
1944	722	18,356	1		
1945	388	5,456	7		
Total	**3,584**	**104,792**	**178**	**10**	**15**

CW/CE Convoys

Year	Convoys	Total Ships	Losses in Convoy	Straggler Losses	Losses out of Convoy
1940	33	550	13	3	3
1941	84	1,276	5		1
1942	159	2,559	1		
1943	179	2,208	3		
1944	76	1,504	2		
Total	**531**	**9,097**	**24**	**4**	**3**

WP/PW Convoys

Year	Convoys	Total Ships	Losses in Convoy	Straggler Losses	Losses out of Convoy
1941	176	2,833	1		
1942	357	6,137	12		2
1943	372	5,406	2		
1944	162	2,170	3		
Total	**1,067**	**16,546**	**18**		**2**

BTC/TBC Convoys

Year	Convoys	Total Ships	Losses in Convoy	Straggler Losses	Losses out of Convoy
1944	37	864	2		
1945	290	5,738	11		
Total	**327**	**6,602**	**13**		

***Kleinkampfverbände* and *Schnellboot* Operations January-May 1945** (after Tarrant, *The Last Year of the Kriegsmarine*, 1994)

Type	Sorties	Losses	Ships Sunk/Mined
Seehunde	142	35	8
Biber and *Molch*	102	70	7
Linsen	171	54	-
Schnellboot	351	10	31
Totals	**766**	**169**	**46**

Appendix II

Convoy Prefixes used in Coastal Waters

(After Hague, Allied Convoy System, 2003)

ATM	Antwerp to Thames, a late 1944 and 1945 series
BB	Belfast to Bristol Channel, 1940 to 1943
BE	Clyde to Bristol Channel, 1945
BTC	Bristol Channel to Thames, 1944–5
CE	Channel Eastward, i.e. St Helens Roads to Southend
COC	Late 1944 and early 1945, Plymouth to Brittany series
CW	Channel Westward, i.e. Southend to St Helens Roads
EBC	Bristol Channel coastal convoy to France, June to Oct 1944
EBM	Bristol Channel MT convoy to France, June 1944
EC	Southend to Oban via Firth of Forth, 1941
ECM	Falmouth to France, June and early July 1944
ECP	Portland and Solent Personnel convoys to Seine Bay, June to October 1944
EMM	Two convoys only; Belfast to France, June-July 1944
EMP	Two personnel convoys Belfast to France, July 1944
EN	Methil to Oban via Loch Ewe; two series, interrupted by EC
EPM	Portland to France via Solent Motor Transport (MT) convoys, July to September 1944
EPP	Portland to France via Solent personnel convoys, July to Sept 1944
ETC	Thames to France coaster convoys, June to October 1944
ETM	Thames to France MT convoys, June to October 1944
EWC	Spithead to Normandy beaches coaster convoys, June 1944
EWL	Isle of Wight to France invasion convoys, June 1944
EWM	Isle of Wight to France MT convoys, September and October 1944
EWP	Isle of Wight to France personnel convoys
EXP	June to October 1944 invasion series
FC	France to West of England convoy series, June-July 1944
FN	Forth North, Thames to Firth of Forth, 1939 to 1945
FS	Forth South, Firth of Forth to Thames, 1939 to 1945

FTC	France to Thames coaster convoys, 1944
FTM	France to Thames MT convoys, 1944
FWC	France to Isle of Wight coaster convoys, June 1944
FWL	France to Isle of Wight landing craft convoys, 1944
FWM	France to Isle of Wight MT convoys, June-July 1944
FWP	France to Isle of Wight personnel convoys, June-Sept 1944
FXP	France to UK invasion series, June to Oct 1944
GS	Humber (Grimsby) to Southend, 1940
HM	Holyhead to Milford Haven
MH	Milford Haven to Holyhead
MT	Methil to Tyne, 1940 & 1941
OA	After July 1940, Methil to Liverpool to disperse in North Atlantic
OA	Before July 1940, Southend to disperse in North Atlantic
OB	Before July 1940, Liverpool to disperse in North Atlantic
PW	Portsmouth-Wales, i.e. Solent to Milford Haven
SG	Southend to Humber (Grimsby), 1940
WP	Wales-Portsmouth, i.e. Milford Haven to Solent

Sources and Bibliography

Unpublished Sources

National Archives

The National Archives
Kew, Richmond
Surrey TW9 4DU

Tel: +44 (0) 20 8876 3444.
www.nationalarchives.gov.uk

ADM 199/2130 Survivors' Reports: Merchant Vessels 3 September to 30 November 1939
ADM 199/2131 Survivors' Reports: Merchant Vessels 1 December 1939 to 28 February 1940
ADM 199/2132 Survivors' Reports: Merchant Vessels 1 March 1940 to 31 May 1940
ADM 199/2133 Survivors' Reports: Merchant Vessels 1 June 1940 to 31 August 1940
ADM 199/2134 Survivors' Reports: Merchant Vessels 1 September to 30 November 1940
ADM 199/2135 Survivors' Reports: Merchant Vessels 1 December 1940 to 28 February 1941
ADM 199/2136 Survivors' Reports: Merchant Vessels 1 March 1941 to 30 April 1941
ADM 199/2137 Survivors' Reports: Merchant Vessels 1 May 1941 to 31 July 1941
ADM 199/2138 Survivors' Reports: Merchant Vessels 1 August 1941 to 31 October 1941
ADM 199/2139 Survivors' Reports: Merchant Vessels 1 November 1941 to 28 February
ADM 199/2140 Survivors' Reports: Merchant Vessels 1 March 1942 to 31 May 1942
ADM 199/2141 Survivors' Reports: Merchant Vessels 1 June 1942 to 31 July 1942
ADM 199/2142 Survivors' Reports: Merchant Vessels 1 August 1942 to 31 October 1942

ADM 199/2143 Survivors' Reports: Merchant Vessels 1 November 1942 to 31 December 1942
ADM 199/2144 Survivors' Reports: Merchant Vessels 1 January 1943 to 31 March 1943
ADM 199/2145 Survivors' Reports: Merchant Vessels 1 April 1943 to 30 September 1943
ADM 199/2146 Survivors' Reports: Merchant Vessels 1 October to 31 December 1943
ADM 199/2147 Survivors' Reports: Merchant Vessels 1 January to 31 December 1944
ADM 199/2148 Survivors' Reports: Merchant Vessels 1 January to 8 May 1945
ADM 199/26 FN Convoys Reports: 3 September 1939 to February 1940
ADM 199/27 FN Convoys Reports: 26 February 1940 to 22 April 1940
ADM 199/28 FN Convoys Reports: 27 April 1940 to 22 June 1940
ADM 199/34 FN Convoys Reports: 1939–1940
ADM 199/39 FS and FN Convoys Reports: 1940–1941
ADM 199/929 CE and CW Convoys Reports: 1941
ADM 199/938 CE and CW Convoys Reports: 1942
ADM 199/42 AN, ANF, AS, BN, CE, CW and WS Convoys: reports 1939–1941
ADM 199/62 Reports of Proceedings of Convoys September to November 1939
ADM 199/212 OA Convoys Reports: May 1940 to July 1940
ADM 199/62 OA Convoys Reports: September to November 1939
ADM 199/585 Miscellaneous Convoys 1943
ADM 199/360 Dover Command War Diary
ADM 178/271 Board of Enquiry into grounding and loss of convoy on Haisborough Sands: Loss of HMT *Agate*, SS *Deerwood*, *Aberhill*, *Gallois*, *Betty Hindley*, *Afon Tawy*, *Taara* and *Oxshot*.
ADM 199/670 Actions with E-boats 1941, 050028/41
ADM 199/1462 Sinking of *U671*

Power 26/407 Minutes of Lord President's Coal Committee 10 October 1940 to 14 May 1941

Imperial War Museum

Lambeth Road
London
SE1 2JH

Tel: +44 (0)20 7416 5320
Fax: +44 (0)20 7416 5374
Email: mail@iwm.org.uk
www.iwm.org.uk

Sound Archive
Tel: +44 (0) 207 416 5342
Appointments: +44 (0) 207 416 5344

IWM Sound 25182 Atkinson, Robert
IWM Sound 13241 Band, Albert
IWM Sound 11111 Barnes, George
IWM Sound 15429 Barnes, Sydney
IWM Sound 20364 Baum, Hans
IWM Sound 13100 Bennett, Ronald
IWM Sound 12424 Bird, Richard
IWM Sound 13300 Bush, Sydney
IWM Sound 17509 Cassidy, Geoffrey
IWM Sound 16843 Chrisp, John
IWM Sound 20939 Clark, Alec
IWM Sound 10936 Downing, Alexander
IWM Sound 13120 Ellington, Albert
IWM Sound 11509 Fellingham, Henry
IWM Sound 2466 Ferris, Henry
IWM Sound 2254 Gardener, Charles
IWM Sound 14238 Gower, Alfred
IWM Sound 14875 Harris, Reginald
IWM Sound 22619 Harrison, William
IWM Sound 16794 Hollinshed, Montague
IWM Sound 10800 Hopper, William
IWM Sound 25525 Hughes, Richard
IWM Sound 9956 Irwin, Hugh
IWM Sound 5194 Laurie, James
IWM Sound 11076 Long, Albert
IWM Sound 9377 Maggs, Charles
IWM Sound 9578 McCurrach, Rob Roy
IWM Sound 12550 Merryweather, William
IWM Sound 28577 Neill, Thomas
IWM Sound 11289 O'Leary, Thomas

IWM Sound 12720 Peters, John
IWM Sound 12245 Punt, Cyril
IWM Sound 20135 Raud, Emanuel
IWM Sound 9970 Richards, Brooks Sir
IWM Sound 12719 Seal, Jack
IWM Sound 11758 Stoves, Robert
IWM Sound 27308 Walsh, Ronald
IWM Sound 21575 Watkins, Dennis
IWM Sound 13242 Wharton, Joseph
IWM Sound 12431 White, Arthur
IWM Sound 13240 White, Frederick
IWM Sound 12818 Wyatt, Peter

Department of Documents
Tel: +44 (0) 20 7416 5221/5222/5226
Fax: +44 (0) 20 7416 5374
E-mail: docs@iwm.org.uk

IWM Docs 95/23/1 Balfour, H.M.
IWM Docs 91/7/1 Blaxell, Lionel H., OBE, DSC
IWM Docs 95/5/1 Blois-Brook, Lieutenant Commander M.S.
IWM Docs 91/17/1 Booth, J.W.
IWM Docs 98/1/1 Cole, Commander P.F.
IWM Docs 91/7/1 Coombs, F.B.
IWM Docs 80/18/1 Constable-Roberts, Air Commodore J.
IWM Docs 76/28/1 Cronyn, Captain St J.
IWM Docs 97/31/1 Dean, Commander B.
IWM Docs 95/5/1 Dennis, Commander J.A.J.
IWM Docs 96/56/1 Ditcham, Lieutenant A.G.F.
IWM Docs 85/44/1 Dobson, Commodore J.P.
IWM Docs 88/42/1 Fyrth, P.K.
IWM Docs 94/32/1 Gower, Captain J., DSC, RN
IWM Docs 90/23/1 King, Captain H.A.
IWM Docs 99/43/1 Lind, W.
IWM Docs 92/50/1 Neale, Lieutenant Commander J.K.
IWM Docs 05/80/1 Nicholls, Lieutenant A.
IWM Docs 91/51/1, Pelley, Lieutenant John G, RNVR
IWM Docs 75/105/1 Phipps, Commander W.J.
IWM Docs 04/2/1 Price, Lieutenant G.R.
IWM Docs 85/10/1 Rutter, Major O.
IWM Docs 87/2/1 Spickett, A.
IWM Docs 01/31/1/ Syms, Commander James Anthony, DSC, RN
IWM Docs 66/277/1 Watkinson, Harold, Viscount
IWM Docs Misc 182/2736 HMS *Wensleydale*

BBC People's War

bbc.co.uk/ww2peopleswar

A4183076, Archer, A.H.
A4197125 Bartholomew, John
A5675538 Clark, George
A9014807 Currie, James
A3130183 Hales, Hilda
A1117964 Marwood, Michael
A3536462 Rouse, Graham
A 6021154 Stanworth, James
A8017102 Stoakes, Charles
A2913068 Walker, Edward
A6178070 Webster, Peter
A4189098 Yeatman, Jack

The Second World War Experience Centre

The Second World War Experience Centre
5 Feast Field
Horsforth
Leeds, LS18 4TJ

Archival / Academic Enquiries: 0113 2589637
Fax: 0113 2582557
E-Mail: enquiries@war-experience.org

Air Commodore John Ellacombe DFC
WRNS Second Officer Penny Martin
Lieutenant Derric A. Breen RNVR

Published Works

Atkin, Ronald, *Pillar of Fire*, Sidgwick and Jackson, London, 1990.
Batten, John, *Call the Watch*, Hutchinson, London, undated.
——, *Dirty Little Collier*, Hutchinson, London, undated.
Bekker, Cajus, *The Luftwaffe War Diaries*, Corgi, London, 1972.
British Coaster 1939–1945, HMSO, 1947.
British Merchant Vessels Lost or Damaged by Enemy Action During Second World War, HMSO, London, 1947.
Burn, Alan, *The Fighting Commodores: Convoy Commanders in the Second World War*, Leo Cooper, Barnsley, 1999.

Coastal Command, HMSO, London, 1943.
Churchill, Winston S, *The Second World War*, vol. I: 'The Gathering Storm', Cassell, London, 1949.
vol. II: 'Their Finest Hour'
vol. III: 'The Grand Alliance'
vol. IV: 'The Hinge of Fate'
vol. V: 'Closing the Ring'
vol. VI: 'Triumph and Tragedy'
Cooper, Bryan, *The E-boat Threat*, Purnell, Oxon, 1976.
Deane Potter, John, *Fiasco*, William Heinemann, London, 1970.
Dear, I.C.B. and Foot, M.R.D., *The Oxford Companion to World War II*, Oxford University Press, 2001.
Dodgson, R.A. and Butlin, R.A. (eds), *An Historical Geographical of England and Wales*, Academic Press, London, 1978.
Deighton, Len, *Fighter*, Pluriform Publishing, 1977.
Donald, Commander William, *Stand by for Action*, New English Library, 1975.
Foynes, J.P., *Battle of the East Coast*, published by the author, 1994.
Führer Conferences on Naval Affairs: 1939–1945, Admiralty, London, 1947.
Galland, Adolf, The First and the Last, Fontana, London, 1975.
Grove, Eric J. (ed.), *The Defeat of the Enemy Attack on Shipping 1939–1945*, London, Navy Records Society, 1997.
Hague, Arnold, *The Allied Convoy System 1939–1945: Its Organization, Defence and Operation*, Vanwell, 2000.
Hancock, W.K., (ed.), *History of the Second World War: UK Civil Series – Coal*, HMSO, 1951.
His Majesty's Minesweepers, HMSO, London, 1943.
Hessler, *Fregattenkapitän* Günter, *The U-boat War in the Atlantic 1939–1945*, HMSO, London, 1989.
Hozzel, Brigadier-General Paul-Werner, *Recollections and Experiences of a Stuka Pilot 1931–1945*, Ohio Battle Institute, 1978.
Jacobsen, Dr Hans-Adolf and Rohwer, Dr Jürgen (eds), *Decisive Battles of World War II: The German View*, André Deutsch, London, 1965.
James, Admiral Sir William, *Portsmouth Letters*, Macmillan, London, 1946.
Jefferson, David, *Coastal Forces at War: Royal Navy 'Little Ships' in World War 2*, Patrick Stephens Ltd, Sparkford, Somerset, 1996.
Lucas, James, *Kommando: German Special Forces of World War Two*, Grafton, London, 1986.
Lund, Paul and Ludlam, Harry, *Trawlers Go To War*, New English Library, London, 1972.
——, *Night of the U-Boats*, New English Library, London, 1974.
McKee, Alexander, *The Coal Scuttle Brigade*, New English Library, London, 1973.

Merchantmen at War, HMSO, London, 1944.

Militärgeschichtliches Forschungsamt (Research Institute for Military History) (eds), *Germany and the Second World War*, Clarendon Press, Oxford, 2003.

Raeder, Grand Admiral Erich, *My Life*, United States Naval Instutute, Annapolis, Maryland, 1960.

Rayner, D.A., *Escort*, Futura, London, 1974.

Richards, Denis, *Royal Air Force 1939–1945*, vol. I: 'The Fight at Odds', HMSO, London, 1974.

Rodger, N.A.M., *The Command of the Ocean*, Penguin, London, 2005.

Roskill, Captain S.W., *The War at Sea*, vol. I: 'The Defensive', HMSO, London, 1954.
vol. II: 'The Period of Balance'
vol. III: 'The Offensive'

Slader, John, *The Fourth Service: Merchantmen at War 1939–1945*, Robert Hale, London, 1994.

——, *The Red Duster at War: A History of the Merchant Navy During the Second World War*, William Kimber, London, 1988.

Smith, Peter C., *Hold the Narrow Sea: Naval Warfare in the English Channel 1939–1945*, Moorland Publishing Company Ltd, Derbyshire, 1984.

Tarrant, V.E., *The Last Year of the Kriegsmarine*, Arms and Armour Press, London, 1944.

Terraine, John, *Business in Great Waters*, Wordsworth, Ware, 1999.

Turner, Frank R., *The Maunsell Sea Forts*, published by the author, 1996.

Unwin, Peter, *The Narrow Sea*, Review, London, 2004.

Willan, Professor T.S., *The English Coasting Trade 1600 – 1750*, Manchester, 1938.

Wilson, Alastair and Callo, Joseph F., *Who's Who in Naval History*, Routledge, London, 1944.

Winton, John, *Convoy: The Defence of Sea Trade 1890–1990*, Michael Joseph, London, 1983.

Woodman, Richard, *The Real Cruel Sea: the Merchant Navy in the Battle of the Atlantic 1939–1943*, John Murray, London, 2004.

——, *Keepers of the Sea; The Story of the Trinity House Yachts and Tenders*, Chaffcutter Books, Ware, 2005.

Woodward, David, *Ramsay at War*, William Kimber, London, 1957.

Websites

'Web Research' has sadly become synonymous with plagiarism and poor history. However, the experience of this author has been that the web, like a library, contains both good and bad material, and to dismiss it all as valueless is just academic snobbery. The following meticulously researched sites have been invaluable for cross-checking events, ships' names, and so forth. The volume of material contained in some of them could never be published in any 'conventional' format, and anyone interested in naval history should be grateful for the time and effort that has been expended in creating them.

Doubtless they are not without flaws, and should not be relied upon to the exclusion of all other sources, but neither should most books, or indeed most primary sources.

www.convoyweb.org.uk/ – all-encompassing, searchable database of convoy codes, ships, sailings, losses etc.

www.uboat.net/ – searchable database of U-boats, patrols, sinkings, losses, etc.

www.bpears.org.uk/NE-Diary/ – chronology of events in the north-east of England, compiled from contemporary newspaper headlines.

www.naval-history.net/ – wealth of material including databases of ships and casualties, brief service histories of warships, chronology of events by theatre and date, etc.

http://www.battleofbritain.net/ – day-by-day chronology of the Battle of Britain with oral histories and individual aircrew losses.

www.wlb-stuttgart.de/seekrieg/km/sboot/ – German language research project listing *Schnellboot* flotillas, boats and commanders, with chronological tables of sinkings.

Index